BAD MOON
RISING

Contents

FOREWORD

Like many people, I learned about the Rev. Sun Myung Moon after encountering a few of the legions of flower-selling young people his Unification Church unleashed on American streets in the mid-1970s. As a member of the clergy, I could not help but be interested in the phenomenon of what appeared to be a fast-growing church with an emphasis on proselytizing college students.

The emergence of the church raised provocative questions. The civil libertarian in me was wary of how some reacted to the "Moonies" in those early days. There were calls for curbs on the group's right to preach and controversial actions by "deprogrammers" who abducted adults who had freely joined the church and attempted to compel them to renounce Unificationism.

The panic died down as the 1970s drew to a close. Moon's flower sellers largely disappeared from city streets. The church assumed a lower public profile. The deprogrammers moved on to other groups.

But even as this was happening, events were unfolding behind the scenes that would prove to be a more interesting chapter in the Moon saga. Slowly but surely, Moon began to ingratiate himself into the conservative power structure of Washington, DC. Moon used his considerable fortune to bankroll the *Washington Times*, an ultraconservative daily newspaper that began publishing in 1982. President Ronald Reagan called it his favorite paper.

Moon also created a dizzying array of right-wing organizations that became conduits for his cash and vehicles to buy influence. He became a type of giant ATM for the far right. Several conservative leaders were unable to resist the lure of this funding stream and drank deeply from it. Over the years, Religious Right leaders like Tim LaHaye, Jerry Falwell, Gary Bauer, Ralph Reed, and others have taken large checks from Moon. Political leaders like George H. W. Bush, Gerald Ford, Jack Kemp, William Bennett, Dan Quayle, and others have taken Moon money to appear at conferences.

Ironically, at the very time Moon was at the height of his power and influence, most Americans thought he was yesterday's news. Yet Moon groups continued working quietly on a number of projects—always with the agenda of promoting Moon's theology and politics. Even something as innocuous sounding as the Moon-backed "Parents' Day"—ostensibly a national holiday to honor America's parents—takes on a different cast when you realize that Moon and his wife consider themselves the "True Parents" of humankind.

Moon and his minions touch our lives in ways that most Americans don't even realize. As the disputed 2000 election played out, Moon front groups sponsored a series of "unity rallies" that were really designed to get people comfortable with the idea that George W. Bush was the legitimate winner. Moon-backed organizations relentlessly promoted Bush's "faith-based" initiative. In what might have been a quid pro quo, a Moon division called Free Teens received federal faith-based funding to teach young people to remain abstinent. Thousands of teens have attended this training with their parents not even realizing the Moon connection.

Moon simply buys his way into religious communities all over the nation. His minions have actually persuaded some Christian leaders to remove the crosses from their churches, arguing that the actions of Moon have freed Jesus from that symbol of torture and death. He brings imams and rabbis together for shows of unity at glitzy conferences that receive in-depth write-ups in the *Washington Times* but mostly are otherwise unnoticed.

All the while, Moon's theology has grown more unusual. He now openly refers to himself as the Messiah, although his supporters insist he doesn't really mean to assume the mantle of divinity. Moon operatives conduct sessions in the "Spirit World" during which dead presidents and other famous deceased U.S. and international leaders endorse Moon and call on all people to join his church. (During one such event, Thomas Jefferson is reported to have said, "People of America, rise again. Return to the nation's founding spirit. Follow the teachings of Rev. Sun Myung Moon, the Messiah to all people, who has appeared in Korea. There is no inconsistency between our founding spirit and his teachings. Well-known presidents and kings from history are excited by the greatness of his philosophy of peace.")

Moon can believe what he wants about theology, of course. But in the case of the Unification Church, there is often an attempt to promote a public policy expression for what are, I think most fair observers would concede, fairly esoteric beliefs. This is where the problems begin. It's never enough for Moon and the Unificationists to believe what they want. They constantly labor to convince the U.S. government to endorse those beliefs.

Thus, March 23, 2004, saw the occurrence of a bizarre event at the Dirksen Senate Office Building in Washington where Moon and his wife, Hak Ja Han, were proclaimed king and queen of America. Wearing flowing robes reminiscent of Middle Ages kingly attire, the Moons had golden crowns placed on their heads during the ceremony, which was attended by a U.S. senator and several members of the House of Representatives.

Reports in Unification Church publications made it clear that Moon's followers viewed the coronation ceremony as more than just an award. On Moon's Family Federation for World Peace and Unification Web site a few days after the event, top Moon official Chung Hwan Kwak was quoted as saying, "So in effect, the crowning means America is saying to Father, 'Please become my king.'"

Observed Kwak, "The 'outside' view of the Capitol Hill event was that Father received a crown, an award for his years of dedication and leadership in reconciliation and peace-making. The 'inside' view of the event was that America surrendered to True Parents in the king's position."

The strange event on Capitol Hill thrust Moon back into the spotlight and reminded Americans that his church was still out there, possibly plotting out more curious initiatives. Unfortunately, much of the discussion that followed veered away from Moon as journalists became obsessed with finding out which senator arranged for Moon to use the room in Dirksen. It turned out to be Sen. John Warner (R-VA), which only goes to underscore that Moon is a man accustomed to having friends in high places.

•   •   •

Moon is no sideshow, nor is he a has-been. His theology calls for the merger of all religions under him. Moon is avowedly theocratic and recognizes no division between church and state. Thanks to his vast fortune (the origins of which remain mysterious), Moon has been in a position to create organizations that have influenced conservative political thought in a way that few conservative leaders are willing to admit. Moon won this influence the old-fashioned way: he bought it.

Journalist John Gorenfeld knows this. Long after others lost interest, John continued to connect the dots of the Moon empire, following the money to the doorsteps of various conservative think tanks and into the wallets of assorted right-wing pundits and talking heads. John knows that Moon is capable of strange antics and bizarre speeches—but points out that none of this has diminished his ability to gain influence in the circles of power.

There have been other books about Moon over the years, but no one has pulled all the threads together and explained the significance of Moon and his political church like John Gorenfeld. Read the results of his years of research and be enlightened.

The Rev. Barry W. Lynn
Executive Director
Americans United for Separation of Church and State
Washington, D.C.

ONE

Moon Behind the Curtain

The scene summoned the moment in Robert Graves' "I Claudius" when Emperor Caligula declares himself a god in the Roman Senate; a fawning solon instantly offers a prayer.

—"Lawmakers Scurry from the Light,"
New York Times op-ed, June 27, 2004

All kings is mostly rapscallions, as far as I can make out.

—Huckleberry Finn

One chilly Tuesday evening, strange things were afoot on Capitol Hill. The U.S. Senate was hosting a ceremony at the request of a wealthy, elderly newspaper publisher who wanted official recognition as a majestic, divine visitor to Washington. The Dirksen Senate Office Building made for an unlikely temple: a formidable seven-story block of white marble, looming on a street corner diagonally across from the Capitol Dome, its great marble pediment is inscribed, "The Senate Is the Living Symbol of Our Union of States." On March 23, 2004, U.S. lawmakers were filmed here in a conference room, paying tribute to the enigmatic Reverend Sun Myung Moon, then eighty-four, and his wife, Hak Ja, sixty-four.

As the cameras rolled, two congressmen presented the Koreans with matching royal costumes. Wearing the burgundy robes and shining crowns, which crested into jagged golden pinnacles, the married couple smiled and waved for the cameras.

Who was this self-proclaimed monarch? In the 1970s, the evening news had presented Moon, the ranting, middle-aged business tycoon who wore flowing robes on special occasions, as Korea's answer to L. Ron Hubbard, someone for college students to avoid, luring thousands of young Americans into a cult in which they sold carnations on the street and married spouses he chose for them. But the media had moved on to other nightmares, leaving Moon, forgotten, to reinvent himself. Now time had wizened him into an elderly patriarch, wearing an ashen face for his coronation. An orange Senate VIP name tag was still pinned to his gray suit, peeking out from behind rows of curly gold filigree, as he stood on stage at the head of a red carpet.

The King of Peace, the Lord of the Fourth Israel, the Messiah, he called himself these days—and the publisher of the *Washington Times*. Though over a dozen congressmen attended his pageant, no one spoke a word of it to the press, not at first. By the time the secret was out, and ABC News was broadcasting the strange sights, it was three months later—summertime—and school was coming soon to the States. Grand parade marshals would drive teen queens and their bouquets around football fields, and the helmets of varsity teams would crash through banners. And homecoming would not be so different, insisted two hapless congressmen, from the Reverend Moon's rites, which had become a scandal.

"People crown kings and queens at homecoming parades all the time," the liberal Chicago representative Danny Davis (D-IL) said.

"I remember the king and queen thing," said GOP first-termer Roscoe Bartlett (R-MD). "But we have the king and queen of the prom, the king and queen of 4-H, the Mardi Gras and all sorts of other things. I had no idea what he was king of."

Yes, they admitted, it was them on camera, walking in the procession with slow, worshipful steps, bowing to the stage where the Moons stood. Those were Davis's hands, wearing white gloves to avoid defiling the embroidered pillow he carried, a crown bobbing on it, to be lain on the brow of Mrs. Moon; that was Bartlett carrying the burgundy cape for Mr. Moon's shoulders. Neither seemed embarrassed. The "throne room" itself belonged to the U.S. Senate, whose Rules Committee, under Republican senator Trent Lott (R-MS), had the final say in who booked rooms and whether visitors could be anointed kings in them. The name of the senator who had booked the room, said one of the evening's hosts, the defrocked Catholic bishop George Stallings, was "shrouded in mystery."

• • •

Shortly after the March coronation, I stumbled across the footage in an obscure corner of the Internet. Immediately after March 23, Web sites run by underlings of the Reverend Moon had hummed with accounts of a Senate coronation that sounded too ridiculous to believe. But a search led to a jolly, misleading promo reel that Moon's worldwide organization, the Unification Church, had stitched together from the party on Capitol Hill, for the consumption of the faithful. It misleadingly implied that our stubborn Congress, panged by guilt over Moon's 1984 prison sentence for tax fraud, had succumbed to his teachings. "Senators and congressmen . . . joined in," a narrator says. "The Kingdom of Heaven has now begun."

The Washington media, which rarely covered Moon anyway, wasn't going to touch this one with a pole. But the blogs needled the press for an explanation of a world most people had never heard of. After all, footage of the congressmen behaving badly was flying around the Web with the speed of a YouTube sensation, one of those links e-mailed to thousands overnight, like footage of a dog that plays the harmonica. Then, in June 2004, the media belatedly picked up the story. "There are moments that best play straight," CNN anchor Aaron Brown said of the pageant. "So here goes. Lawmakers welcome a guy to Congress—and the messiah shows up."

• • •

The coronation had been disguised as a Washington awards dinner. It ended with Moon leading the crowd in cheers of *mansei*, the Korean version of *banzai*. But it began with a train of multicultural pilgrims streaming into the Senate offices on the evening of March 23, there to hand out awards with a world peace theme. They called themselves the Ambassadors for Peace, guests of a conservative prowar senator who had modestly kept his name out of the picture. They were a diverse patchwork of inner-city African American ministers, Muslim imams, New Agers, astrologists, swamis, and activists for strange causes, spanning fifty states, the Near and Far East, and beyond.

Their party began normally enough, serving portions of chicken and fish from the buffet and windy politicians' speeches from the podium. But through a bait and switch—and a strange internal logic—room G-50 of the Senator Everett M. Dirksen Senate Office Building, all marble and eagle seals, changed during the course of the evening into a fantasy throne room for the stern monarch of the *Washington Times*, the influential conservative newspaper that warns of immigrants and threats to Christmas—and who also controls United Press International (UPI), the formerly great news agency.

Moon walked from the chilly evening into the marble building dressed in a suit with bow tie and rose corsage. When he got up to deliver his keynote address, it was in a gravelly northern dialect of Korean, a farmer's accent. Gripping the podium, he gruffly admonished the crowd, which included members of Congress, to accept him as "God's ambassador, sent to earth with His full authority."

With a printed copy of the speech before them—headlined *Declaring the Era of the Peace Kingdom*—guests listened to an English translation in radio earpieces. "The time has come for you to open your hearts," Moon said, "and receive the secrets that Heaven is disclosing in this age through me." To prove his credentials, he spoke of testimonials on his behalf— from the lips of the dead, with whom he claimed the power to converse. "The five great saints," he said—meaning Jesus, Confucius, Buddha, Muhammad, and the Hindu prophet Shankara—"and many other leaders in the spirit world, including even Communist leaders such as Marx and Lenin, who committed all manner of barbarity and murders on earth, and dictators such as Hitler and Stalin, have found strength in my teachings, mended their ways and been reborn as new persons."

His boasts were underscored with whoops and cheers from his followers, who had the good seats. To their church, the moment was a shining vindication for years of hardship: for being treated in the press as predators and for seeing their Christ-like hero, the Reverend Moon, forced onto the witness stand by U.S. tax attorneys, Sen. Bob Dole, and others between 1975 and 1984. Behind the gavels of government, these Pontius Pilates had pronounced Moon an enemy of the American family and the advance man for a South Korean dictator. The Reagan Justice Department had even sent Moon to prison. But now Moon was active in family values politics, and members of Congress were as submissive as puppies. *Moon prevailed.*

The cameras flashed. It was all part of the never-ending awards tour that the Reverend Moon led, crossing from the Far East to the West and back, across the fifty states and around the world, wherever he was not banned by treaties as a convicted American felon, to Brazil, Switzerland, the Marshall Islands, the Philippines; to Paraguay, where he owns 1.5 million acres of land in the Chaco region, a plot twice the size of Luxembourg, near where his neighbor and friend, George H. W. Bush, has reportedly acquired a humbler parcel of one hundred thousand acres.

Moon dreams of being middleman to the world, and the organization has discovered that handing out prizes and treats is a fast route to friends from Pakistan to the United States. "[W]e want to have the Governor, U.S. Senators, U.S. Congressmen, Mayors and State Legislators," church leader Michael Jenkins instructed his subordinates in 2001. "Get all the proclamations you can. Each Event Location will receive a Gift of 14 Gold Watches (18K Gold Plated) from our True Parents. These Watches have a value of $1,200."

By playing the game and appearing at his events, the VIPs, in turn, lend prestige to Moon. "When you go get the proclamations in your various cities and you meet the Mayors," he had said in a sermon, "it is easy, because your foundation has been laid. All you have to do is show other proclamations, other letters and say what others have done to honor Father." Fed back into Moon's PR machine, the images impress potential partners on faraway shores and ours.

Believing they were saving the world, Moon's men had faced

desperate pressure to arrange the March 23 dinner. The Senate event's emcee was Michael Jenkins, leader of the American Unification Church, a white, blandly enthusiastic if wooden spokesman for the cause. In the autumn of 2003, Jenkins recalls in a sermon found online, the Reverend Moon had instructed him three times, first in a low voice, then louder, that unless the world enacted Moon's plan for world peace, millions would die in a new Middle East Holocaust. "Not six million," Jenkins said, "but *six hundred million.*"

That fall the *Times* publisher fished for hours on his boat, while his apostles begged him not to strain his health. "You tell me to rest," Moon retorted, "but I'm determining the course of history." When Moon goes reeling off the coast of Kodiak, Alaska—where the church-owned True World Foods cannery annually ships over twenty million pounds of salmon and other seafood—his followers believe his fishing also mends the wounds of the Cosmos. One day, the elderly fisherman accused Jenkins's American archdiocese of taking the mission lightly. Far from it, Jenkins proclaimed from the pulpit. "Our American members are willing to die," he said. "They're willing to die. Once they understand God's will, *they'll die.*"

Had the Reverend Moon's crowning at the Dirksen Senate Office Building not been filmed and photographed from seemingly every possible angle, and broadcast on *ABC's World News Tonight* and Fox, and giggled at by *The Daily Show's* Jon Stewart, and compared in a *New York Times* op-ed with an act of the Roman emperor who nominated his horse to the senate, it might have remained a mad whisper among Senate aides.

• • •

This book is the story of an amazing metamorphosis: how the Reverend Moon, the international man of mystery whose worshippers call him the True Father, transformed himself from one of the most feared figures of the post-1960s cult panic into a major figure in the conservative world, and not just as the man whose newspaper inspires many of the headlines on Fox News Channel. He's also chairman of a worldwide commercial enterprise of truly stunning reach. Living proof of the adage, from the 1974 movie *Chinatown*, that people "all get respectable if they last long enough," the Korean theocrat's embrace by Richard Nixon, the Bush family, and the founders of the religious right sheds new light on the character of the Republican Party—whose friendship, as the rising conservative movement took a fortune from Moon, helped the reverend carve out an eerie political underworld.

The journey we will be taking into this American mystery winds along the strange rivers of influence in our government, on a ride past idealism and con artistry, cruelty and comedy, profit and ambition on a grand scale. At the end lies a door on Capitol Hill that is always open, not for you or me, but for the rich and powerful Unification Church, a foreign organization widely feared by Americans in the 1970s and 1980s for its recruitment of college students and seemingly un-Republican convictions—that Jesus is a failure, that a Washington Messiah has replaced him, and that individual freedom is, as Moon puts it, "what Satan likes best."

Well into his eighties, Moon maintains the ferocious conviction of an avenging angel. His followers have said he hardly sleeps and can still speak for sixteen hours a day, tapping into God for stamina, and that they can listen that long.

His multinational wealth is staggering. If you have eaten sushi in the last few years, there is a good chance you've crossed paths with Moon's monopolistic fishing empire, True World Foods, which stretches from a lobster-packing plant in Gloucester, Massachusetts, to the $3 million shrimp business in Alaska and fleets in the Pacific. In a 1980 speech on tuna, Moon described the plan: "We build the boats, we catch the fish and process them for the market, and then have a distribution network. This is not just on the drawing board; I have already done it." By 2006, the *Chicago Tribune* had discovered that his company, True World Foods, supplies most sushi chefs in the United States with its fishing fleets, warehouses, and delivery trucks. Moon's Bay Area leader, Kevin Thompson, was arrested in 2007 for running a shark-poaching ring, in which babies were ripped from mother fish. The profits were funding "church operations," he said in taped speeches, saying that Moon—who calls himself the "Ocean King" and is an avid fisherman—loved the idea. (The Feds, however, gave Thompson a year in prison.)

Then there's a fortune in real estate holdings stretching from Latin America to Manhattan; a South Korean industrial and armaments firm Tong-Il (whose name translates to "unification"); diamond and jewelry companies; gun factories; TV postproduction studios; health food; software; Manhattan's Hammerstein Ballroom; the New Yorker Hotel; the University of Bridgeport, Connecticut; and the wire service United Press International, which he acquired in 2000. He regards the *Washington Times* as the nerve center of it all.

If the media hasn't bothered to pry open Moon's world for a while, it may be because his group, the Unification Church, presents itself in such a baffling way to the public. Larry Zilliox Jr., a private investigator in Virginia who is among the nation's leading Moonologists, maintains a list, hundreds of entries long, of names under which the Unification Church has staged its events: an alphabet soup of obscure acronyms. The coronation in Washington was put on by something called the IIFWP, or Interreligious and International Federation for World Peace. To this day, the IIFWP lists as its address 3600 New York Ave., NE, in Washington, D.C. That's the *Washington Times* building.

• • •

"Moon can buy a newspaper," Chris Matthews (of MSNBC *Hardball* fame) said in 1982, when he was spokesperson for Democratic House Speaker Tip O'Neill and Moon's editors had just printed their first issue, "but I can't buy the idea he's a newspaperman."

Five years on, the skeptics persisted. "What I don't understand," said *Washington Post* editor Ben Bradlee in 1987, alluding to congressional reports that Moon's aides had been career South Korean intelligence officers, "is how anyone can take seriously a newspaper that is controlled . . . by the agents of a foreign government. No one would take them seriously if it was Bangladesh. No one would take them seriously if it was France."

Today the peculiar newspaper has become an "extremely important paper for conservatives," *National Review* editor John O'Sullivan has said, "because it's in Washington and has great influence within the administration." Its reporting is incessantly quoted on Fox News Channel, on talk radio, and in the Republican Web world, leaving a mark on public opinion. The *Times* originally rolled out in 1982—created by Moon—to counterbalance the critical *Washington Post* with a friendlier treatment of the Reagan administration. The paper's gossip columnist, Charlotte Hays, observed sardonically that the *Times* is a "place for free-market conservatives to escape the free market." The paper calls itself "America's Newspaper," and its orange-red newsstands, studding Capitol Hill, advertise it as the "Bolder! Brighter!" alternative.

Or is it more than just a daily newspaper? Again and again, the reverend has described his paper's role in surprising terms: as a vehicle for God's word; as "our media"; as a mighty ship at his disposal. In 2005, frustrated by his lack of appreciation in the American press, Moon fumed, "How come our media is silent? . . . You have to write correct articles, or maybe we should sell those newspapers. . . . All central nations should understand the Crown of Peace Ceremony."

Moon's messianic view of his paper has made for strange collisions with its official image. In 1997, the paper held a party for its fifteenth anniversary at the Grand Hyatt Hotel in D.C., and it was broadcast on C-SPAN. Bush Sr. sent a congratulatory video. Sen. Orrin Hatch made a few pointed comments about the "liberal modus operandi" and the spirit of capitalism, and he mocked progressives for wanting to "help the poor, quote-and-quote." Then the *Times*'s chief editor, Wes Pruden, spoke briefly about the man who was about to take the stage. He told the story of how that "young seeker" in Korea survived torture, came to America, and now fostered good journalism with his "commitment to objectivity." And then the grim-faced Moon rose from his chair and spoke for about forty-five minutes.

"Free sex is centered on *Sayy-tan!*" he rasped—as *Times* associates shifted uncomfortably in their seats. His tongue drooped lazily over his lips as he let this sink in. He continued. "World literature and the media have often stimulated free sex," he said. "But from now on, you literary figures and journalists should lead the way to prevent free sex. Free sex should completely disappear." During that evening, he also directed *Times* staff to read a speech of his dozens of times for understanding; he smiled to himself at a private joke about the number seven that the audience seemed to find hard to follow; and he even told the crowd, "No one can oppose me."

Chris Matthews no longer badmouths Moon. For several years his syndicated column ran in the *Times*. Seven years after his feisty dismissal of Moon, the fair-haired pundit addressed a 1989 gathering with the Messiah as headliner. It was the annual conference of the Moon-sponsored World Media Association (WMA). The WMA is an allegedly serious panel that meets to think big thoughts on the future of news, behind it the flags of the world's countries, as at a UN summit.

Moon is a newspaperman after all.

• • •

In the old Dutch settlement of Tarrytown, New York, where the early American writer Washington Irving imagined the hoof beats of a headless horseman, it's fitting that there would rear up in 2004 a self-styled King of America, claiming a mandate from the dead. Four months before the Washington, D.C., coronation, on November 25, 2003, Moon held court here at East Garden, his eighteen-acre estate along the Hudson River. He told his flock, "God likes the idea of a monarchy, because it removes the cycles of election after election which can obscure the focus and direction of the nation."

Moon's philosophy is political as well as religious. Just as Karl Marx saw history as a train stopping at one station after the next, he considers his teachings to be not just a new Testament but the final refutation to

Das Kapital ("a religious alternative to Communism" was how his friend Senator Hatch described Moon's Unification Thought). And he envisions the last stop after capitalism to be the monarchy of the True Parents.

But lowering himself to mere king sometimes strains Moon's patience. "I can dream dreams that God himself never dreamed," he'd told his church in Washington, D.C., on May 17, 2003, according to one of hundreds of speeches posted online. "I'm that kind of person. I can believe the things even God can't believe. I can do things even God can't. That's why God hated me more than Satan hated me."

In his rambles, he also made cryptic references to George W. Bush. "We must connect the Bush administration to the religious realm to work together in the U.N. like brothers," he ruminated. He also insisted that his UN policy proposals go into effect ASAP. Specifically, he has lobbied for the Security Council to be joined by a new "religious council," which would, in theory, install clerics of major religions in the East River organization, who could then, his ministers privately hope, declare his majesty to the nations.

With his seclusion, baronial palaces, and personal mystery, the Reverend Moon is a modern-day Citizen Kane. Like Kane—and Kane's real-life inspiration, William Randolph Hearst—Moon oversees a newspaper that whips up popular anger in service to an agenda. Like Hearst's Castle (or Kane's Xanadu), Moon's palaces (in Korea, North and South America, and reportedly Switzerland) are self-built monuments to his greatness. "[W]hen the world was adrift on the stormy waves of the Cold War," he said at a *Washington Times* dinner televised on C-SPAN in 1997, "I established the *Washington Times* to fulfill God's desperate desire to save this world."

For years, in the late 1980s, reporters wondered why anyone at all came to his extravagant dinner parties in Washington. Even though they always ended the same, with Moon giving himself an award, they were reliably attended by Senator Hatch and other politicians. Then the novelty of it faded, and Moon slipped from the headlines while the rivers of cash rolled on.

Moon has never claimed to walk on water, but for decades he has saved important Republican activists from debt and funded their organizations with a purse that has sometimes seemed inexhaustible. He has given millions to the Bush family and spent as much as $3 billion to push the conservative message in the *Washington Times*, a newspaper that has lost money since its start. During the neoconservative Iran-Contra adventure of the 1980s, he even channeled money and support to Central American death squads. "An unsung hero of freedom," writes Paul Gottfried, a conservative scholar who has written a history of the right. "The continued refusal of Beltway conservatives publicly to acknowledge their steadfast patron is, of course, scandalous."

Instead, they had long treated Moon like some creature locked in a mad scientist's laboratory. They threw Moon a bone from time to time with private parties, but they never welcomed him into the conservative hall of fame and never allowed the marriage to stumble into the light, where it would upset the townspeople. If it hadn't been for the Internet, it would not have.

• • •

The powers of the Unification Church almost never grant interviews. Modeled after a royal family, they are the inner ring that includes Moon and his 36 Families, as well as all the palace intrigue of the Tudors. The first officer in the House of Moon is a Korean, the Reverend Chung Hwan Kwak. He's now an American media president as well: he heads the United Press International wire service, which Moon acquired in 2000. Dubbed The Cardinal by one former aide, Kwak, seventy-two, is widely seen as a Machiavellian power behind the throne—Moon's Karl Rove, one ex-member calls him—having overthrown longtime rival Bo Hi Pak, seventy-eight, Moon's devoted longtime sidekick, much loved among the faithful.

Believers say the Moons are the world's first perfect family. In person, some say, Moon couldn't be further from his scalding on-stage persona. Up close, this Moon radiates serene joy, like the Buddha, so that they treasure his small acts of kindness: a wave from a limousine window or the graciousness he showed in losing to an apostle in a game of billiards. Mrs. Moon has given birth to two Olympic equestrians, the president of a Massachusetts gun factory, and a princess voted off the WB reality show *Survival of the Richest* (who joined the cast to alleviate what she described as "chronic boredom" and was praised by critics for being level-headed compared with the rest of the rich cast).

Beyond the Blessed Central Family are the non-Asian officeholders. They include the white American leadership clique: longtime husbands of brides chosen for them by Moon. Beyond them are minor officials and laymen. Some still believe; some are simply drawn to the power; some have simply staked too much to leave a life that's all they have known since the Nixon years, though it guarantees no pension and keeps many in poverty. Even among many who left in the 1990s over dismaying revelations, there remains a bittersweet fondness. And beyond the circle of whites is a wide ripple of African American deacons: Christians who have unofficially drifted into Moon's influence, drawn by $12,000 watches, free trips, financial support, and talk of racial harmony.

A religion founded in the 1950s in South Korea, where it is looked upon as a cult, the Unification Church in America has only a few thousand followers in the United States, fallen from a one-time peak of thirty thousand. But the church's business and political presence has remained strong, despite decades of magazine pieces predicting the end, typically with such punny titles as "Eclipse of the Moon." Waxing poetic about Moon's sunset has always been easier than making sense of what's still there.

The House of Moon is renamed periodically for public relations purposes, giving it a floating sense of anonymity. In 2004, the Americans were being told to call themselves the IIFWP. Keeping their denomination unclear ("They would make it real general," says one ex-member. "You would think they were Jehovah's Witnesses"), they registered as a nonprofit, put up a Web site depicting the IIFWP as a world agency of crucial importance, opened an office upstairs from the *Washington Times* newsroom, and spent as much as $11 million a year, according to tax returns. "There are literally hundreds of these organizations," former Moon operations manager Michael Warder, later a director of the conservative Heritage Foundation, wrote in a 1988 exposé, "which all reinforce one another, with key Moon operatives sitting on their boards" and the reverend's name absent from the "flow charts of this organizational scheme to protect him."

Doves, peace branches, Greek pillars, and serious-looking globes decorated the Web site. Was this the headquarters of the world's best diplomats? It had to be, from the Internet write-up. They handled crucial missions all over the planet—even briefing the United Nations! They convinced former enemies, Muslims and Jews, to hug and make up, crying! And every year, these people celebrated themselves in a soccer tournament held, of all places, in Seoul, the booming, high-tech capital city of South Korea. Among the VIPs who attend its forums, according to its pamphlets, are "elected officials, members of the State Department and other U.S. government agencies, with their international counterparts, former heads of states, Ambassadors, and diplomats who meet in Washington and at the United Nations."

• • •

One participant, who asked not to be named, told me she'd been drawn to the Crown of Peace ceremony in a misleading courtship lasting months. A New Ager and grandma, she had first been scouted out by the Moon church as a likely fellow traveler. It had been her hobby to put on roundtables in her hometown encouraging the idea that all faiths share common ground. This message had appealed to the Moonies, who wanted that common ground occupied by their master and posed as a kind of Amnesty International for world peace.

She was surprised by a state chapter meeting in which guests were asked to drink specially provided "Holy Juice" in a toast to ending all premarital sex.

The juice was a cloudy, wine-colored liquid ritually served at many

Moon events, mass-produced in clear plastic packets the size of a creamer container at Denny's. Embossed on the underside of the cups is the year 1960, the year Moon took his second wife. The liquid symbolizes his blood. The attendees were shown films playing up the achievements of the IIF-WP's founder, Moon. It was after the grandmother attended several such meetings that an invitation to Washington, D.C., arrived in her mailbox, slicker than a sweepstakes promotion, naming her to the Ambassadors for Peace. "They don't say 'you're being honored before Congress,'" she says of the flashy pamphlet, "but it looks like you are."

The colorful brochure features a photo of the Capitol dome and lists impressive sponsors, many of whom work at that building—Sen. Lindsey Graham (R-SC), Rep. Chris Cannon (R-UT), Sen. Mark Dayton (D-MN), and Rep. Curt Weldon (R-PA)—and also Stephen Covey, best-selling author of *Seven Habits of Highly Effective People*, and Bush family strategist Charles Black.

• • •

The Unification Church is the first world religion to claim the blessing of thirty-six dead presidents, which provides some context for its founder's interest in Capitol Hill. Just as the Roman Catholic Church catalogues the miracles of saints, the Unification Church lists the American heads of state, beginning with George Washington and ending with Richard Nixon, who have allegedly spoken for Moon in "Messages from Heaven" that you can read on your computer by going to www.messagesfromspiritworld. info. Similar testimonials from Confucius, Martin Luther, Stalin, and others sporadically appear in full-page, expensive advertisements that the church has taken out in the *New York Daily News*, the *Los Angeles Times*, and at least five other papers, bearing Moon's beatific smile.

A central church tenet is that a "Cloud of Witnesses" comprised of the great figures of history has spoken from the Beyond to assure us that Moon is the Messiah. It's said that Sang Hun Lee, a Moonist theologian who fell out a window in Korea in the 1990s, allegedly while sleepwalking, was able to make contact with dead U.S. presidents in the Beyond. (After his death, according to a transcript on a church Web site, the embarrassed doctor declined to answer questions about the window. "Please, don't ask me any more about that," he allegedly said.)

In heaven, according to Moon, Lee tracked down the presidents of the United States and convinced them to attend "seminars" in heaven, resembling sessions held by the Unification Church on earthly college campuses. Lee argued so persuasively that the presidents came around to Moon's philosophy. Then Lee relayed their words to the living, including, for example, this surprising testimony from President James K. Polk:

> People of America, do you think you know what kind of places heaven and hell are? As long as you are in your physical bodies, you most likely cannot even imagine. If there is one earnest message that I would give to the people on earth, it would be that Rev. Sun Myung Moon, who is on earth, is working based on the theme, "God is the parent of humankind," and that he is the Messiah, the True Parent of all humankind who has appeared to guide us. You must never forget this fact. You must carefully study the True Parents' philosophy and truth. These are the conclusions I have reached in the spirit world.

The church believes thirty-five other presidents have spoken for Moon. To reach the mystical number 36, the list ends at Nixon, the only president known to have hosted Moon in the Oval Office (as former Nixon aide Bruce Herschensohn has confirmed). John F. Kennedy, paying service to Moon's idea that God has entrusted the United Nations with a theocratic mission, is given this mouthful to utter: "Don't ask what the United Nations can do for you, ask what you can do for the realization of the eternal world of peace (the original founding purpose of the UN)."

The endorsements have been treated skeptically by reporters, including *Chicago Tribune* columnist Eric Zorn, who was not persuaded by this message from Lincoln:

Without doubt, Rev. Sun Myung Moon is the True Parent of humanity. . . . While I was listening to the Divine Principle lectures, I had a vision. In this vision, all the souls in this place, including black people, yellow people, and white people, and including Christians, Buddhists, Confucianists and Muslims, all came together and danced for joy. Then I saw a bright light, which is the light of God, and in that instant, I, Abraham Lincoln, wanted to also jump in among them and begin to dance.

"The Great Emancipator is now the Great E-Dancipator," Zorn joked. But there was a practical meaning beneath it all. The dream is that Caesar will render unto Moon.

On December 25, 2001, in the miracle alluded to during Moon's speech at the Senate offices, the founders of the world's great religions had, he said, convened to name him king of kings. His followers assert that the decision was made during a December, 25, 2001, affair, from 12:00 P.M. to 12:00 A.M., as orderly as a Tuesday night zoning board meeting.

With God as mayor, the town hall–style council had passed a unanimous resolution. God himself then spoke to Moon:

My beloved Son! . . . The word "love" is inadequate to express My feelings, but no better word comes to mind. . . . On December 25, 2001, the founders and leading figures of Christianity and the other major religions drew up a resolution and proclaimed unanimously that, along with you, they would participate in the realization of peace and the unity of heaven and earth. Therefore it is only appropriate that you be exalted as the True Parent of all humankind. . . . Thank you, thank you, True Parent!

. • • •

In the old days, the women's magazine *McCall's* had warned mothers about the dangers of the Unification Church, named for its pledge to fuse all religions under one Father, calling it "by far the most successful of the religious cults that have become so prominent and perplexing a feature of the American '70s." A "nettle in the national consciousness," said *People*.

Evangelist Jerry Falwell, Founding Father of the Christian right, cursed Moon in a 1978 *Esquire* piece. The article highlighted the preacher from Lynchburg, Virginia, as the crest of a new wave, a man who might become "the first preacher to become a political leader." Falwell told the reporter, "Reverend Sun Myung Moon is like the plague. He exploits boys and girls, and he should be exported. People like Moon and the healer types, the Elmer Gantry types, are religious phonies who are raping America. They will stand before God more accountable than any criminal on Earth." By then Moon had a head start in the news business. His church published a New York tabloid, *News World*, that was selling briskly during that year's newspaper strike.

Moon had come to build the American *foundation*, as he called it, for his kingdom. He came to California amid a widespread panic at cults. Young people, largely in California, were surrendering their lives to authoritarian men—always men—at a surprising rate. That Christmas, at the height of the phenomenon, director Phil Kaufman released a timely remake of *Invasion of the Body Snatchers*, the 1956 sci-fi classic. Where the 1950s original has been seen as an allegory for Cold War paranoia—the idea that your smiling neighbor on Main Street U.S.A. could be an inside man for communism—the 1978 remake cleverly moves the action to San Francisco, the spiritual supermarket, playing on the dread of the New Age mind manipulator and his power to create crowds, a snapshot of a crazy time.

But the man we think of as the American cult leader—who removes his followers to colonies, dictates their sex lives, and declares our government satanic—is actually a figure dating back at least to the 1830s. That's when Sojourner Truth, the abolitionist, worked as a housekeeper for a New York group, the Kingdom of Matthias. Her boss, the son of Scottish immigrants, "pronounced vengeance on the land," Truth remembered in her old age.

He said "that the law of God was the only rule of government, and that he was commanded to take possession of the world in the name of the King of kings."

A century and a half before King Moon played God's matchmaker, King Matthias asserted similar controls. He assured the flock that "all the marriages in the world were illegal," another contemporary remembered, and that only Matthias, God's matchmaker, could assign perfect "spirit matches." From Matthias to David Koresh, according to historians Paul E. Johnson and Sean Wilentz, men like this have a "remarkable continuous history in the United States." They appeal "to persistent American hurts and rages, wrapped in longings for a supposedly bygone holy patriarchy."

But in 1978, the age of communism, advertising, and mass media, experts warned that twentieth-century methods had allowed a new kind of persuader to multiply his powers. The fear was that the new guru could train your loved ones to become unfeeling husks, deploying them on the streets to pay for his sedans and mansions.

The media made Moon an icon of the craze. While the young slaved for him, Moon was reported to set sail in a fifty-foot yacht, cruise Manhattan in a custom-built Lincoln Continental, and eat from dishes etched in gold. (His church denied that he was rich and said these blessings were voluntary tokens of appreciation from members.) When Moon gave pep talks to members of his young sales force, who were strung out from hustling flowers, peanuts, and toys to pedestrians, he told them they were backing his desperate fight to build God's kingdom on Earth, a living fortress against the devil.

The media didn't see it that way. *Time* attacked Moon as a "megalomaniacal 'messiah'" who pretended to be a Christian minister but had privately confessed the pose to be a ruse, telling the Moonies that "God is now throwing Christianity away." Moon was elsewhere assailed as a demagogue who called the Nazi Holocaust an understandable punishment for the Jewish murder of Christ and who asked for total obedience.

"I am your brain," he'd said. "You can do everything in utter obedience to me. Because what I am doing is not done at random, but what I am doing is under God's command."

Moon became such a phenomenon that, in 1977, *Saturday Night Live* cast comic duo John Belushi and Dan Ackroyd as, respectively, Sun Myung Moon and a deprogrammer hired to exorcise his magic. By the end of the skit, Ackroyd helplessly prepares to sign his belongings over to Belushi.

For many, to join up in those days was simply to continue the quest of the 1960s for a new brotherhood. They weren't so interested in the megalomania. "The world was a different place then," says Glenn Emery, a former *Washington Times* reporter and ex-member. "Joining a cult wasn't so weird. It was just a matter of which cult you might join." The church appealed to his sense of altruism. Down the street from his Moon commune in San Francisco were the headquarters of another New Age group, Primal Scream.

The alteration of the self had fascinated Americans since the sixties, but the seventies brought a new sense that external predators, too, could change you. The $39 million success of the 1973 demon-possession film *The Exorcist*, argues historian Andreas Killen, reflects an era obsessed with sudden personality change. It also happens to be one of Moon's favorite movies. Moon told ex-member Steve Hassan that it is "a prophecy of what will happen to the U.S. if it doesn't turn back to God." Another follower tells me that Moon, as he watched, "laughed a knowing laugh—like, 'Yep, that's what happens!'"

In the public imagination, the fear of personality change grew more impending with the 1974 crime rampage of Patty Hearst, a wealthy nineteen-year-old heiress kidnapped that year by the black revolutionary Donald DeFreeze. Under the tutelage of DeFreeze, who styled himself Field Marshall Cinque and gave her a new name, Tania, she seemed to horrified observers to have traded her brain for someone else's. She spoke the words of the guerilla leader, who claimed to be bringing humanity into "symbiosis" by robbing banks, wished "death to the fascist insect that preys upon the life of the people," and himself died in a flaming house during a shootout with the LAPD. At her trial in 1976, Hearst claimed that DeFreeze's sexually tinged brainwashing campaign created a new person, "Tania." The defense didn't work, but the trial kindled the question: just what can you force a person to believe or even kill for?

For all the paranoid fantasies of cult uprisings, the real revolution around the corner—the 1980 victory of Ronald Reagan—celebrated ideas poles apart from the mass mind creeds of posthippie California. From its origins in the 1964 Goldwater campaign, the conservative insurgency glorified the rugged American individual. It also promised answers for parents horrified by the radical new ways of life chosen by their offspring. Reagan had vowed to "clean up the mess at Berkeley" and its "orgies" in 1966. The pledge resonated beyond just the student protests, taken as a promise that there would be an answer to attacks on tradition.

Eventually, the path blazed by Reagan-era activists would take America down the long road to the Bush dynasty, and the sincere belief in many quarters was that the George W. Bush White House houses not only the commander in chief but the national preserver of old-time religion and family.

Moon had his feet in both worlds: change and backlash. On the one hand, it was his communes that the older generation found frightful; they housed seven thousand American dropouts by the late 1970s, while tens of thousands of others followed Moon. On the other hand, his troops marched in the name of reaction. Clean-cut and sexually regimented, they venerated Nixon, spoke of banishing "free sex," and said they were starting the world's first perfect families.

•   •   •

It's well known that Scientology leader L. Ron Hubbard went to Hollywood to become legit, but hardly anyone has heard that the Reverend Sun Myung Moon has courted Washington for decades. One of his first supporters was Sen. Strom Thurmond (R-SC). In the post-Watergate years, Thurmond's fellow Republican and World War II veteran, Sen. Bob Dole (R-KS), met growing pressure to stand up to the church and its play for influence. Like other erstwhile foes, however, Dole would one day embrace what he opposed.

On January 9, 1976, twenty years before running for president, Dole asked the IRS to consider repealing Moon's tax-exempt status. He wrote in a letter that Moon's empire "is based more on mind control and indoctrination than on religious faith," operating "for political purposes" as much as for God. Dole then held a televised town hall meeting on "destructive cults" attended by three hundred parents from thirty states who fretted about the Moonies and other aggressive sects. Speakers said people and families were being ruined; young people were being taught to lie for cash.

The hearings made some liberals uneasy, as calls for crackdowns bumped up against the First Amendment's guarantee of the right to follow strange gods. A piece in the *New Republic* accused Dole of jumping on national hysteria to jump-start his political fame, just as Richard Nixon had gotten his start attacking accused Soviet spy Alger Hiss.

Meanwhile, former members of the Moon church testified that the movement had deprived them of food and sleep to grease their willingness to swallow an agenda that made Don DeFreeze's look tame. A secret Unification Church publication, *Master Speaks*, had been snuck out of the church by apostate Steve Hassan. It captured what Moon said behind closed doors. *Time* headlined an excerpt: "The Secret Sayings of 'Master' Moon." Moon had said:

- "The whole world is in my hand, and I will conquer and subjugate the world."

- "In restoring man from evil sovereignty, we must cheat."

- "The time will come when, without my seeking it, that my words must serve as law."

- "[W]e will be able to amend laws, articles of constitution, if we wish to do so."

- "[T]elling a lie becomes a sin if you tell it to take advantage of a person, but if you tell a lie to do a good thing . . . that is not a sin.... Even God tells lies very often."

- "The present U.N. must be annihilated by our power. . . . We must make a new U.N."

- "Many people will die, those who go against our movement."

- "I have met many famous, so-called famous, Senators and Congressmen; but to my eyes they are nothing. They are weak and helpless. We will win the battle. This is our dream, our project. But shut your mouth tight."

(The church has often insisted these were mistranslations.)

"I'm fearful of what we found out in Washington," said parent Bob Fanshier after the meeting. "The church has tremendous strength, is better organized, and has much more money than we do." Under the Kansas sun of a seven-year drought, Fanshier was raising alfalfa and cattle south of Great Bend in the summer of 1975, when his daughter Pam, a twenty-three-year-old former honors student, lit out to join Moon's movement, the One World Crusade. To break her out, the Methodist couple hired a kidnapper—an increasingly popular act among distraught parents, though in many cases illegal. When they committed her to an institution, Moon's lawyers sued. Pam told a courtroom her parents saw her as a Satan worshiper. The judge ruled that they had violated her civil rights.

Mr. and Mrs. Fanshier, visiting Washington for the Dole hearings, then bumped into Pam, in town to rally for the cause. The church allowed her to see her parents briefly, and she agreed to join them for dinner the next night. But the following evening, instead of Pam, they found a note on her hotel door. It said she'd "left to go around the country on assignment." They heard no more. "We know they're using our daughter as a pawn in Washington," Mrs. Fanshier told the local paper.

The Moon Children took Dole's inquiry as a slap in the face. It came just as their new Father opened his pocketbook to associate himself with apple-pie patriotism.

The rallies and marches he staged "would make . . . Lawrence Welk and John Wayne salute," author William Petersen observed in *Those Curious New Cults*, a typical paperback priming Christians to confront the seventies explosion of challenges to the Gospel. For months, the Moonies—largely white and middle-class—had knocked on doors all over New York City and plastered the Bronx with slick posters. They invited America lovers to a spectacle at Yankee Stadium. Their Father smiled against a waving flag, his arm raised in a peculiar, vertical salute—to whom was unclear. "If you look at the poster, he's mimicking Hitler," says Donna Collins, the daughter of senior British church leaders. She was six in 1976, a child who still bounced on the lap of Moon, a grandfatherly figure who she says had little patience for the meek or wretched. "He's not the Dalai Lama, Mother Theresa type of leader," she says, "but a Mao, a Kim Jong-Il."

On the afternoon of June 1, 1976, wind blew red, white, and blue balloons over the ballpark. The Moon campus newsletter *Rising Tide* had warned of "Radical Marxist Leninists Seeking to Co-opt Bicentennial." But to the relief of the Moon Children, tens of thousands streamed in. Relief overcame the exhausted disciples, and they brushed from their faces rainwater and tears.

A summer thunderstorm whipped across the infield, crumpling a giant sign exalting Moon's "Bicentennial God Bless America Festival." With a confident smile, Moon took the stage to fireworks and a marching band that played "America the Beautiful." Above hung a banner in a gargantuan font size: "REV SUN MYUNG MOON—Principal Speaker." Behind his pulpit encircled in red, white, and blue bunting, he spoke in his usual style: striking the air with his hand, chopping and grasping and tilting his body, warning of the nation's subversion by Satan, a personal nemesis. "There are critics who say, 'Why is Reverend Moon so involved in America's Bicentennial? It is none of his business,'" he said. "Ladies and gentlemen, if there is an illness in your home, do you not need a doctor from outside?"

But to parents, the good doctor—despite the helpful image he made for himself by marching their sons and daughters around the Washington Monument for the Bicentennial, dressed like Revolutionary War heroes— had prescribed a pill with unconscionable side effects. The reasoning behind the titles of True Parents was that Mr. and Mrs. Moon were a superior replacement for our own flawed, biological parents. Their saintly portraits wobbled on the dashboards of Dodger-Chrysler sales vans on interstate highways, as the recruits inside cursed themselves for not reaching their daily targets of $75 to $100—meaning certain humiliation when they returned to HQ and were screamed at for betraying Father.

After the sun went down on the Washington Monument in 1976, according to a report in the conservative magazine *The American Spectator*, the leaders set afire a nearby vat with blood samples from 2,100 members to ensure "Father Moon's success in America." ("It worked!" joked writer Andrew Ferguson.) " A shameless blasphemer," *National Review* editor Richard Brookhiser wrote at the time, "[Moon] says things about the United States that should not be said about any human creation."

To the believers, the oppression of the Roman Empire had literally returned, and Bob Dole, at that first hearing, was the voice putting Jesus out to death. "We got kicked in the gut on national TV," said Neil Salonen, the American church's leader, who had the glib manner and good looks of a fraternity president.

To congressional witness Ted Patrick, the swaggering Republican deprogrammer from the Chattanooga streets who claimed to have freed hundreds from cults, Moon was running a timeworn ghetto hustle on naive white youth. Patrick alleged that the group had wedded the totalitarian mind-set of Communist China to the old tricks of Father Divine—the Harlem preacher who claimed to be God, gave sermons in made-up words ("physicalize"), and convinced poor blacks to fund his life of luxury. The church considered the renegade Moon foe a monster. "Man," Patrick jived to a *Washington Post* reporter in 1979, "you get that Neil Salonen, he's the president of the whole Unification Church, and I'll deprogram his ass in front of the whole FBI, if they want it that way."

That was when Dole had assailed the Unification Church for a second time, in 1979. This time Salonen tried to leave a better impression, the church having been continually under investigation by Washington since 1976. Outside the Russell Senate Office Building, Moon's squad of musicians blew into tubas and French horns. They struck up the protest anthem "We Shall Overcome." They called themselves Go World and played, they said, because their Father had stressed the importance of music. Mrs. Moon had picked out the cream-and-red uniforms—the reverend's color vision was not so good. Forrest Wright, head of the band, had been humbled at a leader's breakfast when the True Father looked his way and asked, "What American musician was best?" "John Philip Sousa," Wright managed to say. "OK," Moon had said, "some kind of John Sousa band." And Wright buzzed with it all along the Amtrak trip south to Manhattan.

On the Hill, Moon supporters, including pro-Moon parents, wore red carnations, shouted "liar" at witnesses, and said Dole and Sen. James Buckley (R-NY) were using Congress "to stifle religious freedom." The impetus behind Dole's new hearing was the murder of Rep. Leo J. Ryan (D-CA). Another new church had slain the first and only House member to be killed in the line of duty.

Ryan, fifty-three, was a liberal reformer with a flair for rolling up his sleeves to confront social problems—poverty, prison conditions, animal cruelty—firsthand or undercover. Constituents came to him for help with a new controversy: relatives who had given their bodies and bank accounts to sects. Ryan took notice. After the worried parent of a Scientologist appealed for help, Ryan, a former English teacher, wrote back: "It's too bad there isn't a 20th century Charles Dickens to write about the terrible destruction of these 20th century [F]agins who make themselves rich while they destroy the psyche of so many."

Ryan also sat on a House panel probing the ambitious Washington goals of the Reverend Sun Myung Moon. His own interest was the breakdown of families, while his colleagues dug into Moon's web of connections to power. On Halloween 1978, their disquieting findings rolled off the government printing press.

Weeks later, Ryan lay dead on a jungle airstrip. He had been ambushed during a fact-finding trip to Guyana, where another, unrelated seventies savior had built a doomed paradise.

Jim Jones was a white preacher who claimed to be the reincarnation of Father Divine. He had ingratiated himself with Willie Brown and other liberal San Francisco politicians before picking up stakes, in a fit of paranoia, and moving his interracial church to the Latin American jungle. One day Ryan arrived to investigate conditions. On the way back to his plane, the congressman was riddled with bullets by gunmen working for Jones. By now Jones had already convinced nine hundred believers to drink cyanide Kool-Aid.

In subsequent footage of the colony dead, bodies lay beneath speakers on poles that had blared Jones's ravings and now were silent. The dead slumped underneath a sign of Jones's, on which was written, "Those who do not learn from history are doomed to repeat it." It was a message the experts took literally, casting a suspicious eye on groups from the Moonies to the Hare Krishnas for signs of the next mass suicide.

Psychologists scrambled to explain the authoritarian magic of extracting total loyalty from young Americans. One explanation was that in a jaded 1978, the leaders promised something irresistible—that it wasn't too late for a new Summer of Love, when the world could be saved overnight by youth and devotion. Jackie Speier, an aide to Ryan who had been wounded by gunfire, took the stand to tell Dole the new groups preyed on "the breakdown of the family unit."

"The major religious cults in the United States show surprising similarities," she said. "They offer a ready-made substitute family coupled with a very strong charismatic leader acting as a father figure who has the ability to mesmerize his followers." Other speakers drew comparisons between Moon's recruiting tactics and the theory of Communist "thought reform" articulated in 1961 by psychologist Robert J. Lifton. His study of Communist China found that if you cut someone off from friends and family, limit information, permit only "thought-terminating clichés," and teach that the outside world is satanic, you can remake a mind. At the Dole hearings, critics alleged that cult leaders were reshaping recruits using the methods Lifton had identified.

At Booneville, California, and other retreats, Moon's chieftains sought to create little kingdoms of tightly controlled belief, in which newcomers were intentionally surrounded by like-minded cheerleaders, bombarded with guilt, and denied privacy. ("I do not know about outside world," the wife of *Washington Times* corporate president Doug Joo would tell a reporter in 1997.) Ex-Moonies spoke of being taught Heavenly Deception, the doctrine of lying for God, and Love Bombing, the reliance on the most potent of drugs: the feeling of being appreciated for who you are. Replying to criticism of the latter tactic, a church spokeswoman said, "Anybody who's down on love has a serious emotional problem."

The headlines screamed. "What's behind the Spaced-Out Look"; "Escape from the Moonies"; "Mom Warns of Moonie Perversions." But the church said Moon was being crucified by the liberal media bias of hip writers who sniggered at clean-cut, anti-Communist, worshipful young people. Meanwhile, members of Moon's Mobile Fundraising Teams (MFTs) slept few hours in vans that criss-crossed the country. They scrounged for food. They woke to spend day and night selling enough carnations to make their sales goals. The church asked its critics, Was this any worse than Marines training?

Graduation from the sales force brought with it the tantalizing prospect of joining Father's extended family through arranged marriage. Much has been made of how many pairs were mixed-race, though the inner 36 Families have never admitted a black or a white. Wearing a crown at his huge religious rallies, Moon promised to lead his sons and daughters out of the fallen world, his sidekick Col. Bo Hi Pak's English translation echoing into the bleachers. The children marched. Every step cleansed a thousand years of satanic history, it was believed. Every year, Moon claimed to restore some new component of the universe—right a wrong, repair a family value.

Control of sex was big. After the wedding, newlyweds were commanded to remain apart for months or years in preparation for their first sexual encounter. Moon believed that painstaking techniques were necessary for the "blood exchange" that would prevent a repeat of the Garden of Eden. It's not in the Bible, but Moon's revelation to believers is that Eve *misused the love organ* by fornicating with Lucifer.

"We have to drain this Satanic blood, and fill it with God's blood," Moon said in 2002. Working up enough fury to harangue a stadium, he directed it at an intimate gathering of American teens in blue T-shirts. Sired under his plan, created by his pairings, they are expected to live sinless lives. This is all on video: a scene of harsh adult-child relations that could have been a scene in a Roald Dahl book. A pretty girl of about fifteen, her face uplifted as if hoping for mercy, watches as this visitor to our shores stands cocky, collar splayed open across his jacket, before a banner commending him, not them: "Congratulations, True Parents." Twice-married himself, Moon demands chastity. "We still have this fallen blood running through our organs," he says through a translator. "So we have to protect our love organ so that *no more* mistakes can be made there."

A furious command in Korean, then a waving of hands. The translation comes: "If you cannot make your mind and body united, you are *bound to Hell.*" Tears run down the girl's cheek. And the American teens chant a familiar formula along with the newspaper publisher:

True love!
True life!
True lineage!

Another girl, fifteen, sits up front, angry. Moon has been talking like that as long as she could remember: to make them feel unworthy, she thinks. She has drifted away from the church and only attended because all her friends were in the "Blue Shirt Mafia." But this will be the last harangue she comes to. Friends of hers have been shunned by the Family for having sex.

Impure sex, according to Moon, does worse than ruin people—it undoes God's work for generations. On Blessed Children World, an Internet forum for the Second Generation, one discussion is headlined, "*I cannot accept rape = fall.*" "Kill yourself before you ARE raped," posts a Moon teen. "Bite out your tongue and choke on your own blood if you need to. (No joke, that was in Father's speech from some time ago.) Anyhow, I know it sounds totally NAZI of us to say/think/believe such things." For at all costs, women in Moon's view must not relive the primal wrong, the perversion he sees as responsible for the Fall. "There is nothing more important than the new lineage," he says.

To produce sinless children in the 1970s and 1980s had required, of the parents, a group ritual of pain. Before their first sexual liaison, each parent had picked up a hefty wooden paddle, the "indemnity stick," and slammed their spouse three times on the hip. Some crumpled in pain. "When my husband hit me once, I thought, 'maybe I will go sit down now,'" member Betsy Jones recalls in an Internet testimonial. "He used to play baseball, you know. But I think it knocked something right out of me." One *Washington Times* editor reportedly had difficulty walking after a bat chastened her spine by mistake. The stick's scriptural justification is in chapter 32 of the Book of Genesis. Wrestling with Jacob, an angel hits him on the hip: a blessing. According to Moon, this episode pinpoints the Mars and Venus of the war between the sexes. "All men and women in human history have misused the hip bone," Moon says, "and thus man has resentment against woman, and woman against man."

The body of Unification Church thought—combining the filial loyalty of Confucius, the ancestor worship of Korean shamanism, the Book of Genesis, the Gospels, Taoist ideas about humans as microcosms of the solar system, and more numerology than the Nation of Islam—should not be mistaken for typical religious worship in South Korea—a country of forty-nine million Buddhists, nine million Protestants, and four million Catholics. But the "resentment" he speaks of, the *han*, speaks to a major cultural question in that country. The word describes a shared feeling of indignation and hurt at injustice on an epic scale. (That concept is satirized in the brilliant 2003 Korean black comedy *Save the Green Planet*, in which a serial killer suffers delusions of discovering the one alien gene, planted in human DNA, that has made everyone miserable since the dawn of history.) Moon's grudge is that Eve, then Jesus, John the Baptist, and other figures have successively disappointed the world—by failing to save it. "Since this resentment came about through woman," Moon explains of the paddling, "the man hits the woman first."

After the pounding—"The more you love your partner, the harder you will hit!" a Central Figure, or group leader, told former member Yolande Elise Brener—you have sex with the stranger Moon chose for you, in the positions Moon has dictated. This is to be done in front of his photograph and in a church building, if possible. "Men and women should not love each other in a position which brings suffering to God's heart," Moon says. "Father knows the result of that kind of love will be miserable. . . . Thus, there is no room for discussion here."

So: Woman is on top the first night, reenacting Eve's prideful crime. The last night, the man thanks her for "having me reborn as the sinless Adam." Then he climbs on top of her, regaining the domination God intended.

You must then cleanse your privates afterward with a church-supplied Holy Handkerchief dipped in Holy Wine: a mystery fluid believed to contain Moon's superior blood and physical essence. "Hang the handkerchief to dry naturally and keep them eternally," explain the instructions from the Blessed Family Department of the church, an office in Manhattan. "They must be kept individually labeled and should never be laundered or mixed up."

That way the Father will never be far from your minds and bodies. Your children, born without sin, will not need saving. In between sex acts, according to the instructions, you must "sleep in pajamas and nightgown. Do not have a physical relationship outside of the content of the ceremony." Before the rigidly controlled sex, you must separate from your partner for forty or more days of missionary work, depending on what rules the Father has determined for this round.

• • •

Novelist Don DeLillo, inspired by an old photo of Moon at a stadium—hanging his head low as if history lies heavy and sorrowful on his crown, the couples marching to him—begins his 1991 book *Mao II* with a Moon wedding, meticulously constructing the flat jargon of the movement's instructors: "Make a condition. Do indemnity." He uses the photo as a symbol of American life reshaped by something both new and prehistoric. "Here they come now," the book begins, "marching into American sunlight." For the novelist, the rows of brides and grooms mark the death of language, a hunger for group identity, and a chilly foreboding that "the future belongs to crowds."

That pang of disruption runs through Moon's 1970s press. A Montreal reporter rode along while family and friends plotted to restore a young, agnostic Jewish Canadian convert, Benji Carroll, to his former life. The new Benji was frightful to them. Now he refused to see them without a spiritual minder. His new family were the brothers and sisters of his sales force. On the highway, they pounded on the van walls, and he sobbed for God to erase his shameful weakness: "Get out, get out, Satan. Get out of my body, get out of my mind, Satan, Satan."

They kidnapped him, drove him to a safehouse, and stuck him in a room with a cult buster: Aylsworth Crawford "Ford" Greene III, whom the Moonies called the Servant of Satan. As if they needed another sign he lived up to the title, he was the godson of their enemy, Sen. James Buckley (R-NY) from the Dole hearings.

Like some hippie Bruce Wayne, the intense Ford Greene was born into privilege but wounded by past tragedies, so that he fought like a man with nothing to lose. Greene's socialite mother, Daphne, wife of a prominent San Francisco corporate attorney, kept boxes of files on the movement, which had claimed two of her children. There were reams: internal church handbooks, press clippings, and transcriptions from the Moon world of speeches given to his inner sanctum: "The world really is our stage," reads one. "The money is there, and I will earn that money. I will reap that harvest. And you will become soldiers, trained soldiers." And here the royal stenographer has appended, "[Applause]."

While his sister, Catherine Greene Ono, stayed in the movement, Greene walked out, his head spinning. He spent months afterward, he says, waking up in a panic, afraid of being the twentieth-century Judas. Then came what he calls his greatest failing. When the family kidnapped his sister in hopes of deprogramming her, she smashed a juice bottle, cut herself with a shard, and had to be hospitalized, giving her opportunity to rejoin the movement. Newspaper reports said church youth were regularly trained in such tactics.

No Republican, Greene is known today in San Anselmo, California, for the marquee on the building that is his law office, overlooking the main drag in this Marin County town, Sir Francis Drake Boulevard, and beseeching drivers to "defy evil Bushism." But his godfather, Buckley, was the older brother of conservative lion William F. Buckley, whose nephew is conservative media watchdog Brent Bozell III, who would one day sit on the board of a group funded by the Reverend Moon.

In 1978, supplementing his antique dealership, Greene, a commanding presence, charged a flat fee of $750 per mind. Carroll's was his thirty-eighth and one of his toughest—maybe even too intelligent to crack, he wondered. "Love me, Benji," Greene challenged him, forehead to forehead. "Love Satan." He began a cross-examination:

> Your eyes are vacant, your veins are sticking out, your pupils are dilated and your skin is pale. . . . How is selling flowers to a penniless old woman helping to save the world from selfishness? . . . You think you're learning to love . . . but actually you're learning to hate! Hate sex, hate your family, hate yourself . . . all in the name of loving. What kind of *love* is that?

Finally, the ice crumbled: Carroll's parents were no longer Satan's minions but returned to being his loved ones. There were tears. "I feel . . . like my mind was wrapped in an elastic band," Carroll said. That story became the 1981 movie *Ticket to Heaven*, with *Sex and the City*'s Kim Cattrall as a perky recruiter for a thinly disguised re-creation of the Moonies. She leads childlike group bonding activities—"Choo-choo, choo-choo, POW!" the chant at Booneville went—breaking down Benji's resistance to the sermons about saving the world through fund-raising.

In 1982, Moon was convicted of tax fraud. "Obedience to the law of diminishing returns may cost this little king 18 months from his count-inghouse," *People* wrote in the magazine's roundup of the year's most intriguing people. He went to prison in 1984, around which time most people last thought about him.

There was not another Jonestown but instead a new line that the media had oversold the cult panic. The eighties brought backlash. Now it was said America had perpetrated an injustice on an unusual visitor, singling him out for being Asian and preaching unpopular beliefs. Voices from the Christian right and the civil rights movement alike stood at his side, often for a fee. And time forgot the most important part of his story: questions not of religion but of influence.

Continually asking the wrong questions, tying Moon to the fading memories of Jonestown, the media lost interest in Moon just as he was becoming, through an amazing metamorphosis, something more interesting than Jones II: Citizen Moon, Washington billionaire and empire builder. "He's a dynast," says Richard Barlow, a wry, learned Englishman who was among 1,800 couples married in 1975 and who directed church operations in the region of Arkansas, Tennessee, Oklahoma, Louisiana, and Mississippi before becoming disenchanted by the church in the 1990s. "He wants members to be there to serve him. . . . To commit suicide, like Jim Jones, is an admission of failure."

In retrospect, the differences between Jones and Moon might have suggested how divergent their fates would be. Jones was a preacher of modest means, without even an heir. But when Moon made the news in 1972, he already sat on the boards of eight companies in South Korea—heavy industry, ginseng, stone vases, titanium—a Dickensian empire of unpaid workers, living in dormitories and worshiping their own CEO.

Veteran journalist Bob Parry has spent years investigating the pipeline of unexplained foreign capital that has gushed into the *Washington Times* and conservative causes through the Unification Church. In the mid-1980s, Parry broke major parts of the Iran-Contra scandal as a reporter for the Associated Press and then *Newsweek*. Then, when Washington was ready to close the book on it, Parry persisted until he had a falling out with his bosses. The Reverend Moon scandal is another story no one will touch. Moon, writes Parry, "may have the distinction of being the most unusual person ever to gain substantial influence in the U.S. capital."

• • •

Since 2003, as a freelance magazine writer looking for a fun story, I had been trying to understand what it meant when the Reverend Moon boasted that "in the Republican establishment, the only hope for them is to unite with Father." I hoped to find an answer in the gigabytes of videotaped sermons and reprinted Moon speeches online.

What was hardest to reconcile was the gentleness of the people I encountered who were drawn to the church—among the most scholarly, idealistic, and humble I've met—with the harsh tenor of Moon's speeches. On the one hand, fallen-away member Matthew Lohmann tells me, on a walk past the World Trade Center site one day with his two teenage daughters, that he's nevertheless grateful to Moon. "He helped me start a family," he says. Moon's apostles take his command to "live for the sake of others" as a call to be better people.

On the other hand, the American devotional newsletter the *Unification News* reprints one speech after another in which Moon is vowing to pulverize the American system of government. "If the Clinton administration fails to unite with Father, then it will go down the drain," Moon had rumbled in the 1990s. Instead of distancing themselves, various politicians smile and are photographed at his events.

One moment you are reading about Senator Hatch or members of the Bush clan dropping by to give their regards, for the umpteenth time in some cases. The next, Moon is taunting George H. W. Bush, bragging about the power of his *Times* to humiliate his enemies and musing about destroying Western democracy—a system of government, as we learn, that is detested by God. One day in 1999, Damian Anderson, a fervent follower, asked Moon what would happen when the new century came. Moon, according to movement site www.unification.net, "said that he has been criticized a great deal for saying that the era of democracy will end, but it is true. I asked, 'What will replace democracy?' He said, 'It will be some kind of system based on the ideal of the True Family.'" "After the demise of communism and the destruction of democracy," Moon had similarly said in 1997, "all that will remain will be the True Family and True Children system, centered upon True Parents. That is what is happening now."

During the 2000 Gore-Bush recount standoff, Moon told a crowd the "rest of the world is laughing"—and not just at the Florida butterfly ballots but at America's "headstrong, modernized women, who just go after excitement. . . . They may appear attractive, but they are rotten because of the practice of free sex," he told a crowd. "I know how dirty American young women are." His son, Hyo Jin, crows in a 1992 sermon that by blessing Moon events, Senator Hatch and others are helping the church "take dominion over the world" so that "we could cook up the whole country" and "no one would mess with us."

Then there are the R-rated speeches that it is surprising to find in the world of family-values politicians. Moon orders Moonie men to punish their penises ("Keep pliers . . . and when you go to the bathroom, once a day, pinch your love organ. Cut the skin a little bit as a warning," he said in 2001) and claims that all spouses have failed to understand which of them is "owner of the love organ." Could Dr. James Dobson get away with this?

At a 1996 event in Buenos Aires, reported by Reuters, Moon followed up on remarks by the forty-first president (who had put in a highly paid appearance) by asking the crowd to ponder the questions "Why do sexual organs exist?" and "When you defecate, do you wear a gas mask?"

The other political connections—were they all in the minds of his followers? Then again, what kind of religious fantasy involves "key congressional committee leadership posts"? The phrase pops up in recent remarks by top church official Chang Shik Yang, who asserts that lawmakers in said posts "respect True Father's vision and understand America's responsibility."

Miles and miles of hot rhetoric, some of it dating to the early seventies, filled the archives: "If the U.S. continues its corruption, and we find among the senators and congressmen no one really usable for our purposes," Moon had said, "we can make senators and congressmen out of our members."

When word came through a Moon e-mail list that Moon had been crowned the King of Peace before members of Congress, I scoured the movement's Web sites for pictures. Moon's Web sites teem with sights and sounds—just one is puckish former vice president Dan Quayle toasting Moon at his eightieth birthday party, in 2000. He joins Moon in wishing for a century of "true love."

I found, on a Japanese site, a scene out of a David Lynch movie. Against a barren backdrop, a Tokyo church leader described, in halting English, an auspicious development: "a Crown of Peace ceremony at Dirksen Senate Office Building." All that was missing were the red curtains from *Twin Peaks*. The first sight of the rites themselves turned up on a Korean-language Web site. I couldn't read anything but the dates. I dug into the source code for a March 23 URL, which directed me to another URL, and then—I was watching members of Congress bow to the Reverend Moon, a sight that would make the evening news on three major networks. But why? If it was an embarrassing duty to report the *what*, it would be even more awkward to explain the *why*.

TWO

George H. W. Bush and the Desperate Widows

I have come to understand Rev. Sun Myung Moon's idea of peace by partici-pating in a Divine Principle seminar. After coming to know the true identity of Satan, I fell into a deep rage. How could this fact remain hidden as a secret throughout history?

—Warren G. Harding,
twenty-ninth president of the United States
(according to the Reverend Moon)

All the world's a stage, and every country has its role to play, in the scrip-ture of the Rev. Sun Myung Moon. His system of thought casts Korea in the part of the "Father Nation" and points out that it resembles a man's loins, dangling out from the Asian mainland in the direction of Japan, the "Mother Nation," a chain of islands arching away from Korea like a shy lover.

The United States he designates as the "Elder Son Nation," for our younger nation owes its life, he preaches, to the Father who has be-queathed it with a newspaper, moral guidance, and a river of cash to the religious right. Some of that money may flow from the church's invest-ments in Latin America or the $1,200-a-head stadium weddings in Korea that can bring in a tidy $24 million per event. But much of it unmistak-ably originates in Japan, which the church has long acknowledged as a cash cow. "Japan is mother and wife," church spokesman Masuo Oe said in 1996. "So Japan has the mission to support her husband and raise her children."

So let us detour briefly from Capitol Hill to a scene in Japan in April 1988, during George H. W. Bush's run for president. We are in Fukuoka, a southern metropolis where a bereaved mother is attending a séance.

A seer, the Great Teacher Nagayoshi, is concentrating before a statue of Maitreya, the future Buddha, and with great strain, he says, the father of her child is coming into focus.

"Your husband is descending," the Great Teacher says. "I can see your husband's body suffering in Hell. I cannot stop myself from shaking," the teacher says, now really racked with emotion. "Your husband is saying he wants you to donate five million yen."

When her husband had died of a heart attack in the fall, the housewife could not have guessed that half a year later he would return from the Beyond to ask for the equivalent of $40,000. That winter, she and her daughter were alone and distraught. Then one day a visitor knocked on her door, a stranger who extended the deepest of sympathies and persuaded the lonely widow it would be best for her morale to get out of the house and see an art exhibit across town together.

So the new friends strolled the gallery. Then the friend asked the widow, Why not spoil yourself and buy a painting? "That one would look perfect in your child's room," she told the widow. The widow hesitated at the price tag—about $1,600—but felt it would be rude not to play along. So she agreed, the friend beckoned the sales staff, and the widow wired the cash to a mysterious company—Miyabi Co., Ltd.—whose name was the Japanese word for *refined, courtly elegance*, the quality found in those with a discriminating eye for color.

The friends began watching movies together, films with an afterlife theme, and the widow fretted about whether her own husband would migrate into heaven or hell.

In spring, cherry blossoms bloom in Japan, and thoughts turn to the fragility of life. It was then that the widow (Plaintiff A, as she would be known for privacy) learned through the friend of a rare chance to meet a supposedly revered Buddhist sage, Nagayoshi, who could ease her fears about her husband's fate. When she hesitated to pay the five million yen to the Great Teacher Nagayoshi, the guru left the room, troubled.

"Hang in there," her new friends told her after she offended the Great Teacher Nagayoshi. "Just believe."

She did. But when she returned home, doubts nagged, so she phoned up and refused to pay the money, until they convinced her that the screams of the damned would fill her sleep. She relented. So now they helped her violate banking rules by claiming the huge withdrawal was for an insurance policy. She then laid the cash at the feet of the Maitreya statue.

Soon Plaintiff A met a second "great teacher," this one offering her a special deal on a "holy trinity" of religious items, including a Maitreya statue she could call her own and two sets of Catholic rosary beads, for just twelve million yen. She was also persuaded to enroll in classes in the Divine Principle of the Rev. Sun Myung Moon, newly revealed to be the guiding light behind her spiritual journey. Soon the Moon disciples told her that the dead husband was requesting yet another fifty million yen from beyond the grave but would settle for thirty million—the payout on his life insurance policy.

An argument broke out. They weren't making this up, a Moon priestess named Endo insisted emotionally. Endo whipped out a chart demonstrating, as plain as day, that the "the karma of sexual lust" had fouled the family legacy and that in her stinginess she was willing to watch as her husband's family name, built for generations, went up in smoke. "Your daughter's life, too, will be taken," the Moonists said. And now the widow hesitated. "I will do it," she finally said, and they cried in thanks but suggested the widow keep quiet about the money, or else "Satan would close in." Soon, at a shopping center parking lot, outside a retail shop called Goody, she approached a parked car and handed over the cash.

But later, as Plaintiff A considered her free gift—a photo of the *Washington Times* publisher and his wife in a pose of beatific matrimony—she felt ripples of doubt. Would her husband have wanted his life insurance payout given to Moon? In 1989, she hired an attorney and learned that her case was one of tens of thousands like it, sometimes with an element of physical coercion.

No fewer than three hundred lawyers from across Japan had banded together to prosecute the cases the press was calling the "Spiritual Sales" and the attorneys were calling an ambitious, well-orchestrated swindle.

Right here in Fukuoka, a sickly, solitary widow they were calling Plaintiff B had been informed by fast-talking fortune-tellers that she had only until midnight to save her family by stripping herself of the corrupting influence of money: "Heaven is saying two million yen," a soothsayer named Gondo revealed.

The lawyers called it a scam on a large, concerted scale, targeting the vulnerable to feed the Unification Church's hunger for cash. On May 27, 1994, a judge in Fukuoka District Court ruled that Plaintiff A was a victim of fraud and ordered the Japanese arm of the church to return thirty-six million yen.

Moon's church in Japan claims that voluntary "donations" make up the bulk of its Japanese annual profits, which have reached as much as $400 million a year. Between 1987 and 2006, the lawyers say, the victims who've come to them may have lost far more than that. In a country where the people are traditionally hesitant to take disputes to court, the lawyers have registered 13,898 complaints, with tens of thousands more reaching Japan's consumer affairs bureau.

The Japanese Supreme Court held the Moon church liable for fraud in several cases. But Takashi Yamaguchi, a Tokyo lawyer, says lawsuits haven't slowed the missionaries. "They are probably making about thirty to forty billion yen a year," he claims. The church denies wrongdoing, and a Tokyo spokesman told the *Washington Post* that the lawyers were compromised by the "existence of satans standing behind the Japanese Federation of Bar Associations."

●　●　●

In the fall of 1995, King Moon's lucrative Japanese empire risked unraveling. Two years earlier, *The Tragedy of the Six Marys*, a sordid tell-all from a Korean War–era comrade of the reverend, had arrived on bookshelves with a scandalous claim: the Unification Church started as a sex cult in which a man could be reborn as "Perfect Adam" by sleeping with six women. The aged author retracted his story under pressure from the church, but it had left lasting damage. However, it would be the events of March 20, 1995—Japan's version of the Jonestown Massacre—that stoked national rage against Moon and his followers.

Aum Supreme Truth, an unrelated sect whose guru was similarly obsessed with the migration of souls, had poisoned Tokyo commuters with nerve gas, poisoning five thousand and killing twelve. "Our Japanese movement has undergone the most incredible persecution because of the Aum Truth Church," said Col. Bo Hi Pak, Moon's bespectacled first officer.

Because of Moon's status as an American tax felon, he was sometimes barred from the country. In 1992, the same year that George H. W. Bush threw up on the Japanese prime minister, a kingpin of the Japanese right, Shin Kanemaru, pressured the Justice Ministry to let the Moonie leader in. Now, in 1995, to ensure that the pipeline of bills across the Pacific flowed on, the Moons scheduled a series of high-profile rallies at the Tokyo Dome and other arenas and hired an impressive spokesman.

• • •

The three hundred lawyers begged George H. W. Bush not to keep his date with Mrs. Moon on September 14, 1995, at the "big egg," as the Japanese call the translucent, futuristic baseball park. Their protests went unheeded. The litigators were "angry," says Yamaguchi, "but not surprised considering the relationship between Bush and [the] *Washington Times*." Posters went up proclaiming that at the Dome, "Love Will Save the Earth." The fliers didn't mention Moon's church but advertised the event under the banner of the Women's Federation for World Peace (WFWP), an unheard-of group summoned into existence by the Reverend and Mrs. Moon.

The theme: protecting children. Fifty thousand ticket holders filed into the Tokyo Dome, having paid between $80 and $196, meaning over $5 million minus expenses, rolled in with the Bushes' help.

The Japanese weren't the only ones to issue what the lawyers had called an "urgent plea for nonattendance." Bush also defied a coalition of

American mothers, led by Cynthia Lilley of MOM (Mothers Opposed to Moon), whose family had been traumatized when her daughter Cathryn ran away with the Moonies. " They use the films" of politicians and Moon together, she said, "to reassure parents that it's okay that their children are on the streets selling flowers 18 hours a day." During the tour, the newswoman Barbara Walters had canceled her own scheduled appearance. "[W]hen I found out it was associated with the Rev. Moon," she said, "I turned down the appearance . . . and will no longer appear at their events." (The rallies had also featured actor Christopher Reeve and Martin Luther King Jr.'s widow, Coretta Scott King.)

Walters's example was not followed by George H. W. Bush. When reporters for major newspapers presented him with evidence he was helping Moon, his Houston spokesperson, Jim McGrath, would hear none of it. "The sense the Bushes have," McGrath said, "is that these are about family and about building bridges of friendship between the Japanese and the American people." Bush, he said, "strongly believes in the mission of the group." And Bush himself told the *Washington Times*, "Until I see something about the Women's Federation that troubles me, I will continue to encourage them." When that day came, the reverend's roulette wheel of names for his traveling show would have spun, allowing President Bush to accept an innocent-sounding invitation from Moon's "Family Federation for World Peace."

At the Tokyo Dome, Bush stood to applause and gave a canned speech. High time, he said, for U.S.-Japan "bashing" to stop. Minutes after the president walked off the stage, the wig came off the event. "I sincerely encourage you to seriously study my husband's teachings," Mrs. Moon told the throngs of the Dome, explaining that God had permitted the Returning Lord to "stand on top of the world."

The Dome kicked off a series of six Bush-Moon stops in Japan, including one on Kyushu, the island where Plaintiff A had been bilked. In the summer of 1996, after the group swapped its old name for a new one, the forty-first president cheerfully attended, along with ex-president Gerald Ford and the top-billed Reverend Moon himself. Reuters also reported that Bush surfaced with Moon in Argentina, where he was filmed praising Moon for publishing a paper that "brings sanity to Washington."

• • •

The sight of the American president subordinate to a Korean religious leader won over the Japanese, in the view of Moon's sworn sidekick, Colonel Pak. "The people of Kyushu were flabbergasted at Father and Mother's power to tell a U.S. president what to do and plan his schedule," he said from behind a pulpit in New York on January 2, 1996. The Japanese, Pak explained, had a national inferiority complex and could be bowled over by "anybody with a big nose and blue eyes who speaks perfect English," so that the visit "completely changed the attitude of the Japanese government and media towards the Unification community."

Until he was replaced in his capacities by rival Chung Hwan Kwak, Pak, in his trademark horn-rimmed glasses, was second to no one but Moon in directing church operations around the globe. Having pledged body and soul to Moon, it was Pak who defended Moon before a hostile panel of U.S. congressmen in the 1970s, bursting into tears with conviction and grief. Those who have encountered Pak have called him a tiger, a gentleman, zealous, magnetic, stern, theatrical, sincere, capable, and manipulative, with an uncanny ability, one journalist recalled, to make you feel as if you have committed a discourtesy. His admirers include Gen. Alexander Haig, Reagan's first secretary of state, who calls Pak a "longtime friend," "noble," and committed to "a better world for all mankind" in the foreword he wrote to Pak's volume of collected speeches, *Truth Is My Sword*, its book jacket the color of blood. Former disciple and *Times* reporter Glenn Emery calls him "one of the sweetest people I have ever met." Yet one journalist remembers Pak as "kind of a creepy guy"; during a long investigation, the journalist and a colleague would phone one another up, taking turns pretending to be Pak.

Meanwhile, according to reports in major newspapers, Pak has been tortured by mysterious South Korean kidnappers in 1984; beaten bloody by a church psychic in 1987; and sent to prison, between 2004 and 2006, over a real estate deal gone bad. He has also been called the brains behind the rise of the Unification Church from a shanty in war-torn Pusan, Korea, to a modern Pacific Rim conglomerate.

The church maintains different faces in America, where the power is, and Japan, where the money is. Stateside, having learned hard lessons about public relations, the Moonies have lowered the intensity of their recruitment drives, averting such debacles as the 1993 *Today Show* piece "Cathryn's Story," in which an NBC TV crew filmed heartbroken mom Cynthia Lilley, forbidden to see her daughter at a Moon dorm (see chapter 3). But if American headlines no longer tell of American youth whipped into fervor as money-raising dervishes shouting "Smash Satan," Asian reports continue to describe a pressure-cooker environment in which sales teams meet astonishing quotas with a frenzied dedication. "Crazy for God," one churchman calls Moon's fever pitch.

In Japan, the Unification Church has also founded a counterpart to the *Washington Times*: the *Sekai Nippo*. Just as the *Washington Times*'s editors are nostalgic for segregation (see chapter 3), the *Nippo*'s apparently pine for the invasion of Manchuria. With ties to Japan's own far right, the paper has advanced such slogans as "exporting weapons is moral." Editor Seojima Yoshikazu, an ex-Moonie, resigned and wrote a 1984 tell-all article, "This Is the Secret of the Unification Church," only to be wounded by an unknown man with a knife. According to Seojima, the church explicitly pressured the Japanese to raise money for the *Washington Times*, a newspaper he called "the top priority of the entire Unification Church worldwide" for its access to American politicians. Back then, he said, $2.5 million a month in Japanese income was so earmarked.

The 1995–1996 Bush-Moon tour also found the odd couple taking their show to Washington; Asian disciples paid as much as $11,260 for the privilege of tagging along. During the tour, George and Barbara Bush were photographed presiding casually over a birthday cake with red, white, and pink candles that was being sliced for the True Mother. Looking on was Colonel Pak, smiling. Barb, according to the church's enthusiastic reports, went so far as to join a "Bridge of Peace" ceremony in which she hugged a Japanese lady, one Mrs. Sugiyama, to heal scars of World War II. The church claims to have made "sisters" of twenty thousand women in this fashion, encouraging "sincere repentance for wrongs in the past . . . centered on heart," in the clunky jargon of Moon. Bush, as if remembering his time on the aircraft carrier USS *San Jacinto*, "had tears in his eyes," asserted longtime member Betsy Jones in a 1996 account.

In Illinois, the estranged mother of a Unification Church recruit wrote to Jack Kemp, Bob Dole's running mate that year, pleading with him to stop attending Moon events. "I just wanted to let you know that I agree with you," Kemp replied, and he promised to break off his affair with the True Father. Then he took $52,000 to speak at three more Moon events. His conservative policy group Empower America, formed with Reagan education secretary Bill Bennett, was shortly thereafter headed by Josette Sheeran, a longtime church VIP recently tapped by the George W. Bush administration to direct the UN World Food Program.

• • •

Just who is taking advantage of whom in the ongoing relationship between America's favorite Republican family and the Moon clan? If the elder Bush has put one over on the True Father with his many gestures of support, it would be in keeping with the treatment of evangelical Christians, in the view of David Kuo, the younger Bush's disgruntled former faith-based czar. His recent book *Tempting Faith* accuses Karl Rove of seducing religious folk for cash and support, while privately disdaining them as "the nuts."

Even so, a mold is broken by the gracious lengths to which George H. W. Bush has been willing to go for Moon, all the while being the butt of the reverend's humiliating insults. Southern Baptists repay their debts to the GOP by selling *Faith in the White House* DVDs and urging that a Prayer Shield hallow the younger Bush. But the *Times* publisher has a different style. On February 21, 1991, in the last week of the Gulf War, Moon went to the New Yorker Hotel, his dingy landmark in midtown Manhattan, and rhymed, "Push Bush!"

He continued. "Father always said from the beginning that [George H. W.] Bush doesn't have a trunk, so he has no guts. So somebody has to push Bush," he said. "Who can tell Bush what to do? . . . The only one who will say 'Bush, do this' is Reverend Moon." Months later the *Times* owner was claiming to have received a plaque from Bush on the occasion of the Gulf War victory, "giving thanks to God," in what Moon decided was a gesture of gratitude for his advice.

Moon's checkbook had produced tidy sums over the years, mostly not directly to politicians but to the political scaffolding behind them. During the 1988 campaign, he gave $5 million to help found a $15 million conservative coalition, the American Freedom Coalition, which sent out thirty million political mailings in 1988 and staged marches in support of the first Iraq war. On the board sat Richard Viguerie, the "founding funder" of the Reagan revolution.

Four years on, as if unhappy with the service he purchased, the reverend lashed out. On December 6, 1992, one month after Bill Clinton won the election, Moon grew disheartened that President Bush had failed to get on board with specific proposals that would have glorified the Unification Church. For example, he said, he'd asked Bush to sign one simple proclamation naming Korea "the eternal country of peace," supreme over 160 other nations. "But Bush didn't listen and he rejected my idea, which was God's will," the *Washington Times* publisher said or imagined. "Where is he now? He is out of office." The only explanation for Clinton's victory, he said at another appearance, was that the United States "has been turned into almost a model nation for Satan."

•   •   •

Today, Moon's Japan crisis has passed, thanks to help from Bush and others, and his Japanese operation survives. It has even weathered the 1997 Asian economic crisis. In 1998, Elliot Abrams, a pardoned Iran-Contra felon who became George W. Bush's deputy national security advisor, was listed as a guest at rallies held in Brazil by the church's "International Coalition for Religious Freedom." Abrams, the movement's old ally in the Cold War mischief of the 1980s (when Moon created CAUSA, essentially a networking organization for Latin American anti-Communists), spoke to cheers.

A program for the conference laid "urgent contemporary issues" on the table. Roughly paraphrased, they were as follows:

1. Moon still banned from European nations due to criminal treaties

2. Worried Japanese hiring "deprogrammers" to snatch over two hundred Moonists in Japan a year—government letting it happen

3. Reverend Moon banned from Japan

And number 4: "A continuing atmosphere of prejudice and suspicion against Unificationists as 'cultists,' fed by hateful stereotypes and media sensationalism."

• • •

The financial power behind the Republican newspaper continues to innovate. A 2006 Japanese TV report revealed that Moon clerics were snagging Japanese tourists at Inchon International Airport in Korea, then taking them on two-hour trips into the mountains, to Cheongpyeong Lake, east of Seoul, where Moon has built his final palace. The buildings here are the domain of his priestess, Hyo Nam Kim, lady of the Heaven and Earth Training Center.

It opened around 2006 in a shower of confetti and with a royal procession of limousines, women marching in pink, courtiers in tall hats, and King and Queen Moon in their crowns waving loftily, as shown on a

Korean Web site. Above, a mountain road wound to a domed building completed in 2005, the so-called Original Palace. There is something familiar about it, so that at first glance it leaves a peculiar impression on the eye. In a land of pagodas, it is neoclassical. In fact, it seems patterned after the U.S. Capitol dome. Go up Moon's faux Capitol Steps, and you stand beneath a rotunda that spirals away in magnificent imagery of the True Parents.

In the 1990s, a priestess assigned to a nearby training center began claiming to channel the soul of Mrs. Moon's mother, Dae Mo Nim. This advanced her considerably within the movement, so that children lined up to have their evil spirits liberated by her. Soon her channeling became a focal point of the church. On Mr. Moon's death, followers believe, he will dictate his orders through such spirit mediums.

The Japan News Network reported on June 11, 2006, that women lured to the site were shown the Hollywood afterlife fantasy *What Dreams Will Come*—to encourage them to consider whether their families might suffer in hell, like Robin Williams's dead wife in the film—and were repeatedly told their uterine health problems resulted from the spirits of Korean women raped under Imperial Japan, but they could be cured with cash payments (which reached $260,000 in one case) and arm-flapping exorcism ceremonies. An "Ancestors Liberation Blessing Form" provided by the center offers a complex payment scheme per ancestor freed from hell.

The cash continues to bless the Bushes. In 2003, $1 million dollars from church interests flowed into the George H. W. Bush Presidential Library, doubling the $1 million or more that the forty-first president took while visiting Japan, the United States, Argentina, and Uruguay with the Moon family in that Clinton-era speaking tour. Other Moon funds have gone to a business owned by presidential brother Neil Bush (see chapter 9) and to Bush family charities. In 2005, $1 million was donated for Hurricane Katrina relief via Moon's group, the IIFWP, through Bush's Points of Light Foundation. During the 2005–2006 fiscal year, the church gave another $100,000 to a Barbara Bush reading charity.

If the church has not completed its long-standing mission of winning a presidential pardon from the Bush family, it has, at least, coaxed tender moments of access from the powerful family. Michael Jenkins, the top American Moonie, claims astonishingly to have convinced the elder Bush on a visit to the presidential library at Texas A&M University to drink the church's "Holy Wine," without informing him of the cocktail's significance to Unificationists as a symbol of the Reverend Moon's blood and body.

The story is hard to swallow. But I'm watching Windows Media video of Jenkins preaching on May 20, 2007, and would welcome alternative explanations. From behind an IBM Thinkpad laptop, Jenkins, upbeat and wearing a spotted red tie, is sharing a secret with a giddy audience. One midnight, before Jenkins was to visit the Bush Sr. library with a gaggle from the Women's Federation, the phone rang. It was Moon. He had these orders: "Bring the holy wine. . . . Jenkins, you give the Holy Wine to President Bush."

Jenkins claims:

> When you give Holy Wine to someone, you've just changed their destiny.
> . . . We went to Texas, to the Library, [with] the Women's Federation and
> Rev. Kwak . . . and the moment came and I said, "Mr. President, these
> women . . . have a special presentation for you."
>
> He said, "What's this?" And they brought out two little cups of
> Holy Wine. . . . He took the two cups and he shook it, like "This is cute,
> what's this?"
> [The crowd laughs, anticipating.]
>
> Then I said, "It's a blessing for your family, Mr. President. We're
> ending divorce in America."
>
> He goes, "Divorce? Barbara and I aren't gonna get divorced! At
> this age!"
>
> "No, Mr. President, your family's a model. . . . Here." And we opened
> it for him.

Bush studies the unsettled liquid, as trepidation grows on the face of chief officer Chung Hwan Kwak that they have gone too far this time. The tension is unbearable. Jenkins hints again. Finally, the ex-president tells Jenkins, "Oh, this looks like communion. OK, so you want me to drink this?"

"*Yes!*" Jenkins says, sharing his turmoil—but then imitates Bush going *gulp*. "He drank it right down!" And the crowd goes wild at the coup. And remember, Jenkins reminds the flock, that "at the *Washington Times* gala [Bush] called out Father's name and praised Father and it made the front page of the *Washington Times*. . . . Times have changed, my brothers and sisters. We have come of age. We have the power. *We are the chosen people.*"

That, at least, is the yarn spun by Michael Jenkins on video. Secret Service protocol doesn't allow mysterious fluids down a president's throat. Days later, however, in a separate sermon in Korea, a Moon priest, Chang Shik Yang, was filmed delivering a PowerPoint presentation exhibiting Jack Abramoff–style photo ops, featuring not only Dick Cheney and George W. Bush (posing before evergreen trees with cherubic church president Chung Hwan Kwak and then with *Washington Times* president Douglas Joo—"As Koreans, does this not make you proud?" Yang says) but also a flock of ladies cozying up to Bush Sr. Yang once again mentions Texas A&M and notes that the women "received such special attention," before screening Moon's greatest hit, the 2004 Senate coronation.

A public relations person for the Bush Sr. library told me he "vaguely" remembered "a women's group having a luncheon here," but then he passed along my question to Bush's spokesperson, Jim Appleby, who said that "the Office of Former President Bush cannot justify such a ridiculous question with an answer."

The *New York Times*'s columnist David Brooks, who began writing for Moon's *Washington Times* in 1984 at the age of twenty-three, has called it a "bizarre assertion" that Moon "has been close to the Bush family." That contention is made in two recent books by former GOP insider Kevin Phillips, whom Brooks called an exemplar of the "paranoid style in American politics" for saying such things.

THREE

WHAT DOES GOD NEED WITH A NEWSPAPER?

They asked me how much it would take to get me. . . . I rattled off some crazy figures . . . and they said "sure." . . . But I figure I'm worth the price. Before I came, they didn't get invited to anything . . . they were persona non grata. . . . Now they're legit.

—HARRY J. STAPHOS OF THE NEW YORK DAILY NEWS,
AFTER JOINING A MOON PAPER IN THE 1970s

With the Washington Times as the core, we are establishing preeminence in the American print media. . . . By doing so we can include all fields of intelligence. Today we have in this area surpassed the liberal New York Times and Washington Post, and are continually gaining important confidential information not only from America but also from other governments all over the world.

—SUN MYUNG MOON,
QUOTED IN HIS UNIFICATION NEWS, DECEMBER 1986

"No one can completely control another person's mind," says Cathryn Mazer.

Rather than *brainwashing*, that word swirling with Manchurian Candidate fantasy, she prefers "undue influence" to describe what she fell under as a teenager. In 1993, her brother and mother Cynthia, a music teacher, turned to a private detective to track down the lost eighteen-year-old, accompanied by a crew from NBC's *Today Show*. The expedition brought them to the gates of the Reverend Moon's grandiose estate in upstate New York. Cynthia Lilley finally found her only daughter elsewhere, at a dormitory in the woods of northern Long Island.

When they got there, a follower of the *Washington Times* publisher answered the door—"You're Mom, right?" the young woman said—and then arranged a short audience with Cathryn. But the girl they encountered had drastically changed her priorities, newly fearful of betraying Moon. She could not go with them, she said. Outside, shut out, her family cried and called up to the window: "Cathryn, we love you."

Gordon Neufeld, a Calgary writer who spent a decade in the church, has his own way of describing the Unification Church's influence: "placing roadblocks in the mind." Thoughts such as leaving, he says, simply become too awful to contemplate.

The word *brainwashing*, for all its bad press, remains in the *Diagnostic and Statistical Manual,* the handbook for psychiatrists, in which it is associated with the mind-set of war prisoners. Whether the concept can be applied to an ultracontrolling religion is hotly debated among sociologists and other experts, some of whom have been financially rewarded by new religions even as they have ridiculed the "anticult" line as un-PC, un-American, unscientific. (Both Scientology and Unificationism, however, teach that people's minds *can* be controlled, respectively, by extraterrestrial spirits and Satan.)

One day, the pretty, dark-haired Cathryn had been walking Broadway in New York when a kindly couple invited her to complete a survey on God. They got to talking. The survey workers' exhibition of simple, forthright faith seemed like rain from heaven. Cathryn, who had lost a father and struggled with addiction, had been taught in Alcoholics Anonymous to go find a Higher Power to which she could surrender. But looking back, she calls those people recruiters for a cult. "If I had one ounce of sense in me," she says, "I would have known."

During her stay, her behavior changed. She swears that her politics did, too. She had never considered herself Republican, having grown up in a liberal Los Angeles household. And yet she found herself doing the strangest things after joining their Long Island camp: not just going hungry for God, taking twenty-minute-long showers to apologize for the Fall of Man, and selling pictures of clowns on the streets, but also joining a group prayer for Republicans to win midterm elections in 1994.

Hard to believe, but former regional church leader Richard Barlow finds it sadly typical. "Moon's take was that the Democrats were immoral," he tells me. " He goes on about secular humanism." Mazer remembers her new friends crying and yelling for the souls of the Spirit World to intercede against the party that had just retaken the White House after twelve years of Republican rule. "A little voice inside said, 'This is a cult,'" she says. "But more powerful was the fantasy that this might be an oasis for me."

• • •

The Clinton victory was no good thing in the eyes of the Reverend Moon. Though Moon would seek influence under any administration, the change swept the White House of long-nurtured connections. At Moon's training institute in Tarrytown, December 6, 1992, he decried the just-defeated Bush Sr. as "dog-like," and rued America. " Such a country should be destroyed," Moon said, according to a transcript prepared by the church. "It should never be respected."

In the years since his 1976 God Bless America Festival, the United States seemed to Moon to have betrayed his patient investment in it. Increasingly he spoke of America as "the kingdom of Satan."

Cathryn Mazer and other members were shown merry films on Moon and his photo opportunities with political allies. "For me it legitimized [Moon's] role in the world as a significant person," she says. With the endorsement of Bush, Dan Quayle, and others, Moon seemed less like a fringe figure and more like a Dalai Lama or Gandhi—someone she could be proud to join. She recalls watching "a lot of video reedited to make Democrats look really buffoonish and make Republicans look heroic."

During this era, the Moon church, which had risen to influence by campaigning against communism, was shifting gears to align with the right's new priorities: fighting a "Culture War" declared at the 1992 national party convention by candidate Pat Buchanan, ex–*Washington Times* columnist.

One figure who came under special attack was Hillary Clinton. In public life, the most powerful First Lady since Eleanor Roosevelt had been assailed for pushing Bill Clinton's universal health care plan. Father Moon and his aides had their own reasons to detest her. "They hated Hillary because she was not following the Divine Principle," Mazer says. She represented a "satanic reversal of the male-female role."

The Reverend Moon preached that until his arrival on Earth in 1920, no one understood the true place of man, woman, and child. Women must not reenact Eve's uppity behavior by doing things a man should do but rather submit to motherhood. To him, their sexuality is a dangerous force when unchained from God's plans. "A woman's reproductive organ is concave," Moon told the Canaan Baptist Church in Harlem on May 8, 2001, "like the wide-open mouth of a poisonous snake with fangs."

Mazer didn't stay in the church long enough to be assigned a husband but does remember begging for donations for Moon. The seed of manipulation, she says, was the abuse of her idealism. "It's not rocket science," she says. "'Push the guilt buttons. Make the little kid sell.'"

Her mom, Cynthia Lilley, finally pried her loose by hiring Steve Hassan, a licensed counselor and ex-Moonie youth leader, to talk her out of it. Then, in 1995, Lilley turned her attention to severing the first President Bush's relationship with the Returning Lord. Under the spell of Moon, she told the press, "the previously vibrant, curious, loving young woman had become robotic and cold and obsessed with protecting herself against me."

· · ·

What kind of national American newspaper is published by a man with a reputation for inspiring sudden personality change?

To find out, I take a taxi from Capitol Hill. Unlike visiting the *Washington Post*, which is five blocks north from the White House, trekking to the brick *Washington Times* HQ means a long trip through the drab slums of Washington Northeast to an outlying neighborhood known for tire stores, fast food, and poverty. The cab driver, a Jamaican immigrant who recalls the old mass weddings, is flabbergasted to hear who owns the newspaper.

We pull up to the curb of the converted paper warehouse on New York Avenue.

Nervously, I open the doors, which are done up in Italian travertine marble, and head into the fancy lobby, wondering if the *Times* will live up to what Moon says about his $20-million-a-year baby. He makes the newsroom sound as if it is one half intelligence agency, one half imperial fortress. "Many comfortable Washington political bureaucrats who have had their beautiful offices inside big marble buildings considered Reverend Moon and the Unification Church as insignificant as peanuts," he said January 1, 1983, months after the paper began publishing. "But now," he said, "they are reading it and trembling at the stories. They find themselves having to take advice from the *Washington Times*!"

I ask the receptionist if conservative TV personality Tony Blankley, or another *Times* editor, might be able to talk. She dials. I wait, eying an internal company directory that I hold in my hands. Incongruously, it lists Blankley side-by-side with projects of the Reverend Moon, including the Interreligious and International Federation for World Peace (IIFWP) that put on the Dirksen Senate Office Building coronation in 2004, and the Summit Council, which tends to the church's North Korean interests. The Moon groups are listed on the third and top floors.

Superficially, the place reminds me of my old paper, the *Modesto Bee*, only ritzier. There's the elevator to the newsroom, company swag in glass cases, and mounted blow-ups on the walls of notable editions. One front page plays up triumph in the Iraq war. One showcases a feature on Hollywood producers who are blinded by liberalism.

The editors won't talk. So I ask the lady to connect me to the Summit Council for World Peace, whose dealings with dictator Kim Jong-Il I'm investigating for *The American Prospect*, the liberal magazine. No luck. We try paging the IIFWP.

"Has Reverend Moon been here lately?" I ask while we wait. (I'd read of how Moon would show up at company dinners in a Rolls-Royce to ask his staff, "Do you like me? Some people don't like me. You don't like me, do you?" and asking if they would like to see more of him.)

"He was here a few months ago," she says, bored.

"Kind of a big deal. He says he's the Messiah."

"Mmm-hmmm."

Finally, after dialing another yet another Moon religious group in the building, I am accidentally connected to the World Media Association, which shares the number. It's been around since 1978, founded by the True Father—as he told a Senate panel in 1984 at the Dirksen, that same building where he would be fêted in robes twenty years later—"to set a standard of responsibility in the communications media." In a piece of PBS interview footage from 1984 that must be seen to be believed, then-*Times* corporate president Col. Bo Hi Pak, that most slavish of aides, describes how the WMA will help lower the boom on the Soviet Union.

"It is a total war," Pak says. "Basically a war of ideas. War of mind, the battlefield is the human mind. This is where the battle is fought. So in this war, the entire thing will be mobilized. Political means. Social means. Economical means and propagandistic means. And basically trying to take over the other person's mind. That is what the third world war is all about—the war of ideology."

The WMA has the same phone number as other groups. In the confusion, the woman on the phone seems to think that because I am a journalist, I must be here to learn about an upcoming luncheon—to be held here at the *Times* building. Asked what it's about, she says something about how news producers should become "not watchdogs but guide dogs." There must be a misunderstanding—doesn't everyone agree journalists are watchdogs? She says I'll understand after I see the flyer. She sends someone down.

The doors, through which a number of nondescript *Times* staffers have been passing this whole time, open to produce a middle-aged Caucasian lady with a long stare, as if she has been deep in meditation. She wants to give me the flyer but also to chide me for visiting the *Times* unannounced. After I repent, she hands me the invitation, and with an amazing document in hand I hop the famous "Lunar Shuttle," the employee bus, back through the slums to the Hill. In the shuttle has been posted a stern notice that the bus must not skip a single stop—by direct order of church official Douglas Joo.

The flyer reads:

WORLD MEDIA ASSOCIATION

"NEEDED: A NEW PARADIGM FOR NEWS."

It goes on.

> News is available through more media than ever before and for 24 hours a day. Yet much of it sounds the same. Are media giving people the facts they need? In the 21st century, is the media's traditional role of reporting 'facts' still relevant? Is it time for media to become 'guide dogs' instead of 'watch dogs?'

The logic of the World Media Association seemed to have sprung fully formed from the satirical mirror universe of comedian Stephen Colbert—the world in which truthiness trumps truth. In fact, it predated Comedy Central's *Colbert Report* by months.

DATE: Wednesday, May 25, 2005
ADMISSION FREE
12:00 Noon – 2:00 PM (Lunch provided)

PLACE: *The Washington Times* Auditorium
3600 New York Ave., NE

The flyer promises that experts will be on hand to address the news-sounding-the-same crisis, including Jan Schaffer of the respected Pew Center for Civic Journalism and a journalism professor from Howard University, and two Unification Church officials, Larry Moffitt and Michael Marshall, the chiefs of United Press International.

Rory O'Connor, producer of the 1992 *Frontline* documentary on Moon, soon phoned Schaffer to ask why she would grace such an event. "Clearly you have a point of view," she told him and hung up.

• • •

Surely Tony Blankley, the *McLaughlin Group*'s genial English explainer of Bush policy, would be able to make the pamphlet in my hands seem less mad—and to explain why the functionaries upstairs have claimed to use "our media power" (as the Reverend Jenkins has described it) as a bargaining chit in deals with Stalinist North Korea and other entities.

Blankley declined to answer questions. While employed by Moon, Blankley had recently completed a book, *The West's Last Chance.* In keeping with the paper's unkind view of immigrants, the book would issue the scary message that Muslims with WMDs and fertile wives might reduce white people to conquered slaves, subjugating Europe in ways the entire German and Soviet war machines had failed to achieve. (In 2007, Blankley left the *Times.*)

Not deigning to address the Moon issue, Blankley passed on the query to editor in chief Wesley Pruden, the force behind the paper's fierce defenses of all things Old South—and "all things" is not used lightly here. In the *Times*, the only major paper with a Civil War section, Pruden was the only editor to front-page the charge that PC liberals are out to tarnish the legacy of Confederate general Robert E. Lee—but stood virtually alone in burying news of Rosa Parks's death on October 24, 2005, letting it wait on the inside pages until days later.

"I have the editorial independence that Bill Keller of the *New York Times* or Len Downie of the *Washington Post* can barely imagine," Pruden said in a statement declining an interview. "Certain critics of the *Times* imagine that there's a magic key hidden in a magic banana hidden somewhere in the basement, that once found would open up all the secrets. There are no secrets."

• • •

Which is actually what is so strange. It has long been known to Washington insiders that this "lively conservative voice—at vast expense," as *Post* publisher Katharine Graham describes the *Times*, is Moon's gift. "Presumably," she writes in her memoirs, "its backers feel that their presence in the nation's capitol and access to the government are worth the price."

The paper has bled billions since its start in the 1980s, when spokespeople for the paper still clung to the story that the *Times* would become profitable. "I can see us being in the black . . . three years down the road," editor Arnaud de Borchgrave predicted in 1986. For years, naive media observers have seen the catastrophic sales figures and predicted downfall for the paper. Perhaps the *Times* will not survive to the publication of this book. But circulation has never been the point.

Though the *Times* has sunk to the third-place paper in D.C., behind the new *Washington Examiner*, its articles and commentators remain far more widely quoted—out of proportion to how few people actually want to read it. Even though *Examiner* publisher Phil Anschutz (net worth: $7.8 billion) is a Christian right activist whose op-ed page proudly swings right, the *Examiner*'s news coverage itself is calm, measured, and mainstream next to that of the *Times*, whose publisher Sun Myung Moon (net worth: unknown) funds obvious, spin-room crusading. A study by the *Columbia Journalism Review* in 1995 said "no major paper in America would dare be so partisan."

Take, for example, a June 11, 2007, story, "Suit to Decide Workplace ' Hate Speech,'" describing a case facing the Supreme Court. The story strongly suggests that the high court was considering whether "the words 'natural family,' 'marriage' and 'union of a man and a woman' can be punished as 'hate speech' in government workplaces." On closer look, the headline was a lie, and the story misleading, describing a vaguely interesting First Amendment case that had been ginned up to sound ominous. A group of Christians employed by the city of Oakland, California, claimed the management trod on their free speech rights by removing a pamphlet of theirs from a workplace bulletin board, in which they had alluded to their fight against gay marriage. But no one had been "punished," the lower courts merely having tossed out the Christians' case against the city of Oakland. And no one had invoked the concept of "hate speech" until an evangelical group, the Pro-Family Law Center, had come late to the case and issued a hysterical press release, dutifully written up in the *Times*.

• • •

The version in Moon's paper was soon arousing outrage in blogs, on conservative news sites, and on talk radio. That night, Fox News's Brit Hume reported in his "Political Grapevine" that the terms *marriage* and *union of a man and a woman* could be punished as "hate speech." Columnist George Will, on June 24, devoted a column to the idea that marriage itself could become "something akin to hate speech."

Stronger ripples were felt from the paper's coverage of the Mexican border. A 2006 study by the American Civil Liberties Union (ACLU), "Creating the Minutemen," analyzed 581 articles and editorials behind the hyping of the Minutemen Project, a small group of border watchers who took center stage in the national media, especially on Fox News, in 2005. The first reports that an army was forming to stop Mexican immigrants came in the *Times*, a paper credited by the ACLU with absurd exaggerations of the group's size—complete with predictions of a Minuteman air force. It swept a fringe movement into the media spotlight, transforming "a relatively small band of extremists into the armed vanguard of the anti-immigration movement." In reality, there were never more than two hundred minutemen, despite predictions in Moon's paper that as many as four thousand were on the way. TV producers and editors across the United States took cues from the *Times*, and Fox News Channel fell in love with the story that the Moon press had created.

• • •

There is a photograph in which young Craig Maxim, a handsome blond boy, is posing behind Moon's throne in the 1980s, as a favorite in the royal court. Today, living in Atlanta, he considers Moon a cult leader. He's a life-long musician who considers himself a small-government conservative. He says he's embarrassed by the media "stranglehold" of his old master. "On a daily basis just about any Christian radio station, on average several times a week, will quote the *Washington Times*," he tells me. "It just sickens me as a Republican and a Christian."

He used to sit at Moon's feet, believing he was as lucky as those who lived in the time of Jesus. He also remembers that Moon spit in someone's face at a wedding ceremony. Another time Moon raged at an autograph seeker for being in the bathroom when everyone else had their chance at his signature. "You lose," Moon shouted, dismissing everyone from sight.

Maxim and his mother, who introduced him to the church, served Moon as human exhibits of his influence on America: living, performing mannequins to impress visiting guests from afar. Dressed up in Korean robes, the twenty-year-old and his mom could sing the songs of the Fatherland, with perfect inflection, in the native tongue.

> *Arirang, Arirang, Arariyo . . .*
> *I am crossing over Arirang Pass.*
> *The woman who abandoned me here*
> *Will not walk even ten li before her feet hurt.*

When Maxim joined the church, already married, Moon had reassigned him a new wife, calling the old match satanic. The new woman's parents, alarmed by this matchmaking, snatched her from the group. Maxim, too, eventually left the church. It was not an easy decision—the church had taught him his family would pay the price for generations. He nevertheless protested outside Moon events with a sign: "Mom, Please Come Home." As if in revenge for Maxim's exit, he says, his mother was assigned a new, abusive husband.

When Maxim and other members go public with such incredible stories, Moon's apologists don't question their facts but their motivations.

"I'm not calling them liars," said spokesperson Phil Schanker on Fox News in 2000. " I believe that . . . Craig Maxim had a snapshot experience based on [his] own perspective, background." Schanker suggested Maxim couldn't handle an environment where "ideals were being expressed, high goals were being challenged." Online, Moonies call Maxim "bitter."

• • •

From John Podhoretz to David Brooks, a good many conservative commentators have done time at the training grounds of the *Washington Times* before attaining national prominence. Today the *Times* is a major Web presence with as many as two million viewers a month. Its real pull, however, is in transmitting stories into the bigger national media. In the Web, radio, and cable TV news world of conservative talkers, there is a demand for news reporting that fits into existing agendas, and Moon's paper provides a diet of reassuring news.

An example of the paper's power to shape national stories is found in the strange saga of "Pastor Joseph," who has not been rediscovered in the painful national reassessment of how we were led to war in Iraq.

The story begins at the desk of "The Short Count," Arnaud de Borchgrave, editor-at-large at both the *Times* and UPI, having joined the Moon media empire in the mid-1980s. De Borchgrave, the insomniac descendant of Belgian royalty, is a veteran correspondent; he collected battle fatigues from twelve wars, in some of which he was wounded. He slept in the old days in an office above the newsroom, in a deluxe fold-out bed, often covered with clippings, a bust of Lenin kept ironically over his toilet, and a .45 pistol on the wall bearing the royal seal of Jordan. "More like the *Times*'s maître d' than its editor," recalled former employee Charlotte Hays, a Mississippi belle who wrote a tell-all for the *New Republic* subtitled, "I Was a Moonie Gossip Columnist."

De Borchgrave speaks in a rich, high English, dresses to the nines, cultivates an aura of mystery, travels first-class, and spits acid at those he feels have betrayed him ("After shooting yourself in the foot," he wrote an editor who quit over Moon's influence, "I can understand how embittered you must feel"). He has seemed at times to be a one-man intelligence agency. He has published a $1,000-a-year newsletter of "ultraconfidential" information, *Early Warning*, and has annoyed a former Senate Intelligence Committee chairman, Sen. David Durenberger (R-MN), who was peeved in 1987 that the count, having won Reagan's ear, seemed to be interposing himself between CIA analysts and Reagan. The senator accused him of "an effort to control political decision-making in America." And when Reagan gave way to Bush Sr., de Borchgrave boasted that an even closer friend sat in the Oval Office.

De Borchgrave has done double duty working at a foreign policy think tank, the Center for Strategic and International Studies (CSIS). In 1980, he was canned from *Newsweek* for reasons that remain unclear. (De Borchgrave cited an elaborate conspiracy involving a vendetta by Katharine Graham of the *Washington Post*.) The fired count then wrote a sexually explicit spy novel, *The Spike*, envisioning liberal editors as Soviet dupes and liberal think tanks as nests of Soviet influence. Lately he has also become a critic of Bush foreign policy.

However, on March 21, 2003, when the Shock and Awe bombardment commenced over Baghdad, de Borchgrave committed to print the unlikely conversion experience of a man named Kenneth Joseph. Joseph, the story went, was an Assyrian Christian "human shield" who came to Iraq to oppose the war at the cost of his life, if necessary. But what he saw, the Belgian assured his readers, changed his mind—and would change anyone's.

An emotional personal essay followed in UPI by Joseph, recalling how his mind spun around when Iraqis actually told him "they would commit suicide if American bombings didn't start."

> "We want the war, and we want it now."
> "What in the world are you talking about?" I blurt.
> Thus began a strange odyssey that shattered my convictions. At the same time, it gave me hope for my people and, in fact, hope for the world.

Two days after the first Pastor Joseph story in UPI, de Borchgrave recycled the subject in a *Washington Times* piece, describing the protester as a "young American pastor of the Assyrian Church of the East." That's when it exploded. None of the media outlets on the right dared miss what seemed proof of their ideas. You could read about Pastor Joseph in WorldNetDaily; NewsMax.com; Free Republic, the conservative message board; *Human Events Online*, part of the venerable anti-Communist magazine; Powerline, the blog that would topple CBS anchor Dan Rather; *National Review Online*; the writings of *USA Today*'s Jack Kelley, soon to be fired for inventing stories of demonic Arab children and vigilante Israelis; the writings of Jeff Gannon, soon to be exposed as a male prostitute with White House press access. And it ran on the "Liberation Update" section of the White House Web site.

The message rang loud and clear: War protesters were "beginning to get it," "shocked back to reality." "Disillusioned human shields," said Reed Irvine. Remarked *Powerline*'s John Hinderaker: "These guys are obviously slow learners, but at least they were willing to admit they were wrong. No matter how well the war goes or how much it improves the lives of Iraqis, we won't see much of that."

Soon the story seeped into the mainstream: the *Los Angeles Times*, the *Seattle Post-Intelligencer*, and *USA Today*. Capitalizing on his fame, Joseph continued to appear in the media in 2003 and 2004, assuring viewers that the "bad news" from Baghdad was exaggerated ("The stores are full of supplies," he said). "A former human shield who is now grateful for the war," Fox News's John Gibson said in introducing him.

But Carol Lipton of the left journal *Counterpunch* talked to "human shield" groups and couldn't find anyone who had heard of Joseph. Somehow, when other human shield groups had been turned back, Joseph was let in. And far from dreading the war, Joseph had written for a right-wing newsletter, in which he seemed downright eager for the attack. (Today on his Web site he calls himself a "modern-day Indiana Jones" and makes no mention of his priesthood.)

Joseph continually claimed to be on the verge of airing fourteen hours of amazing videotape, proving his story, claiming it was slated for airing by Barbara Walters. It wasn't. "It transpires that Kenneth Joseph was probably a bullshitter," conceded Johann Hari, an eloquent proinvasion Brit, apologizing for pushing the phony story in his column.

Then there are other stories of fake news at the *Times*. In 2002, the paper launched a full-blown campaign against "scientific fraud" after wildly claiming that forest rangers had planted fake wildcat fur in forests to stop logging. The paper ran ten news items, two editorials, and an opinion piece as part of its crusade, which was echoed by a half dozen mainstream newspapers. "Lynxgate illustrates the power of the *Times*," wrote Paul Tome of the progressive watchdog group FAIR, ". . . to promote a conservative agenda and feed it into the mainstream media environment."

As if crusading in the name of bogus cat pelts wasn't daft enough, Moon's ad department turned around and phoned up an environmentalist, Andy Stahl, offering him a deal: for $9,450 Stahl could buy rebuttal space in the paper, printing his side of "the lynx issue" and ensuring that "every member of Congress, the President, his cabinet and those who work for them will have seen your message." They had already created a mockup. "I'm very chagrined," said editor Wesley Pruden afterward, claiming the idea hadn't originated in the newsroom. The *Washington Times* seems able to withstand an infinite number of such humiliating episodes without losing its TV presence.

Other national stories the *Times* has pounded into existence include the shocker in 2002 that the National Education Association was an "affront to Western civilization" for suggesting teachers blame America for 9/11. Nothing of the kind was true. Then there is the War on Christmas, typically consisting of a few incidents magnified into a national crisis. On November 29, 2005, wrote Felix Gilette in the *Columbia Journalism Review*, "the editors at the *Times* began adorning the pages of the paper with a classic as perennial as popcorn strings 'round the tree—stories about how

Christmas is purportedly under attack from politically correct liberal heathens."

A few days later, radio host Bill O'Reilly hung up on a caller who phoned to ask why the War on Christmas coverage didn't mention that the publisher behind many of these stories had "paid black ministers to throw crosses into Dumpsters." "Because I don't know anything about him," said O'Reilly, "and I didn't even know the *Washington Times* was involved with this, and I wouldn't smear Sun Myung Moon anyway, the way you just did, Stanley. I mean, you're taking it right out of the left-wing playbook: can't win the debate, smear the person. You ought to be ashamed of yourself."

. . .

One of the oddities of the Unification Church is that while it tries to link Moon with the legacy of Martin Luther King Jr.—having drawn King's late widow to his events and even winning a $80,000 federal grant in 2005 to promote King Day—it also finances the newspaper world's most devoted opponents of black equality.

Nation reporter Max Blumenthal spoke with no fewer than twelve sources who told him of a pervasive climate of newsroom racism. Former *Times* reporter George Archibald told him that the Unification Church had become concerned and wanted a bigot purge. The veteran newsman said his boss liked to get high and complain about the "niggerfication of America." In 1995, Coombs had been pressured into firing from the paper his friend Sam Francis, a distinguished prose stylist accused by the Southern Poverty Law Center of being "one of the most important voices of America's racist right" but remembered in a *Times* obit by Coombs as "the voice of the Founding Fathers speaking down through the ages."

Most outrageously of all, Coombs's wife, Marian Kester, has opined in the pages of the *Times* that the American borderlands are like Tolkien's "White City," implicitly comparing Mexicans to the filthy orc hordes from *Lord of the Rings*. She has even written in to neo-Nazi Web site Stormfront, geeking out together on Peter Jackson's film adaptation; she and the site's e-brownshirts see the films as groundwork for a new white supremacist myth ("Loved your review. . . . And here's mine," she wrote in).

Then there is the case of Robert Stacy McCain, an assistant national editor and member of the League of the South hate group—kept on at the *Times* even after the *New York Press* reported that his were the fingers behind a series of racist Web rants. One described interracial romance as triggering "natural revulsion . . . THIS IS NOT RACISM, no matter what Madison Avenue, Hollywood and Washington tell us."

One fellow who claims McCain is "a pretty good friend of mine" is Bill White, a Maryland Nazi. The thirty-one-year-old white supremacist leader wears Third Reich uniforms and leads protests against black people. Before coming out of the closet in full Nuremberg Rally regalia, White contributed four pieces to the *Times* in 2000 and has been quoted by the paper's John McCaslin (see chapter 4) as an authority on "Liberty Dollars," a seedy alternative-money scam that White claims could erase the national debt. On White's racist Web portal, Overthrow.com, he claims to attend the same up-with-white-people American Renaissance conferences as McCain and Mrs. Coombs, who, he tells his readers, confided that the management won't let her attack Jews the way she ought. In 2007, the FBI investigated White's site for encouraging racist death threats sent to *Miami Herald* columnist Leonard Pitts Jr.

And then there is longtime chief editor Wesley Pruden himself. Like Mel Gibson, he is the son of a father with foul views—Wesley Pruden Sr. protested integration at Little Rock, Arkansas, in the 1950s, calling out, "That's what we gotta fight: niggers, communists, and cops"—whose own career has done anything but distance himself from the hate.

At the *Times*, the son seems to have led a mutual admiration society of antiblack writers. He has employed science columnist Fred Reed, who has written *Times* pieces on "the coming race war." Reed, a cigar-smoking "keyboard mercenary" who patterns himself after Hunter S. Thompson, is an outspoken segregationist who complained bitterly in non-*Times* writings about having to "[suffer] through another Martin Luther King Day," calling the holiday Orwellian.

Reed, in turn, receives fawning treatment in the work of Steve Sailer, another frequent *Times* source who has, in print, compared the unfunny Reed with P. J. O'Rourke, the funny libertarian. An ex-correspondent for UPI, the hobbyhorse of this cheery, bearded writer—practicing what the Anti-Defamation League (ADL) has called "genteel racism"—is using Web and media outlets to float new ways of seeing African Americans as inferior.

Sailer, who has only a bachelor's degree, heads a tiny pseudoscientific think tank, the Human Biodiversity Institute, which promotes 1930s-ish ideas about improving the human race through eugenics. He has written the odd piece for the *Washington Times*, where he has been quoted as a serious expert by Fred Reed ("The evolution of the human race is about to accelerate almost unimaginably!" he ejaculates). Sailer's writing often pushes the work of Canadian scientist J. Philippe Rushton, the head of the white supremacist Pioneer Fund. His scientist friend has devoted a great deal of energy to the proposition that African Americans' larger penis sizes allegedly correspond with reduced intelligence.

Rushton has frequently been quoted in *Times* pieces by Robert Stacy McCain, including in this August 31, 1998, contribution, "Whites Ponder Future of Their Race," highlighting a convention attended by David Duke: "'We stand in defense of our people,' Jared Taylor, editor of *American Renaissance* magazine, told the crowd Saturday at the Dulles Hilton. 'We owe it to our children, who must not become despised minorities in their own land.'" These are voices it would be hard to imagine in a major American newspaper without the charity of Sun Myung Moon.

• • •

Every now and then, the mainstream press will report that tensions have grown so between the racists at the *Washington Times* and the world peace promoters of the Unification Church that we are on the verge of war: a bigot purge, an installation of normal Republicans. At press time, the Confederates have retained control. On June 20, 2007, the *Washington Times* was the only newspaper to report a press conference by "Hispanic and black groups opposed to immigration," failing to mention that the groups' money and office space were supplied by white supremacist John Tanton.

According to ex-*Times* reporter George Archibald, the Peace King's son has blinked in the staredown with the Coombs-Pruden duo, because he fears losing their connections to the White House. They "have somehow convinced the South Korean owners," he says, "that the sycophant relationship with George Bush I has translated into being able to get President George W. Bush, Condoleezza Rice, and anyone else they want in Bush II's administration on the phone, or at an editorial board luncheon, any time they want."

But it seems hard to imagine the church's inner circle being kept awake nights by racism. The group, after all, spent years helping France's version of Wesley Pruden and Fran Coombs: Jean-Marie Le Pen of the National Front, one of the most virulent anti-immigration movements in the West (see chapter 4). And the storyline of the two factions at war can only help both. The *Times* staff gain the illusion of independence by being at odds with Moon. Meanwhile, the American church, out to entice the inner city, can only gain by distancing itself from white supremacy.

●   ●   ●

Is there a wall between the *Times* and its patron, or just a floor? Or is that even the point?

After a few eye-opening early lessons in the 1980s, where several editors quit over interference, church leaders seem to have learned the lesson that controlling the news is of secondary value to access. Without the *Times*, how could Moon preside over a 1997 event where Ronald Reagan himself sent a video message of thanks? It went as follows:

The American people know the truth. And you, my friends at the *Washington Times*, have told it to them. It wasn't always the popular thing to do. But you were a loud and powerful voice.

Like me, you arrived in Washington at the decade of the most momentous decade of the century. Together, we rolled up our sleeves and got to work.

And—oh, yes—we *won the Cold War.*

At these *Times* anniversary parties, the church always insists that its pontiff receive greater or equal stage time to the ex-presidents. And so it was, in 2002, that an audience of squirming Washingtonians listened as Moon told them that the paper "will become the instrument in spreading the truth about God." By this time some *Times* journalists had fled to the bar. Earlier in the evening, Laura Schlesinger, the radio moralist, led the Reverend Moon and his staff in a toast "from one survivor to another," saying she and the *Times* had something in common. They'd both weathered "belittling attacks."

· · ·

On April 14, 1987, opinion editor Bill Cheshire walked into the office of Arnaud de Borchgrave, with a secretary and three writers, each carrying letters that read, "I hereby resign . . . because of the breach of certain agreements of which you are well-aware." Managing editor Josette Sheeran, the paper's liaison to Moon, turned pale. When the first editor and CEO, Jim Whelan, had quit in 1984, it was easy to explain as a personality clash. But five people leaving? "They thought we would be dutiful little conservatives and do what we were told," says editorialist John Seiler, the last to hand in his badge. "Good riddance," he remembers de Borchgrave shouting after him.

Essayist Sam Francis had asked them to reconsider. "I figured all along the Moonies were running the show," Seiler recalls his saying, but why not play along, since the church was paying for everything? Cheshire, for one, had tired of the game. The last straw: After they wrote a piece denouncing the dictator of South Korea—whose 1980 crackdown had killed 207 democracy protesters—the count said, "Let me check this out upstairs." He dropped in on San Kook Han, a Moon officer and former Korean government man, then returned downstairs convinced they had to spin the op-ed 180 degrees, prodictator. (De Borchgrave denies this account of events.)

Editor Wesley Pruden called the reasons for the exodus "fanciful" and ran a replacement op-ed, taking sides against the reformers, who would be redeemed the next year with Seoul's move to democracy (and 1996 death penalty for the dictator in question, Chun Doo-hwan, who received clemency in the name of national healing). The *Washington Times*, however, justified the crackdown by asking Americans to imagine that the United States had been invaded by Communists. If so, "Americans might appreciate more the Damoclean sword under which South Koreans habitually live."

Later Cheshire said of his old workplace, the *Times*, "No one appears to care very much that the American political institutions have been subverted by foreign interests." After he left the paper, a journalist named Tony Snow, thirty-two, considered taking the job. One of the departed writers, John Seiler, warned Snow the newsroom was under the influence of the Reverend Moon. Reportedly, Snow listened, smiled, and became opinion page editor between 1987 and 1990. He then became George W. Bush's press secretary.

• • •

UPI, the reverend's wire service, is not the predictable right-wing animal that the *Washington Times* is. In 2003, years before the Walter Reed scandal, it earned awards for a series exposing the misery in which wounded U.S. troops were being kept. On the other, it has pushed the Kenneth Joseph story and other *Times* themes.

Today, the *Times* galaxy includes a number of connected media projects of even lesser journalistic accountability, whose coverage is fueled by big links from the *Drudge Report* and attention from Fox News Channel. They have included the *World Peace Herald* and the often ironically titled *Insight* magazine, which runs pieces without bylines. Most famous was the uncredited item on January 17, 2007, claiming that Democratic candidate Sen. Barack Obama spent four years at an Islamic madrassa. "Barack's Background: Ancient History or Madrassa Matters?" asked *Fox and Friends* afterward. "The madrassa bomb," said Fox News's John Gibson on January 19, "dropped on Barrack Obama." The story became most famous for being discredited by CNN and other outlets. Somehow, despite the outcry, Moon himself kept out of the discussion.

• • •

Moon has bent the media laws of physics, as if existing inside a bubble where time and space do not exist—or at least the unspoken rules of coverage, sensationalism, and accountability.

Take, for example, the Louis Farrakhan law of distance—the force that tends to repel politicians from Nation of Islam events, in direct proportion to his outbursts at "wicked Jews" and claims of UFO travel. After attending a Moon event in 1997, Farrakhan told CNN he wouldn't shun the Returning Lord just because he has "been vilified and demonized in the press, as I have." But national-level officeholders who wouldn't be caught dead at a Farrakhan rally have flocked to Moon's parties.

There is also the George Soros law of international donations: that if a billionaire dumps a fortune into U.S. politics, explaining he wants to "guarantee" a Bush loss, or announces, as Moon did in 1984, that "several hundred million dollars have been poured into America, because this nation will decide the destiny of the world. These contributions are primarily coming from overseas."—criticism of him will follow on *The O'Reilly Factor* and other programs, as a troubling hand behind the scenes, making outrageous statements. Not so with Moon.

Finally, there is the Don Imus law of accountability: that when a media figure has had an off day and described American women a "line of prostitutes" whose wombs "should be sealed with concrete;" or pined for a holy fire, a "purge on God's orders" that would cleanse the world of gays and lesbians; or harangued Christians at the company dinner for leaving their crosses on the walls—all of which the *Times* owner has done (see chapter 4)—an apology, however insincere, is forthcoming for "those who may have misconstrued." Not so with Moon.

Aside from a handful of rare interviews, Moon has simply not been available to the public and goes mostly unmentioned on television. A search of the TV news archives at Vanderbilt University in Nashville suggests that coverage of Moon dropped off steeply between 1985, when he left prison, and 2004, the year of his coronation.

On January 20, 2000, after Fox's Paula Zahn aired a report that was critical of Unification Church purchases of seventy-five thousand acres in Brazil, the anchor, reacting to "a lot of feedback saying we fell short," invited on Moon's Rev. Phillip Schanker to refute charges. "Critics say this is just another plot to make millions off his church members," she said. After Schanker explained that the group did not believe in mass suicide, Zahn said, "Thanks for setting the record straight." The group believes in victory.

• • •

There was another young woman who joined the Unification Church, like Cathryn Mazer. But this one did not leave, at least not for several decades. Cathryn would stay for only a few months, during which time she witnessed what she described as "hard-core Korean conservatism." But Josette Sheeran, twenty-one when she joined in 1975, stayed in the group. The training put her on a fast track to power.

"I have seen personality changes in my daughters," announced her father James Sheeran, New Jersey's insurance commissioner, in 1975. "They seem to think that there's a communist under every bush," he said, "and they're seeing God all the time." Sheeran's heartbreak was sometimes credited with pushing his fellow World War II vet, Bob Dole, to launch an attack on the Rev. Sun Myung Moon. Not one but three of his girls had become children of a new father through what Sheeran called "cruel and exotic entrapment of their minds, souls and bodies."

Josette, twenty-one; Jaime, twenty-four; and Vicki, twenty-six, had all joined during a rise in church recruitment that swelled Unification Church numbers to thirty thousand that year. "The church seems to suit many of them," the British *Economist* reported. "They become transformed into starry-eyed believers with perpetual smiles." On August 28, 1975, at five in the morning, Mayor Sheeran, an ex–FBI agent, charged into an International Training Center in upstate New York, convinced that his daughters were being held there. With him were his fourteen-year-old son and his wife, Sarah, fifty-one. Then, he said, ten to twelve male disciples between the ages of twenty and thirty stuffed rags into his mouth and beat him for an hour until he lost consciousness. "I was assaulted very viciously," he said.

After the church filed charges of its own, and the FBI failed to establish a violation, both sides dropped the matter. Over a year later, Dad and his Moon-loyal daughters were again on speaking terms, but James Sheeran said of the church leaders, "Why don't we flush them out and make them pay taxes? How sick can we be to permit that to continue?"

In those days there was no *Washington Times* but only the *News World*, Moon's New York tabloid and his entry into American journalism. (It was later renamed the *New York Tribune* and folded in 1991.) Josette Sheeran wrote stories for the *World*, which Moon was determined to use to topple his enemies on Capitol Hill the way the *Washington Post* had brought down Richard Nixon. She joined the team of writers striking out at mild-mannered Rep. Donald Fraser (D-MN), who had followed up on Dole's hearings by opening a full-blown investigation into Moon's hustles in Washington. An ex-Moon leader who became a administrative director of the Heritage Foundation, Michael Warder, told *Frontline*:

Moon wanted a whole series of articles going after poor Congressman Fraser. And so we would assign reporters to dig up all the dirt we could find . . . and of course I would say to Moon, I said, "On one hand, we're supposed to be doing this—but on the other hand, we're competing with the *New York Times*. And so there's matters of credibility here." And he would, you know, bluster and get angry . . . and say, "Just do what I'm ordering you to do and don't ask so many questions," and that sort of thing. And of course Colonel [Bo-Hi] Pak would reinforce these messages from Moon.

Craig Maxim is one of two sources close to the church who say Sheeran—whose byline appears over a piece attacking Fraser—worked closely with Moon, despite the official "church and state" wall between the *Times* and the Moons. "I have watched Josette come and give a full report about things the *Washington Times* was doing, and make sure [Moon] knew everything that was going on," Maxim says. "And similarly, Moon would respond to her comments and make decisions based on what she told him."

Sheeran told the rival *Post* that her master's church was something "not yet understood by society." Glenn Emery, a former church member, says he was present at the ceremony where her Moon-arranged husband, Whitney Shiner, struck Josette with the ceremonial Indemnity Stick. During the ceremony he "managed to connect with Josette's coccyx with full force," Emery says. "The poor woman collapsed in agony on the floor . . . it's a wonder she wasn't paralyzed."

In 1997, the year Sheeran cohosted the *Times* get-together in which Moon railed against "free sex," she left the newspaper, where she had become managing editor, well liked by the staff, even among those who playfully called her "The Ice Queen." The *Washingtonian* now pronounced her one of the city's most powerful women. As she reinvented herself as chief of William Bennett's free market think tank, Empower America, she now claimed to have become an Episcopalian in early 1996, divorcing her husband and disassociating herself with the Unification Church.

So had the Messiah himself, oddly enough. Church promos exulted that on August 1, 1996, the reverend had retired the very name "Unification Church," with all its baggage, in favor of a "Family Federation for World Peace and Unification in 1996." No longer was he calling the world to his church, but his church was going into the world, stressing the power of uniting with other religions.

But the mid-1990s were also a time of disillusionment for many long-time Moonies, as revelations of violence and drug abuse from the inner circle, as well as charges of infidelity, cut into membership. Some insist that Sheeran has severed all ties. Other sources say word from deep inside the church is that Moon has groomed political loyalists, possibly including Sheeran, to leave the church and fight for his cause, as in the case of anti-Darwin warrior Jonathan Wells. Says Craig Maxim, "Josette Shiner may be out of the church, but if she hasn't firmly slammed the door on it in her mind, they may still be able to manipulate her."

It seems fair to ask, at least, if the values of Moon's True Family have made it into the White House, just as the lessons of Boston's First Families made it into the Kennedy administration. Sheeran was appointed by George W. Bush in 2001 to the position of undersecretary of state for economic, business, and agriculture affairs. A State Department phone directory listed Paula Gray, now Hunker, underneath as "senior adviser." Both Hunker and Sheeran were named in a 1982 Bo Hi Pak speech, as part of a special "spiritual counseling team," along with Sheeran Pak aide Jim Gavin and others.

In November 2006, she left to lead the UN World Food Program, backed by then-ambassador John Bolton. Fearing embarrassment, a Bush official pressed the *Washington Post* not to report the connection, which it did anyway.

Ironically, according to Robert Boettcher, the congressional staff director of a 1978 House probe into Moon's goals, the reverend "envisioned a food crisis in the future when the world would come begging to him." Asked whether Sheeran still subscribes to Moon's public policy ideas, her press secretary at the Office of the U.S. Trade Representative said it was an offensive question. If I had a license to practice journalism, he said, it should be revoked.

• • •

There is a story that in the 1980s, *Times* scribe Jack Knarr awoke to chanting. On most nights, he slept in his car in the newsroom parking lot. One night it became so cold that he sought shelter in the Reverend Moon's newsroom.

Later he related what he saw to disbelieving colleagues. At 4:30 A.M., the voices begun. He stirred and directed his gaze to the mezzanine balcony. Josette Sheeran Shiner, managing editor, was up there, Knarr said, with a group holding candles in a predawn vigil. He watched, speechless, while they ambled down to the basement for an early morning prayer breakfast.

• • •

The Reverend Moon's dream of an obedient media is revealed in a transcript of a WMA "journalism workshop" presided over by the *Times* publisher in 2003. Michael Marshall, then the editor of Moon's magazine *The World & I*, had this striking exchange on the topic of loyalty, according to a transcript, dated months before being tapped to lead UPI.

> MOON (addressing Marshall): Are you with *World and I*. Can you follow what I'm saying, do what I'm saying, the contents? For how long?
>
> MARSHALL: I will commit to follow forever.
>
> MOON: Forever, for life. Great.

(UPI has replied that the transcript is "garbled" and should not be trusted.)

The parent company of both UPI and the *Washington Times* is an entity called News World Communications, headed by Chung Hwan Kwak, an elite member of Moon's inner circle, and directed for some time by early *News World* employee Larry Moffitt. It took a B-movie fan to write the best account of what it's like in Kwak's world: a media *Rocky Horror Picture Show*.

UPI columnist John Bloom, an accomplished investigative reporter in his own right, is best known for his TV alter-ego, Joe Bob Briggs, the midnight movies host. At a company "World Media Conference on World Peace" in 2003, he writes, one minute you saw celebrity guest Sam Donaldson, the news anchor, rumbling in that famous voice about being "a real toughie when it comes to telling it all." Then Kwak, Bloom's boss, took the stage:

> At this point he displayed a diagram of the human body with a slide projector and posed a question that perked everyone up: "What is the most important part of our physical body?"
>
> Of course we all searched the body, and I think most of us probably thought, "Uh, heart? Brain?"
>
> No, said Dr. Kwak. "It is the sexual part."
>
> . . . He then said that the family should openly discuss the sexual organ, both its use and misuse, and make sure that in marriage we present ownership of the sexual organ to our spouses. "Because our spouse has the key to our love organ," he said, "we can have great joy in marriage. This is a cosmic law." . . .
>
> [H]e was especially agitated by the distribution of condoms in order to stop the spread of AIDS.

Briggs says the audience was divided between journalists who were church members and those who weren't. The first group, watching a presentation on various "Messages from the Spirit World," reacted with amazement. The others asked, "Have these people lost their minds?"

• • •

Here's how this whole mess started.

James R. Whelan's nightmare experience as first publisher and editor of the *Washington Times* begun in the fall of 1981. A Harvard-educated historian of strong anti-Communist convictions and a veteran UPI Latin American correspondent, the Irish American was preparing the next edition of the *Sacramento Union*—the conservative rival to the *Sacramento Bee*—when friendly strangers entered the old building, situated near the sequoias and redwoods of the California capitol. The visitors passed the bust of an old employee, Mark Twain, and came up to see Whelan without an appointment.

Larry Moffitt, one of the two, reminded Whelan of Dennis Day, the boyish, singing TV sidekick from the old *Jack Benny Show*. He wanted to know: Could Whelan spare a half hour?

Moffitt, a Unification Church leader, wanted to persuade Whelan that Washington needed a paper to replace the *Washington Star*, a paper that three months ago had breathed its last after 129 years, leaving the world's most powerful city a one-paper town. It had groaned under debt for years and failed to be revived by *Time*'s last-minute investment of $85 million in it.

"This is going to be an antidote to the *Washington Post*," the visitors said of their new venture, according to Whelan. "Don't you owe this to your country?"

"I don't remember to what extent the name 'Moonie' came up in the conversation," Whelan says of that first meeting. "But it came up sufficiently that I asked our librarian to do a search and produce for me some clips on these people. And so he produced a batch of clips which were disquieting. But not alarming at that point. They were disquieting."

He turned down the offer. They persisted, and by the Christmas season he was lying in bed recovering from a mild heart attack, brought on by the stress. When the doorbell rang at 10 P.M. one night, he suspected immediately that it was Col. Bo Hi Pak.

The colonel wanted a man like Whelan at the helm, a Harvard-educated historian and Latin American correspondent of firm right conviction. Whelan had given stern orders: "admit nobody." But his wife let in Moon's delegates anyway.

Taking a seat by the fire, they impressed upon Mrs. Whelan the reasons why her husband should join them—"trying to persuade her that it was my patriotic duty," he said, "and that I would never again feel at ease with my conscience if I were not to do it." So his wife roused him, saying Pak was making a good case. "I really think you ought to do it," he remembers her telling him.

Reached at his home in Chile, Whelan speaks in a dignified English, never dangling a preposition, as he remembers the campaign to hire him and the 1984 flame-out in which he held a press conference and said he had "blood on my hands" for empowering Moon. He had been promised complete control over the newsroom and company but "could not stand by . . . while a compact of trust was turned to ashes." The *Times*, he said, "is firmly in the hands of top officials of the . . . Unification Church movement." Bo Hi Pak, having replaced him as CEO, had taken "direct, on-site, executive control of all noneditorial functions of the newspaper on behalf of the newspaper's owners."

The paper fired back at its departed editor/CEO. Arnaud de Borchgrave and others claimed Whelan had been fired for excessive salary and benefit demands: a new Cadillac, a better deal on his company-owned house in McLean, Virginia, and membership in country clubs. But *Times* officials confirmed to *U.S. News & World Report* that it was a matter of church control.

From the start, outrageous salaries had been a way of life at the *Washington Times*—for prized journalists, if not for the church's low-cost grunt laborers. Columnist Charlotte Hays recalled an *Insight* anniversary dinner costing about $500,000. To ease the strain on the church of the $250 million start-up fees, church followers were reportedly encouraged to sign their checks back to the movement and live on a tiny allowance, while Bo Hi Pak harangued them for slow sales. "Father is very angry at this situation," one peon recalls being told. Washington, D.C.'s $15,000/year minimum wage law was part of the "satanic D.C. government."

On the other hand, it became standard operating procedure to lure professional journalists with giant dollar figures. The cash would compensate for the early stigma of working with the "Moonie paper." "The money was fabulous, just fabulous," Jan Ziff, a BBC correspondent who was offered a job, told a *Vanity Fair* reporter. " It was very, very tempting but the more I thought about it, I just couldn't work for the Moonies."

• • •

In Reagan, the conservatives had a new president, but they feared that the man who famously said "government *is* the problem" was a sitting duck for the Washington Establishment—including, as they saw it, the *Washington Post*, the newspaper that had doomed Nixon.

In the old way of seeing things, the *Post*'s reporting lay in the middle of the road. Its reporters saw their work as neither left nor right. The wealthy family that published the *Post*, led by matriarch Katherine Graham, was close to the Kennedys but dined with Republicans as well as Democrats. The conservative view, however, was that the *Post* was so invested in the old, liberal premises about the world that it could never be as fair to Reagan and his policies—prioritizing anticommunism ahead of human rights enforcement, building "Star Wars" missile defense. To them it was a matter of national survival.

"The Moonies operate under a cloud of suspicion," *National Review* publisher Rusher would later say. "But whether they're any worse than the Graham family is a matter of personal taste." To James Whelan, it was, at least, his belief that "the capital of the United States needed, deserved to be served by more than a single newspaper voice, and one which itself has a strong ideological bent."

The *Times* rode in on a reaction to "liberal media bias" that had not yet become a cliché. Among the first to push the idea that the news media was hopelessly left-wing was Reed Irvine, a former Federal Reserve economist who devoted his retirement to war on the press. For years, Irvine tried to have CBS's Dan Rather fired; he hounded the *Washington Post* with complaints it was unfair to conservatives, to the point of endorsing communism. *Post* editor Ben Bradlee finally wrote back that he was a "miserable, carping, retromingent vigilante," a note that Irvine kept as a trophy for his dedication. Ads for his newsletter, *Accuracy in Media* (AIM), asked potential subscribers, "Mad at the Media?" That ad ran in *Rising Tide*, the anti-Communist biweekly passed out by the Moon Youth on college campuses.

By the time Moffitt met with Whelan, the True Father had already graduated from *Rising Tide*'s open ideological attacks to seminormal New York journalism. His paper the *News World* wasn't (at least officially) the terrible sharp sword of Moon's prophetic decree but something you read with your morning bagel. From the church's point of view, its greatest achievement might have been getting Ronald Reagan to pose for a photograph clutching an Election Day edition of the paper, carrying an accurate prediction: "Reagan Landslide: Will win by more than 350 electoral votes and carry New York as well." In 2002, Bo Hi Pak claimed the encounter went like this:

> When Ronald Reagan was campaigning for the presidency, I was publisher of News World in New York. I went to see him in Ohio with Josette [Sheeran] Shiner. I met with him. I told him, "Mr. President, you are going to be the President of the United States." He said very humbly, "No, I am not your president, I am a candidate. . . ."
>
> "No, you are the President of the United States. I want to convey a message to you."
>
> "Whose message?"
>
> "Reverend Moon. Reverend Moon got the revelation. You will be chosen by God to dismantle Soviet Union."
>
> He was shocked. He was shocked! He shake hands firmly with me: "I need Reverend Moon's prayers, and I need Reverend Moon's support, and I will do the mission."

The latest idea was to make Mr. and Mrs. Moon the cross-town rivals to Katherine Graham and her family. At the very least, Whelan's visitors had said, he should fly to New York to discuss the prospect. So he went.

He phoned diplomats who could vouch for the Unification Church. One was Douglas MacArthur III, nephew of the Korean War general. "I wouldn't join their religion," one dignitary told Whelan, "but I find them to be very purposeful, very decent people."

And so, canceling a planned holiday in San Diego with California politician Pete Wilson, Mr. and Mrs. Whelan flew to talk to Pak. He came away from a four-hour meeting impressed but not persuaded. "Bo Hi Pak was a very charming fellow, very gregarious and very persuasive," says Whelan.

He described the overtures afterward in Dallas, at a meeting of the new conservative leadership group, the Council for National Policy. "And almost unanimously, they said, 'Jim, you have to do this,'" he remembers. "'This is our chance to have our voice heard where it matters most.'" He agreed but returned to Sacramento to think it over.

The warriors of the right might be enthusiastic about the *Times*, but would they stand with Whelan if the experiment failed and he took flak for editing "the Moonie paper"? That part, he was less sure of. "I talked it over with my wife," Whelan says, "and I decided—no!" After all, they were settled in Sacramento, at a house that won an award in an architectural magazine. He phoned the churchmen to turn them down.

"They continued to persist," he says. By this time Richard Mellon Scaife, his boss, had caught wind of their persistence. And in the conservative world, the last thing you wanted was for Scaife to be disappointed in you.

• • •

Scaife, a forty-nine-year-old Pittsburgh banking blueblood, had for years been handing out slabs of his own fortune (today worth $1.2 billion). For the conservative movement to control the debate in Washington, as they saw it, would mean more than just a newspaper of their own, fighting the liberal Establishment. It would mean their own Establishment—their own experts, think tanks, law societies, magazines, councils, committees, centers, studies, position papers, and training grounds. A good many entities—from Heritage to the Federalist Society—would owe much to Scaife's philanthropy.

Scaife reportedly grew uneasy—would his editor in the California capitol leave, and so soon after Scaife had paid dearly for a bigger stake in the *Union*? "Dick is a man of, how shall we put it, decisive temperament," Whelan says. ("Mr. Scaife," *Wall Street Journal* reporter Karen Rothmyer asked him on the street in 1981, "could you explain why you give so much money to the New Right?" Replied Scaife, "You fucking Communist cunt, get out of here!") Scaife phoned Whelan from a publishers' association and reminded him of the expensive 1977 buyout. "And I did that counting on you, my friend," Scaife said. "And I would look upon you very unkindly if you were to let me down by walking off."

Shy of media attention, Scaife had earned a reputation among his colleagues for wrath and long memory. "I have some influence with conservative organizations across the country," Whelan recalls being told. "And I can assure you that you will be supported by *none* of them."

"Dick, I have no intention of doing this," Whelan told him. But after he hung up, the pressure on him was tightening and tightening, and he needed to get free of it. So he told the *Union* he'd be unavailable for a few days. With the family, he drove south down the coast of California, under the black cloud of a Scaife genie that couldn't be put back into the bottle.

He made it five hours south to Santa Maria, which was choked with fog, and then pain cut suddenly into his chest. Whelan checked into an emergency room, was released, and told to go to a hospital. But he decided the heart problem wasn't as grave as he'd feared. So he drove back to Sacramento.

Before going to sleep, he checked in with his subordinates at the *Union*. They told him Pak had camped out at a Holiday Inn there in downtown Sacramento, from which he was deploying representatives to the Whelan home every few hours to see if he'd returned home.

So it was not surprising when the doorbell rang this latest time. He and Pak stayed up until 2:15 A.M., talking. "And in the deep and dark of evening," Whelan said, "I agreed to do it."

He only asked for $75,000 a year, he said, at a time and place where he might be expected to make $150,000–$300,000, so that "nobody could say I was doing it for money." But first he extracted a firm promise from the Unification Church. "I said, I will not go as editor. I will go with all the power in my hands and that will guarantee our independence. Because the only way you can change it is by firing me. Otherwise, I will control *all* of the newspaper. In *all* of its dimensions. Editor, publisher and CEO."

• • •

According to church lore, it was just nine days after the *Washington Star* went out of business that Josette Sheeran had had asked Col. Bo Hi Pak if he had considered moving into the vacuum with a paper run by the church He said he had. The next month, a meeting with Pak was convened at the summer getaway of the Sheehan family in Manasquan, New Jersey. Present were Moon's Young Turks: a clique of leaders under thirty-four who included Sheeran; her "Team Mother," Paula Gray Hunker; Ted Agres; and Jonathan Slevin. In one old photograph, they lean over blueprints for remaking the warehouse of the Frank Parsons Paper Company into the ritzy conservative newspaper.

In 1982, the *Washington Star*'s state-of-the-art mainframe computer hummed back to life in new hands. On the morning of March 1, 1982, promises given, Whelan landed in the light snow of Baltimore-Washington International Airport, having left behind California and Scaife—"who for about six months or so was a very powerful enemy," he says. Two months later, on May 17, a date that the Reverend Moon has celebrated ever since, the editors put the first edition of the paper to bed.

• • •

"Who the hell are you to stand in judgment?" Whelan asks during an interview in his office. "No, they're not zombies."

That was Whelan talking to a *Post* reporter in 1982 when the paper came out. The story gives no indication that, two years later, he would become one of the only men in Washington to question Sun Myung Moon's second life as a politician.

"It is the *Washington Times* which has given him the high visibility and the clout that he's got," he says now. "Because almost everybody wants to be either published in the *Washington Times*. Or they surely don't want to be attacked in the *Washington Times*. They want the *Washington Times* on their side.

"And so a lot of people might otherwise and maybe do hold their nose while they're endorsing, backing, blessing Moon. They don't want to cross him, because they want the favor of the *Washington Times*." That, he says, explains why black liberal congressmen would have anything to do with the publisher from the other side—let alone bow to him.

What about editor Pruden's claim that the paper is so independent from the church, even the *Washington Post* is secretly jealous?

"Well, there's an expression in Spanish that you can say even mass," Whelan says, then explains: "You can say anything if you're brazen enough, I suppose. You don't have to be a priest to say mass."

What about the claim by congressmen that they were surprised into attending Moon's honors as Peace King?

"Humbug. Humbug!" he says. "I mean, anyone who has bothered to look at events sponsored by the Moonies, including those sponsored by the *Washington Times* for the last twenty years or so, knows perfectly well that *Moon presides*."

• • •

Whelan's personable visitor, Larry Moffitt, went on to direct operations at UPI. He has written an essay grappling with one of the Rev. Sun Myung Moon's more controversial interventions in the Spirit World: to free Hitler from hell.

In Tarrytown in 1998, Moon tantalized his flock with dishy information. "God sends out special emissaries in [the] spirit world to get information for Father," he said, according to a church account. "Do you want to know all the details, or just the rough summary?" "The details," they called back.

What they heard was Moon's *Inferno*—a vision of how his personal enemies and world tyrants had met fitting fates in the next world. The messages had been relayed to him by Sun Hun Lee, the theologian responsible for the Messages from 36 Presidents. Lee had explained his mysterious 1997 death plunge as a screw-up. "Nobody would go through a window if one knew that it was a window," he said.

On a mission beyond the grave, Lee had to search far and wide for Karl Marx, so drastic was the *Das Kapital* author's exile from God. Marx was found stubbornly preaching communism to the miserable masses of a shantytown. Two days of arguing, and Lee had made a serious dent in his philosophy. And Marx "felt embarrassed to have all his followers see that he was wrong." (During his lifetime, Lee liked to argue that Marx's dialectical view—that forces clash and then merge into something new—is disproven by the example of the egg, and the harmonious relationship between the struggling chick and the shell it pecks at.)

Then Lee searched for Stalin. The Soviet monster had barricaded himself in a high-security house surrounded by mud huts. His sentries beat up Lee. The missionary also located Mussolini, reduced to a pathetic drifter. General Tojo was found living in narcissistic loneliness at a house where he'd erected a Shinto shrine to himself. He cried and recanted after hearing of the True Parents. Reflecting Moon's affinity for Japanese nationalism, the leader of the wartime empire had gotten off light, considering his war crimes, which included enslaving Koreans as "comfort women."

Faring not nearly so well was Mary Pak, a South Korean women's university chancellor (no relation to Bo Hi Pak). The church detested her for working with local Christians to jail Moon in 1955 on morals charges after a scandalous affair at Ehwa Women's University that made the Reverend Moon a laughingstock in Seoul. Pak was trapped in a castle for maimed souls: "eyes missing, limbs missing, their head split open . . . deformed, crippled spirit men." Her hands were glued to her mouth, preventing her from eating. The grudge was that Pak had ruined a crucial seven-year phase after the Korean War—between 1954 and 1961—when, like the coming of a comet, conditions had briefly been right for Moon's kingdom, the Third Israel. Instead, she set him back for decades, and the lord of the *Times* refused to forgive her until 1998.

For his part, Jesus was in grateful spirits—glad that Moon had reportedly put on a ceremony matching him to an elderly woman, the wife he never had. But Christ remained troubled that Christians were distracted by his crucifixion, rather than admiring the feats of the *Washington Times* publisher. He relayed a "particular thank you for the beautiful apartment for my wife in the physical world. . . . I apologize that my name is so much worshipped in the physical world. It shouldn't be that way, and I am sorry for that."

And then there was Der Führer. "He killed over six million Jews so I thought he would be among evil spirits," said Lee. "But he was not to be found there."

The wanderer followed the blood and smoke, the rattle of chains, and shouting voices. He finally found Hitler tied to a tree in the Spirit World, spread-eagled.

A sign pinned to Hitler's chest read "King of the Nazis." Jews, resentful of the Holocaust, lined up to fling bricks at the naked German ruler. That's before the True Father intervenes.

What Moffitt points out is that Moon, by freeing Hitler, also liberated an innocent soul: a virgin female Jew, trapped in Hitler's force field of limbo.

Moffitt considers:

Maybe there's even a sign as you approach the tree, about five feet tall with a horizontal line drawn on it and the words, "You must be this tall to smash Hitler's balls." . . . Hitler, by his evil deeds, not only consigns himself to hell but becomes like a big constipating cork in the colon of spiritual upward mobility. Millions of people are just stuck there in that awful griminess, unable to get past the blockage of Hitler's evil. . . .

If that young Jewish woman could have all that sorrowful crap lifted off her shoulders, . . . then it is so well worth forgiving Hitler.

The man who would have been Helen Thomas's boss, at what was once America's greatest wire service, is also a stand-up comic and beekeeper.

FOUR

THE NIGHT THEY REPLACED JESUS

People of America! Life on earth is a fleeting moment. I hope you will start now to prepare yourself for life in the eternal world. Do not forget even for a second the fact that Rev. Sun Myung Moon is the Messiah.

—PRESIDENT ANDREW JACKSON
(ACCORDING TO THE REVEREND MOON)

The night of the coronation, May 23, 2004, ABC News Senate correspondent Luis Martinez, new on the job, remembers his interest being piqued around 8 p.m., when he spotted a man of some local infamy, lingering outside a Senate event with various holy men and catering carts. It was the Rev. George Stallings. What on earth could Stallings possibly be doing here?

Stallings was a flamboyant D.C. priest whose sordid fall from the good graces of Pope John Paul began when reports reached the Vatican that this preacher, so often swamped by autograph seekers, had abused an altar boy. He was told to enter counseling. Instead, he rebelled, launched a failed boycott against the *Washington Post* for reporting the allegations, formed a Swahili-themed breakaway sect that spiced up the liturgy with dancing, and adopted a high-rolling lifestyle. The Catholic Church was simply racist, he told *Ebony* magazine, and "my blackness could no longer tolerate it."

In his new life Stallings took to wearing a gold watch, a gift from the Rev. Sun Myung Moon, for whom he had become ambassador to the wider black clergy. Moon had also handpicked a wife for him. The D.C. priest angered his parishioners when he told a local paper that he appreciated the Japanese ethnicity of his spouse, because Asians "don't party all the time." It was all part of the Unification Church's drive to associate Moon, the marriage impresario, with the rebellion in the Catholic Church by priests asking for the right to take wives. Moon had also snagged Archbishop Milingo, a Catholic faith healer from Zambia. In 2001, Milingo, in his seventies, had been assigned by Moon a forty-three-year-old wife, a Korean acupuncturist, but then recanted, telling the press the next year he had been drugged or brainwashed into violating his oaths and succumbing to her skillful massages. But then Milingo returned to the Moon fold and was excommunicated by the pope.

Martinez had just finished covering a protest by the disabled rights group ADAPT. Its members, who had defied the limits of cerebral palsy and other severe conditions to come to Washington, would have killed for the kind of unfettered government access now being enjoyed by the Reverend Stallings. Tired of bad health care, they lay on the Mall all morning with signs reading "It's Cold, It's Freezing, but ADAPT's Not Leaving." They blew their breath tubes to steer wheelchairs into the Senate offices, where they refused to leave a committee room until the Capitol Police began removing them in handcuffs. After Martinez interviewed a man who could only spell out his grievances one letter at a time, pointing to an alphabet board, he called it a night.

The ABC reporter asked what the big to-do was. A tall man regarded Martinez's press badge, unimpressed, and said, "This is a closed event. You're going to have to leave." "Just wanted to take a curious look," Martinez said, but that didn't wash. He went home, shut out.

• • •

Meanwhile, in the Senate hall, the Reverend Moon, sitting near the front with a red flower pinned to his tuxedo, beamed and soaked up praise from the lectern, where his cheerful American deputy, Michael Jenkins, ushered in a successively more cosmic and arcane series of lecturers to celebrate his reign on earth. Listening to the droning speeches, the various Americans who'd traveled here from across the country to win world peace awards drank Diet Coke and picked at the remains of their dinners.

Within the Moon world, Jenkins is considered a white man with a gift in reaching African Americans. It's his voice—nasal, not mellifluous, but that monotone will climb all the way up to a yell that a nonnative English speaker might conceivably mistake for the passion of the old black gospel style. His cadence, however, is sometimes tripped up by a translated jargon that is at war with English: "We must make a condition for Father," for example.

One weekend before, he had privately told a congregation that the event at the Senate would mark the "absolute culmination of the mission of Christianity." "We are one," you can hear him saying in the speech, which was recorded and posted on a religious site. "One movement, one family, one heart, one mind-set, one body." He boasted that the movement was "educating the White House and the U.S. State Department" on Mideast policy and then added, "Oh, and by the way: Everybody who is on the stage, every politician and every religious leader that brings forward the crown and the robe? They are gonna believe that Father is the second coming, the savior, and the Messiah. No one's gonna be up there just out of ceremony."

Now that the "culmination" of Christianity had arrived, Jenkins was more discreet about the meaning of the event. He turned over the microphone to Chung Hwan Kwak, chief officer of the church—a kind of Mr. Spock to Reverend Moon's Captain Kirk on their journey through the cosmos—who regaled dinner guests with talk of a "Fourth Israel." According to a confidential source, one confused witness, invited from Texas to win a peace award, remembers thinking, "I thought we were still working on the first one."

Four Israels, and one Moon to rule them all. Within the church, it's believed that Man has disappointed God three times so far: first, in the Garden of Eden; then, at the time of Jesus, whom Moon considers a bitter failure; next, in the 1950s, when the world could have united under the world's young new savior, the Rev. Sun Myung Moon, but had lost the moment, increasing the mess for God.

Early in the night, Congressman Curt Weldon (R-PA), winner of a $3,000 honorarium from the Unification Church, had delivered a show-and-tell presentation on his recent diplomatic trip to meet with repentant Libyan dictator Muammar Khadafy, as part of his duties on the House Armed Services Committee. Weldon held up a photo of himself, pinning a flag pin to Khadafy, Reagan's nemesis in the 1980s. Normal enough. But after Weldon accepted a gaudy "peace award," slung around his neck like an Olympic medal, Kwak and the other holy men took the stage.

Too embarrassed to be named, a U.S. senator later said through a spokesman that the politicians fled as the nature of the party dawned on them. One after another, speakers on stage testified that the tumblers of unknown prophecies were falling into place tonight on Capitol Hill. A Detroit rabbi, Mordechai Waldmann, even blew a shofar, normally reserved for high Jewish holidays. He blurted out that this party, where "people come together for peace," was a "miracle" worthy of the Torah.

The speeches picked up speed . . . rolled toward an overwhelming question. *Could the Messiah be among us? Here in Senate room G-50?* Now Stallings, the fallen preacher, rose to speak with a fire in his eye, working up the audience and bellowing full-steam: "Now is the time for America . . . to receive this gift from God who has come among us!"

To applause, Moon took his place at the head of the deep red carpet that rolled off the stage. Soon he stood flanked by his wife, the solemn Hak Ja Moon, and bearded clerics in Christian and Islamic garb. They were hangers-on from around the world, picked up in his travels, wearing grave faces, like priests about to open the Lost Ark or Bible characters in a Renaissance painting.

The hosts announced a letter of congratulations the Republican Speaker of the House. Congressman Danny Davis got up to read a poem written by Moon at sixteen, composed after he saw Jesus and learned he was the Second Coming. It began, "When I doubt people, I feel pain."

Davis continued through the verses.

Even though we are deceived, still believe . . .
Oh Master! The pain of loving!
Look at my hands.
Place your hand on my chest.
My heart is bursting, such agony!
But when I loved those who acted against me
I brought victory.
If you have done the same thing,
I will give you the Crown . . . of Glory.

It is important to understand where crowns enter Moon's dream.

Photographs of one of his Korean temples appear to depict a glass museum case full of gold and jewel-encrusted headpieces that would shame Napoleon.

The styles are as varied as the heads of chess pieces, evoking all the kings who ever ruled on Earth. Some are metal and pointy, with Far East influences, or jeweled and bulbous, like the King of Bavaria's. The "Russia" crown is domed and Slavic, like the czar's. They are labeled by index card: "Russia," "Thailand," "U.S.A." On special occasions, courtiers carry them to him, one at a time.

The "U.S.A." crown stands apart with its design, its spires hooking upward like golden stalks of wheat, as if celebrating that the reverend's most abundant harvest—of political friends—is here in the States.

• • •

In 1986, Moon's daughter-in-law Nansook Hong witnessed a private ceremony in which the reverend dressed up like "a modern-day Charlemagne," in her words. The robes were of the finest fabric, gathered by Mrs. Moon, who, according to one source who has been close to her, studies how a queen should comport herself by watching Korean historical soap operas.

Seeing her husband's father dressing up like the king of the Franks gnawed at Hong. Mr. and Mrs. Moon had imported her at fifteen into the United States for an arranged marriage to their troubled son, Hyo Jin. She was led to believe he held the divine status of Perfect Adam for having been born to the world's first perfect family. A less well-connected clan might have been troubled by federal prosecutors, who sent Mormon polygamist Warren Jeffs away for fifty years for marrying adults to young girls.

When Hong went public, she told the BBC that her media mogul father-in-law had "crowned himself as 'Emperor of the Universe.' At that point," she said, "he became God, in his eyes."

Deciding she lived in a world gone mad, Hong eventually fled Moon's New York palace in the dead of night, bringing her children. She prayed for God to protect her from their father, Hyo Jin. Having tortured animals as a child, Hyo Jin had grown into an aspiring Jimi Hendrix with an arsenal of sixty guns and very little discipline. Some of the pistols had been manufactured by his brother Kook Jin, president of the church's Kahr Arms concealable weapons factory in Massachusetts. Hong describes Hyo as a druggy bully who threatened to break all her fingers and beat her bloody one day, when she was pregnant with his child and tried to flush his cocaine down a toilet.

But when a crowning, like the one that terrified a young woman behind the gates of East Garden, was held on federal property, compliant congressmen didn't complain to the press but took it in stride. The one news company permitted to attend the ritual was News World Communications, the little-noticed firm behind the *Washington Times*, United Press International, *Insight*, the *Middle East Times*, *Tiempos del Mundo* (which closed in 2007), and other outlets around the world. WashingtonTimes. com would report of the sights using only the blandest possible description: "Several dozen religious and civic leaders were honored last night in

Washington for their 'exceptional dedication as peacemakers,'" wrote the *Times*'s Cheryl Wetzstein, a Unification Church member.

• • •

John Judis reported in *U.S. News & World Report* as long ago as 1989 that "almost all conservative organizations have some ties to [Moon]'s church." But, he said, "conservatives fear repercussions if they expose the church's role."

A number of sociologists have urged that the word *cult* be jettisoned as language from an ugly past, and replaced with the friendlier term *new religious movement*, or NRM. The word *Moonie*, coined by the press and casually used within the church, is now officially condemned by the grown-up, PR-savvy Unification Church. Members ask to be called Unificationists, a name that rings few bells and invites confusion with Unitarians. There was a period when the group retained the late civil rights legend Ralph Abernathy to proclaim the M-word the new N-word, laden with Yellow Peril race hatred. It was as if to say the force behind the Moonie panic of 1978 had been that which drove nineteenth-century Americans to accuse Chinese immigrants of plotting to enslave white women in opium dens.

Were that true—in one sense, it was Asiaphobia that first led U.S. anti-Communists to *embrace* the Reverend Moon and his demonstrations against what Moon called the satanic evils of Ho Chi Minh—it still wouldn't explain why the Capitol's conservative paper, allegedly fighting to defend Republican values, would work with an NRM so preoccupied with stamping out democracy and "individualism"—which, Moon has said, "is what God hates the most and Satan likes the best."

His followers have told me they see no controversy in the claim God wants an end to voting by ballot. "How is it going to shock anyone when a religious leader says that God should rule the world rather than democracy?" asks Peter Elliffe of Crystal World, a church-owned company in New Jersey that manufactures translucent sculptures of Snoopy, teddy bears, and the Capitol building. Another young believer tells me "democracy is only a temporary system" until civilization has gone heaven's way. When Moon has blessed everyone on Earth, he says, we will be living in the Kingdom, or *Cheon Il Guk*.

In anticipation, the church publishes laminated orange Cheon Il Guk "national citizenship cards" to keep in wallets. "The world should follow and resemble me," Moon explained, "so we are issuing the Cheon Il Guk card, which has True Parents' photo." On the flip side, the divine husband-and-wife team smiles in cosmic guidance.

• • •

But Moon's influence must be measured in more than just the names at his peace parties or the zany congratulations cajoled from such politicians as Rep. Charlie Rangel (D-NY), whose office acknowledges signing a proclamation on official letterhead in 2004 reading, in part, "I, Charles B. Rangel . . . do recognize you as 'True Parents' exemplifying self-giving service and leadership and as 'King of Peace.'"

Regardless of how seriously anyone in Washington treats the philosophy of this wealthy benefactor, and his stated intention "to influence the entire American society," he has voted with his money, and those dollars favor conservative politics by an immense margin.

While the rare Democrat has spoken at Moon-sponsored rallies (his right-wing coalition CAUSA claims to have snagged Sen. Al Gore one night in the late 1980s), there is simply nothing on the left to compare with the array of conservative characters who have come to Moon or the stunning $3 billion gift to them of the *Washington Times*, not to mention the life-sustaining millions for the right's mail-order dynamo (see chapter 5), a $3.5 million endowment to Jerry Falwell's Liberty University, and the fortune given to the Bushes.

And when the Unification Church surfaces behind issue campaigns, it's never for liberal goals—funding government health care, raising the minimum wage, protecting gay rights, withdrawing from Iraq. Instead,

Moon's influence has surfaced in campaigns for abstinence-only education, creationism, opposition to gay rights.

Salon.com writer Michelle Goldberg revealed in 2005 that Jonathan Wells, a prominent creationist who had been appearing in Kansas antievolution commercials, had confessed to being assigned his life mission by Moon: "Father's [Moon's] words, my studies, and my prayers convinced me that I should devote my life to destroying Darwinism, just as many of my fellow Unificationists had already devoted their lies to destroying Marxism," he wrote. "When Father chose me to enter a PhD program in 1978, I welcomed the opportunity to prepare myself for battle."

Moon's dedication to the hard right is true to his early background in nationalist, anti-Communist Japanese circles. In fact, the symbol of the Unification Church—interlocking arrows ringed around a bursting red sun—defies the onlooker not to think of the 1940s. As early as 1967, Moon, then known as an enigmatic CEO-prophet, was linked to Ryoichi Sasakawa, a wealthy gangster of the old Japanese right: the faction in Japan that believes in celebrating the military might of the 1930s empire, dealing with organized labor at the end of a bat and paying homage at shrines to war criminals.

Since the end of the Cold War, Moon has abandoned the anti-Communist image to cut deals with Kim Jong-Il and others. But historically, that original strain of hard right politics has determined his bewildering collection of friends around the world. The Paris press has found evidence that the *moonistes* gave at least $800,000 in 1984 to the National Front of Jean-Marie Le Pen, the "France for the French" candidate who alarmed much of the world in 2002 when he finished second in the race for prime minister. Le Pen has been fined for Holocaust denial, hates mixed marriages, and wants to expel all immigrants. And yet Moon's Bo Hi Pak was allegedly impressed by his vision of a "Christian Europe," assigning two hundred Moon disciples to work tirelessly for his 1988 campaign, *Le Monde* reported.

On November 21, 1987, a reporter for France 3 television had asked the charming Pierre Ceyrac, a Unification Church official, if it wasn't "a little bit disturbing" that Moon had spoken of global dominion. "No, it is not disturbing," said Ceyrac. "I think that the goal of all religion—the Catholic religion too—is to have the most possible influence, so its ideas, its ideals, triumph. It's completely normal." Running on France's National Front Ticket in 1989, Ceyrac won a seat in the European parliament, just as another Moon deputy, Gustave Pordea, had in 1984. Justifying how the multicultural Unification Church could find itself in bed with a white supremacist, Ceyrac said in the 1990s that the movement had been "deceived" by Le Pen. But Moon's hand "helped to keep them away from extremism and racism," Ceyrac said, "and surely had a good impact on their future development."

• • •

All this, and the March 23, 2004, ceremony had left a minor Democrat, the Rep. Danny K. Davis, inexplicably holding the crown.

Davis told me he met Moon through inner-city ministers. Several of the black deacons in Moon's circle have sought funds from the White House under George W. Bush's Faith-Based Initiative, which distributes cash to churches—a government policy that the first head of the faith-based office, Jim Towey, promoted at a 2002 conference paid for and broadcast by the Unification Church.

While the church funds white nationalist voices at the *Times*, Moon has inspired black civic leaders across America to hail him as a modern-day Martin Luther King. Some have nodded at comparisons between two men who dealt with race issues and faced IRS hassles. "Is there a better icon for people of color than the Reverend Moon?" asks an East Texas preacher, William Reed, in an essay calling the Father a victim of bigotry. But Tony Norman, a writer for the *Pittsburgh Post-Gazette*, says black ministers have been bamboozled by a man who should be "excoriated for a series of scams stretching back thirty years."

Recently Moon has even paid ministers with gold watches as part of an unusual but ambitious "Tear Down the Cross" tour he staged, nationwide, for Easter 2003. The premise was that God wants Man to abandon the cross (the symbol of Jesus's death) and bring on the crown (the symbol of Moon's success). "There will never be a shortage of black preachers mopping their brows and calling down God's wrath on gay marriage and other 'abominations,'" Norman wrote. "But I think I would tear my eyes out in shock at the first sign of a jeremiad by a black preacher about the pernicious influence of the Unification Church on congregations in urban America." In the Reverend Moon's hierarchy of race, Koreans are first, blacks last. "Little by little the color of black people will gradually become lighter," he said in 1991.

The central and visible role of Davis in the Crown of Peace fiasco guaranteed, whether by design or accident, that the Democrats would not use the crowning as campaign ammunition—against the party that has relied on Moon's newspaper and accepted the lion's share of his donations.

Without partisanship, a scandal runs out of steam. That's the premise behind a February 3, 1989, memorandum from Moon's Washington strategist, Gary Jarmin—the lobbyist who arranged the coronation. While Group A would campaign for right-wing causes, Group B would invite Democratic speakers. The presence of liberals, Jarmin says in the memo, "helps protect our Conservative Republican friends at elections time," he says. "In other words, the Democrats will be reluctant to attack the 'sponsors' . . . if their own participated in the same delegation."

The mastermind of Moon's crowning, it turns out, is an important pioneer of the Religious Right who has been serving two masters: the Christians and Moon.

• • •

Gary Jarmin, the conservative lobbyist with two hats—as Washington point man for the Reverend Moon, whose church he left in 1973, and co-director of a Christian right organization, Christian Voice—is not a household name but has impressive connections. Former colleague Louis Desloge, an ex-Moonie who worked with him on a U.S.-Cuba trade project, recalls that Jarmin, whose office was full of pictures of him with Reagan,

Goldwater, and others, would casually remark, "I'll talk to Karl," meaning Rove. Recalls Desloge, "A typical D.C. guy who sees the rest of the country as peasants."

Early in the year Jarmin had written a letter to Sen. John Warner (R-VA) requesting use of the Senate hall for "awards dinner," without mentioning Moon or the planned spectacle.

Jarmin, who has complained that "moral decadence is a very serious problem today and politics is a big reason for these problems," is frequently named in newspaper stories on mail scam artists who bilk the elderly. The *Charleston Gazette* reported in 1999 that an eighty-five-year-old grandmother had sent $4,000 of her yearly $5,000 income to Christian Voice after receiving two to three terrifying letters a week. One read, "[O]ur children are in desperate trouble. . . . Because the Militant Homosexual Lobby [*sic*] has unveiled a dangerous new scheme to shove their evil agenda through Congress."

Her family tried to get her off the list, but the junk mail kept coming. Said a daughter-in-law, "She was so confused. Every time they sent her a letter, she sent them a check." She speculated that the grandmother had ended up on the mailing list by donating to the Christian Coalition and the Dole campaign.

But Christian Voice is no mere boiler room. Or at least it wasn't in that fateful year 1978, the year of *Invasion of the Body Snatchers* and the rise of the New Right. That's when a *60 Minutes* piece featured the group as the sign of a sea change in America. "Millions of Christians appear to be coming together to form a new powerful force," the report said. "In the vanguard is Christian Voice."

In 1980 and 1982, the group's Fund for Moral Government raised more money than other Christian political action committees. To bring home the bacon for Reagan, whom his group praised as "the only Republican presidential candidate committed to Jesus Christ," he drew on a mailing list 187,000 names long, including 37,000 ministers. It was the first time the Christian right made a dent in a presidential election. Jerry Falwell's Moral Majority PAC, just getting started, raised only $22,089 that first year, while Christian Voice, already at full speed, trucked in $494,722.

Like MoveOn.org today, Christian Voice had won a reputation for using the latest tools—computerized mailing lists, for example—to turn conservative unrest into a force powering the Reagan Revolution. In 1980, it targeted thirty-two races, defeating twenty-three incumbents. Its innovation: the "Biblical Scorecard," sent just before Election Day.

Sent by the millions, the Biblical Scorecards graded office seekers on support for school prayer and opposition to gay rights and abortion. Seeking the White House in 1984, Democratic candidate Walter Mondale said the scorecards raised the specter of "moral McCarthyism." That year Jarmin, speaking for the Christian world, said, "We've taken over the GOP in many areas. . . . We intend to use the Republican Party as a political vehicle."

This was a radical idea then. Critic Doug Bandow of the libertarian Cato Institute protested that in Jarmin's approach, "believers will be tempted to substitute a temporal, flawed agenda for the eternal gospel of Christ." Others pointed out the absurdity that Father Robert Drinan, a Democratic congressman and Catholic priest who opposed prayer in school, received a 0 percent score from Christian Voice's moral proctor, while Rep. "Slamming Dan" Crane, a Republican censured for bribery and sex with a Senate page, had carried a perfect rating.

By 1996, when the Christian right was in full swing, Ralph Reed, chief strategist of the influential Christian Coalition, had credited the lobbyist (in his book *Active Faith*) with strategic tips: "Gary [Jarmin] encouraged me to build a pro-family student network on the nation's college campuses."

The reverend's lobbyist is linked to a host of powerful direct-mail players. Jarmin's "militant homosexual" spam relies on a Virginia-based contractor, Response Dynamics, which has committed similar postal assaults on behalf of the National Center for Public Policy Research (NCP-PR). The NCPRR is a think tank that sent 160 "scare letters" in just one month to eighty-six-year-old Faye Shelby, the *San Francisco Examiner* reported in a 1998 piece, "The Fear Merchants." "I didn't know that I could just turn them down," Shelby said. "I thought if I didn't correspond with them about Social Security, I wouldn't get my checks."

The NCPPR, whose board has included Jack Abramoff, was named in a Senate report as a group through which that felonious lobbyist laundered payments for a congressman's golf trip with Ralph Reed. As it happens, NCPPR director Amy Moritz Ridenour is one of a few conservatives ever to acknowledge the conduit of influence between their world and the fantasies of Moon. "Most people are afraid to address the issue," she told *U.S. News & World Report*, "because they don't want to publicize the extent of the church's involvement." That was 1989; soon, the discussion became even more hushed.

• • •

Moon's faithful servant, Col. Bo Hi Pak, had tasked the humble lobbyist with bringing Moon's Kingdom to Washington.

On Pak's sixtieth birthday, on August 26, 1990, Pak called Gary Jarmin "someone who can do what Father needs" and "a political strategist like I have never seen. He has a precise and most acute mind. He makes things happen. . . . I have asked him to reserve that strategy and power, so that someday he can pull off something very big for the sake of Father's great providence." Just how big a "something"? The name of one Jarmin project signals large ambitions: "Global Dominion Communications."

In 1989, a Jarmin memo found its way to the *Washington Post*. It a proposed "sub-rosa travel service" so that politicians could travel with Moon, while keeping it a secret.

> It would greatly increase the prestige, credibility and influence of the Movement [MVT] in Korea. . . . [M]ost U.S. politicians would probably refuse to participate if the MVT openly admitted it funded the visit. . . . I believe we must find some indirect way of sponsoring this program which would not expose politicians to any unfair or malicious attacks. . . .
>
> Politicians could easily defend participating in a trip funded by the WT [*Washington Times*].

The travel service plan may not have been enacted, but the tack of using the *Washington Times* as cover for Moon events has persisted.

• • •

Jarmin worked to win gestures of support for Moon, the small, manageable gestures that the True Father will appreciate and the public will not notice: a snippet of language here, a coded salute there. A few newspapers took note of Mississippi senator Trent Lott's oddly phrased proclamation of July 27, 1993. From that day's *Congressional Record:*

> I rise today to offer remarks on "True Parents Day," which will be celebrated officially on July 28, 1993. . . . I urge my colleagues in the U.S. Senate, and all citizens of our Nation to recognize and support True Parents Day and the restoration of God-centered families in our society. . . . Parents, by the example of sacrificial love and transmission of moral and cultural values, play a crucial and determinant role.

This was on the heels of a bizarre national campaign, led by Jarmin and a Moon group calling itself the American Family Coalition, on the pretense that Father's and Mother's Days were not enough. We needed a new holiday, Parents' Day.

Several major media outlets reported the connection to Moon. Hallmark, Pat Boone, and *The Brady Bunch*'s Florence Henderson had been persuaded to get behind his plea for a holiday that would honor "true parents." Or True Parents. Parents' Day had been a religious holiday in Moon's world. But it was sold as a nondenominational thing. It was pared down to just "Parents' Day," without the "True," when it was signed into law by Bill Clinton as a generic salute to Mom and Dad.

"On July 28, 1993, Mrs. Moon . . . made an historic speech on Capitol Hill before U.S. senators," Colonel Pak said three years later, describing an event hosted by Orrin Hatch in which the Mormon called Mrs. Moon a dear friend. "It was a landmark speech on family issues. The U.S. Congress was so moved and inspired . . . that both houses passed unanimously and enacted the Parents Day Resolution." His master put it differently. "Men and women in the American Congress didn't know what they were doing," Moon said, "but as you know Congress passed the resolution of

Parents Day." The genius of the Unification Church, says Louis Desloge, who remembers fellow members smirking at the secret meaning, is in inculcating members to "exist in several different worlds at once."

• • •

Behind the 2004 crowning was a similar game of double meanings, to keep congressional friends out of the soup. "We have no king but Jesus," former attorney general John Ashcroft has said. There is no tradition of naming kings at the Dirksen, a white marble hall for elected officials and their staff, named for one of the last of the old-fashioned orators, the Republican minority leader Everett Dirksen, who made the Top 40 with *Gallant Men*, an LP of readings on the American Revolution, in which kings were overthrown, not anointed.

So the church's master theologian, Dr. Kwak, had his work cut out for him. He explained (in a memo obtained by Rob Boston of Americans United for Separation of Church & State) how Capitol Hill could host the ceremony—a "total offering" of the country to Moon, he called it—while pretending to host a dull awards dinner.

> The "outside" view of the Capitol Hill event was that Father [Moon] received a crown, an award for his years of dedication and leadership in reconciliation and peacemaking. The "inside" view of the event was that America surrendered to True Parents in the king's position . . . . So, in effect, America is saying to Father, "Please become my king."
>
> It is only now, after Father's thirty years of investment in America, through America recognizing him as king, that his investment is for "his" America. This was a very emotional moment for Father because only now, after all those years of investing his blood, sweat and tears, that he is beginning to see "his" America responding.

Kwak, the writer of this passage, is also president of an American news service.

The turn of the twenty-first century found United Press International in a long decline. It had once been a thriving news wire with origins in the old Hearst press, counting among its thousands of employees such journalistic legends as Helen Thomas, Walter Cronkite, and William Shirer (who wrote *The Rise and Fall of the Third Reich*). But by 1999 it was reduced to one barren newsroom on the seventh floor of the Washington head-quarters. Working there, weekend editor Ken Layne recalled in 2000, felt like being a "security guard at an abandoned building. . . . The shabby remains of United Press are now in the hands of the Moonies, and nobody who claims to be a journalist will come anywhere near it."

By then, reporters had been laid off. In 1992, UPI had fallen into the hands of absentee Saudi businessmen—and now the not-so-absentee True Father. After fifty-seven years at UPI, Helen Thomas, last of the fabled "unipressers," quit rather than serve the True Father. Kwak was installed as corporate president. The new UPI provides content for the *Washington Times* and prints the occasional plug for a church rally at the United Nations Plaza.

•   •   •

"Now it's right I received the crown," Moon crowed at the Sheraton National Hotel the day after the coronation, according to notes taken by follower Debra Gertz. She is the wife of Bill Gertz, the author and influential national security reporter for the *Washington Times*.

"True Father spent thirty-four years here in America to guide this country in the right way. Yesterday was the turning point. Now I'm going back to Korea." But there remained signs the USA continued to fall short of his standards. He cited "homo marriage." And he belittled a follower for being overweight. In a final, surprising segue, he urged the Moonies to "welcome Rev. Kwak as president of UPI in your heart," shortly before finishing his talk. "I have no more to teach," he said.

The Washington crowning was still on his mind on August 20, north of Seoul, Korea, near the lake where he communes with the souls of the dead, and his summoners, like the medieval pardoners of Chaucer's time, charge per ancestor freed from hell.

"What has been the source of God's anguish?" he asked rhetorically. "There was never a person God could affirm as His own historically victorious son." As proof that he is "historically victorious," unlike Jesus—in Moon's eyes, a carpenter who turned in substandard work as the first savior—he cites two momentous occasions: not just March 23, when Moon was crowned, but February 4, when, as it turns out, a lower-key dinner at the Ronald Reagan Federal Building honored him.

I found a videotape of this, too—and a photograph of Moon reviewing the Crown of Peace literature at his mansion. The Capitol dome dominates the imagery spread out on his table. His most loyal leaders stand stiffly at attention, longing for their Father's approval of the pamphlets.

• • •

Weeks after discovering Washington's habit of crowning Moon king, I was having trouble finding an editor willing to publish the story. *Mother Jones* said Moon just wasn't a fresh subject. The producers of an NPR show had commissioned a piece about the *Washington Times* but didn't seem surprised by the mention of the ritual. They left me to work on it while they took summer vacations.

Doubt grew. If the East Coast media didn't think a coronation was important, maybe it wasn't, and didn't they understand this stuff better than I did? Maybe anointing donors as gods happened all the time in Washington, like logrolling or gerrymandering.

Meanwhile, I needed a pro-Moon quote from a conservative. I e-mailed a past defender of the Unification Church: Joseph Farah, Rush Limbaugh's cowriter. Farah, I learned, does not consider himself a conservative but a Christian. He presides over the—for lack of a better word—conservative news site WorldNetDaily, among the biggest independent news sites on the Internet. When Helen Thomas quit over the UPI buyout, he had raced to the defense of the reverend. "Those who are making the sideways comments about UPI's new owners are, cut to the chase, racists and bigots," Farah wrote.

Sent the March 23 video for his consideration, he booted up Windows Media Player and watched the show.

[Montage: People pound taiko drums. CG energy beams whoosh around the planets. Children frolic. It all builds to a climax.]

UNCTUOUS MALE NARRATOR:

The great march of human history towards peace!

[Choral music. We see a forest. In a window, footage of famous authoritarians appear: Stalin, then Kim Il Sung of North Korea. Finally: Sun Myung Moon.]

NARRATOR:

The twentieth century was a dramatic turning point in history, when humanity crossed through the Pass of Freedom and traversed the Sea of Equality, to finally approach the Gates of Peace.

[Airlines, people going to work, making phone calls, using the Web. Then: Action music. Footage of important 1990s world events. Then sentimental music soars.]

NARRATOR:

The Cold War has come to an end, and now: a new world of peace, without national boundaries, so longed for by all people and nations, is about to dawn. . . . The era of the Eternal Peace Kingdom, one global family under God, is upon us.

[In slick computer animation, Moon's logo swirls around a number of scenes, including a picture of him as king. Title card:

TRUE PARENTS' CROWN OF PEACE CEREMONY.
The music becomes jaunty as the Washington Monument appears.]

NARRATOR:

On March 23, 2004, in the Dirksen Senate Office building, in Washington, D.C., in the U.S., 81 U.S. Senators and Members of Congress . . . 26 ambassadors to the United States . . . and some 450 leaders from various fields . . . came to participate in an Ambassadors for Peace Awards . . . and Crown of Peace Ceremony. The program for the evening was presided over by the respected Baptist minister and civil rights leader Rev. Walter E. Fauntroy, who served in the U.S. Congress for some twenty years.

[We see Fauntroy, founder of the Black Congressional Caucus, then Rep. Curt Weldon. Soon, Chung Hwan Kwak takes the stage.]

KWAK
(triumphantly):

True Father and True Mother are sure the champions of peace . . . the King and the Queen of Peace, and the King and Queen of the second and third Israel!

[People move into position for the crowning ceremony, as wedding-ish music takes over.]

NARRATOR:

The highlight of the occasion was the Crown of Peace Ceremony. . . .

[Someone is narrating the details.]

MICHAEL JENKINS:

The fruits of their labor . . . Muhammad, the Buddha, and all the saints have proclaimed that True Parents are now receiving the mantle. Religious leaders will present the mantle of anointed. . . .

NARRATOR:

God's painful heart was eased. And hope for humanity elevated. Indeed, it was a moment engendering great optimism for the future.

[People are bowing and bringing the Moons the bejeweled crowns.]

JENKINS:

. . . The honorable Roscoe Bartlett, representing the United States . . .

NARRATOR:

An announcement to God was read aloud. . . .

[Sappy music again.]

NARRATOR:

With delegates from the world's nations . . . regal robes and crowns were offered to Dr. and Mrs. Sun Myung Moon by prominent Protestant and Catholic religious leaders and Congressmen of the United and States followed in procession by Islam, Judaism, . . . and the world's religions. This was greeted by thunderous applause.

[Moon has taken the stage. He speaks fiercely,
his speech dubbed over in English.]

MOON:

I am God's ambassador, sent to Earth with his full authority . . . [etc.]

NARRATOR:

The declaration of God's fatherland and the era of the peace
kingdom, the realization of God-centered families, and true
peace. A flood of emotion filled Reverend Moon's heart as he
proclaimed the fundamental, concrete, eternal plan for peace.
Tears came to his eyes. He had invested thirty-three years of
his life in America and had rose from the position of servant of
servants to become the King of Peace. Like the Roman Empire,
two thousand years ago, America, a Christian nation, stood
with the mission of realizing God's ideal, and spreading this
ideal to the world. Knowing this, Reverend Moon was able
to endure the racial discrimination and religious persecution
he encountered, overcoming these with love and devotion.

[Heartfelt looks from the audience. The crowning ceremony proceeds.]

NARRATOR:

Senators and Congressmen and representatives of all the families
of the world joined in.
    God's fatherland is the ideal heavenly kingdom of Cosmic
Peace and Unity. From the beginning of the universe and on into
eternity . . . the kingdom of heaven has now begun. . . .
    In the twenty-first century, our history is going to melt away. . . .

[This goes on for quite a while.]

NARRATOR:

Like a candle that burns down, sacrificing itself to give light to the
world, the light of wisdom and hope will shine from the headquarters of world governance—the "Peace United Nations"—into all
realms of life. This light will radiate beyond the high barrier sepa-
rating nations and nations and will illuminate the road to peace,

the path to fulfillment of humanity's hopes . . . and dreams. Now is the time for global governance centered on God. Rev. and Mrs. Moon, together with world leaders, *will* take the lead in creating a world without boundaries. Filled with true and lasting love. . . .

Farah e-mailed back, asking me to appear on his radio show. It wasn't standard procedure to discuss an unfinished story, but it didn't seem like it was going to air, and would another journalist beat me to it? So I came on the radio, expecting to be excoriated as a racist and a bigot, and wondering if I wasn't one. Then, to my surprise, Farah agreed with me, on his syndicated radio show, one of the first media outlets to break the news.

Even if it meant sacrificing his weekly *Washington Times* column, he wanted to crusade against the event. "Do you think this is an appropriate event to take place in your U.S. Capitol?" he asked listeners. "Does this disturb you at all?"

In a separate interview, Farah recalled his own experience, in 1990 or 1991, standing on a stage with Moon. "I'd never been to Korea," he says. When Moon's group, the World Media Association, invited him on a free trip, "I thought, 'Well, why not.'" An evangelical Christian who had succeeded Jim Whelan as editor of the *Sacramento Union*, his fears that he might be seen as endorsing a false prophet were assuaged when WMA representatives assured him that the reverend didn't literally claim to be the Messiah.

So there he was on stage, with more than forty dignitaries, VIPs, and diplomats, when the reverend took to the podium. He read a translation of the speech, handed out at the last minute. "It was typical Reverend Moon stuff until about"—he laughs—"halfway into the speech, when he proclaimed himself the Messiah."

What could he do? Just walk off? He wanted to respect other people's beliefs. But the Christian in him was troubled. "Am I lending credibility to this speech?" he thought. "Sweat, perspiration started dripping down my face," he says. "What options do you have in that situation?"

• • •

While news editors steered clear, video of the Moon coronation was bubbling up online. Then the *Washington Post*, which had hesitated for months to touch the story, gave it front-page treatment.

It must be that the networks rely on the *Post* to verify what is real. For now they leapt on the story. Luis Martinez of ABC News produced a segment that ran on that night's *World News Tonight*. His piece showed a clip of the video. *Like a candle that burns down . . . .*

Legislators scrambled from the report—all but for Representative Davis, who said he'd worked with Moon for a decade and admired his peacemaking. Representative Weldon's spokeswoman insisted that he never attended the event, until being furnished with photographs. It turned out he and Davis shared a past with Moon. They'd praised his initiatives on the floor of Congress in 2003 ("We are grateful to the founders of Ambassadors for Peace, the Reverend and Mrs. Sun Myung [Moon]," Davis had said, describing an upcoming awards ceremony June 24, 2003, in the Rayburn Room). Both had traveled abroad with the IIFWP and taken Moon's money.

Oddly, while Davis eventually agreed to sever ties with Moon, Weldon refused to rule out attending future IIFWP festivals. His spokesperson suggested his past participation had something to do with his diplomatic trips to North Korea. He was voted out of office during the anti-Republican backlash of 2006.

• • •

While the identity of the mysterious Moon-coronating senator became the "talk of Washington" (according to the *New York Times*), the faithful feared a new crucifixion was coming.

In Florida, on or about June 29, 2004, according to the church newsletter, a Korean woman took it upon herself to fast for forty days, taking

120 bows every day to apologize to God for America's rejection of its king. Our country was "blinded because of the fall," and the news media was "stirring up public opinion against True Parents" because of the "coronation as peace king in the Senate office building."

In Washington, the American leaders met to film new explanations of the coronation that would quiet the clamor. Michael Jenkins was now claiming Moon wasn't technically *the* Messiah but that *messiah* is a generic term, meaning "anointed one." A twenty-year-old follower, bred and raised to believe Moon was the savior of the world, says he was interning at the church's TV studio in Washington, working the video camera. "I was going through turmoil," he told me. "I had to sit there and film these guys while they lied to my face."

June 30 at the National Press Club, thirty Moon defenders pushed the new line. "No one was 'duped' into attending," said spokesperson Mike Leone in a press release, begging to differ with members of Congress. The blog frenzy was "pure politics," he wrote, "taking aim at Reverend Moon's pro-family, conservative positions."

In Des Moines, Iowa, the Reverend Moon's Web site manager, David Payer—also a local GOP officer—was so incensed that he bought the domain name Gorenfeld.com and erected a protest site.

"I want people to know a little about John Gorenfeld," he said when I phoned him a year later, with a breezy menace that was more John Malkovich movie character than heartland politician. He said I ripped the crowning out of the context of love and Korean tradition, which justified the Moonie *kyung bae,* or bow to the filial father. "You gave it a perspective, or a view, that was cast so diabolically," he said, "as if there was something to do with becoming the King of America or something."

Some messages gently encouraged me to see the light. Not so the e-mail that arrived from the former director of the Manchester, New Hampshire, Unification Church, Rev. Gunnard Johnston, fifty-nine, now a missionary in Lithuania:

So tell me, John. . . . [A]t night do you hear the voices of those who clamored for Jesus' head on the platter? Do you hear the snarls of the Inquisitors apoplectic over someone questioning the authority of the status quo? Do red-faced screams of "blasphemer" and "false messiah" fill your head? . . .

Being skeptical is one thing. I'm cautious myself. But when you start a hate-war, a disinformation campaign, an all-out attempt to murder someone else's public image, and you ride that train day and night without end, you make yourself a loser destined for a very dark and smelly place. And the more you ply your trade, the darker and smellier it becomes for you.

As it turns out, this pundit had been quoted at some length in the *Washington Times*. On February 5, 1998, "Inside the Beltway" columnist John McCaslin had rang up one Gunnard Johnston to give what was supposedly a neutral, third-party sense of how the fresh new Monica Lewinsky scandal was playing in Europe.

Among the women of Lithuania, Johnston detected "intense embarrassment":

Will I ask them to my private office 37 times, strictly for "business" reasons (as Monica Lewinsky's lawyer put it)?

Will I use my position of American prestige for my own personal pleasure and gain? Will I throw them aside, like last week's dirty laundry, when I am through with them?

These, and other questions, are in the eyes of most of the women I meet these days.

This was only nine days after Hillary Clinton had made her remark that a "vast right-wing conspiracy" was after Bill. And a year after the First Lady had come to a sort of truce with the paper that had done so much to play up the Whitewater scandal. "Hey," she told Moon editor Josette Sheeran at an invitation-only "Renaissance Weekend" retreat for a wide variety of bigwigs in Hilton Head, South Carolina, "I want you to think about running my column." And so for some time her "Talking It Over" pieces joined Chris Matthews's in the *Times*.

• • •

The only Republican who questioned Moon's *influence*—and not just the crowning—was fired for doing so.

Ken Grubbs Jr. had been director of the National Journalism Center (NJC), a farm system for training and placing young Republican journalists. The NJC is an arm of the Young America's Foundation (YAF), a prominent leadership outfit for winning the debate on college campuses. YAF arranges for Ann Coulter, David Horowitz, and other famous TV conservatives, as well as prowar army officers, to visit universities. Its e-mail list encourages students to pressure professors to celebrate the fall of Saddam and complain if their professors are contemptuous of military service.

On July 2, Grubbs observed mildly in the *Wall Street Journal* that the coronation of Moon "has got to be freshly embarrassing to the many fine journalists who work at the Times." He defended the paper as "never a mere lapdog" to its owners, but then he made the mistake of questioning a *Times* piece that gave heavy credence to the church's spinning of what he called a "profane self-exaltation" by Moon. Before Grubbs took a job with the *Times*, he said, he "consulted a Christian clergyman, who gave me a tentative green light. I don't think he would do so today."

Grubbs was axed by YAF president Ron Robinson—one of the "seasoned generals of the right," according to *Time*—who told the *Post* that the writer was out of line. He never should have been "criticizing the media, writing commentaries attacking the media. I didn't expect Ken to do it." And if attacking the media crossed the line, it went without saying that attacking the owner of D.C.'s conservative newspaper was beyond the pale.

• • •

The next month, Sen. John Warner, warhorse Republican from Virginia, confessed to being the one who was "deceived," as he put it, into allowing this imperial ceremony to happen. Unhappy with the *Post*'s treatment of this revelation, Gary Jarmin wrote in on August 14: "We never deceived the senator or tried to misuse his good name. John Warner is an extraordinarily honorable and decent man who deserves better." Explaining the mix-up to the *Post*, Warner's staff had said he'd merely agreed to sponsor an "annual awards banquet" on February 4—not March—only for it to be rescheduled on account of a bioterror scare. But that's not the way it happened.

As early as February 7, the movement's Web hummed with reports that "members of the Senate in USA offered a crown to True Parents," as one bulletin from February 7 said, over a month before the ceremony that made the news. And so, as has never been reported, Capitol Hill had been used twice that year—February 4 *and* March 23—to celebrate the True Parent. *Fool me once . . . .*

I purchased a videotape of the February 4 event held at the Ronald Reagan Building. It hadn't been canceled. It was being peddled by a group calling itself the American Clergy Leadership Conference (ACLC). We see Michael Jenkins on stage, inviting "outstanding Jewish leaders" to crown Jesus as King of the Jews, a prerequisite, Moon says, for his own supremacy. So a pudgy, yarmulke-wearing man strides awkwardly across the stage with a crown. "Welcome home, Jesus," says Jenkins.

But Jesus's simple crown is a consolation prize next to the sensually plush ornaments brought forward for Moon and wife, maroon and purple diadems. Jesus, Jenkins says, is watching "before Congress, before the White House, the United States of America . . . anointing Father and Mother Moon as king." In Moon's absence, one of his sons accepts the crown.

Mormon representative Chris Cannon (R-UT) inexplicably takes the podium to say, "We are only going to have peace in the Middle East when people of faith gather together. And it is *this* kind of process that will make that happen." The church claimed an astonishing forty-one other federal and state legislators in attendance, including Minnesota GOP senator Norm Coleman. Not one has spoken publicly of it.

• • •

How long have U.S. politicians honored Moon, and what can it mean?

The trail leads to Charlie Black, an advisor to Bush 41 and Reagan, and listed as a host of the coronation. His public relations firm, BKSH & Associates, has represented, in addition to major U.S. corporations, such exotic clients as Ahmed Chalabi, the Iraqi exile leader. It also has handled PR contracts for the Pentagon.

Before the crowning became a scandal, I e-mailed Black questions about his role. "I lent my name and sent invitations to a few friends," he replied. "Unfortunately, I had a conflict and couldn't go to the event." Was it a common kind of "event"? Black said, "I don't know if it is annual, but they have done similar events. I don't know Reverend Moon, but work with the management of the *Washington Times* and their foundation occasionally on conservative causes. I think the dinner committee list included a number of us "secular" conservatives." "Similar events": as it happens, the church newsletters cheerfully claim other recent honors for Moon. If one is to believe the *Unification News*, on May 15, 2001, a *Times*-affiliated "National Service Award" was held at the Rayburn Building, and the church called it the "Coronation of God's Kingship."

Another event was at the February 2, 2000, at the Cannon House Building Caucus Room. The *Times* called it the American Century Awards, but Moon used it as a platform for his speech "The Cosmos Is Our Hometown and Fatherland." It may not have included costumes, but the "Fatherland"-themed event alone should have telegraphed fair warning to congressmen claiming to be caught off guard by the 2004 rhetoric.

This time the cosmic con had whirled around handouts of $2,000 American Century Awards to celebrate the year 2000. The operators of a Chicago homeless shelter declined the cheap gift, not wanting to be linked to the Moon organization. Those who did not complain included Dennis Hastert, the House Speaker, who had nominated the shelter, and other sponsors whose names were used for the event, including Sens. Strom Thurmond (R-SC) and Orrin Hatch (R-UT), Rep. Henry Hyde (R-IL), and Rep. Dennis Kucinich (D-OH).

Pastor Yang of the Moon church has called the 2000 awards an "event that led up to" the Dirksen ritual. During the affair, according to a church newsletter, Moon stood to explain the geometry and morality of his Cosmos . . . a network of vertical and horizontal lines . . . rotating spheres . . . a chain running through Man, Woman, Child and God . . . the Christ-like ideal of "living for the sake of others," to which he credited himself. He explained that he'd loved his enemies into submission:

> I lived for those who opposed me because of their inability to understand the truth, and invested myself for their children, and lived for the sake of governments that persecuted me. They eventually came to respect me. From this, we can learn God's strategy in contrast to Satan. God's strategy is to take the blow and initial loss, then regain everything in the end. Satan often is the first to strike, but he loses in the end.

Retribution: a theme of his for years, according to his archived sermons. Even in his boyhood, Moon would remember in 1978, he was a "hot-tempered" youth. "I'd never forget if someone slapped me once," he said, "and I couldn't sleep all night for thinking of revenge . . . not just on that boy, but on his whole household. I was considering setting the house on fire and harassing his parents in order to bring great trouble to that home." And in 1987: "[T]his government put me into prison. History will reveal the truth in the future and the American government and people will realize what an evil thing they did. What will they do then? They will bow down." They did in 2004.

. . .

Reports of "deceived" senators didn't prevent powerful partners from sending video congratulations to another crowning that took place December 13—this time in purple robes adorned with silk collars and lily patterns. This one, at the Marriott Hotel, was put on by the American Clergy Leadership Conference (ACLC). Sun Myung Moon's *Times* reported congratulations from George H. W. Bush and his son, the newly reelected president of the United States.

With the election behind them, it was a safe time for Bush Sr. to pay his respects. "Your theme is right on target," he said in a recorded message that was quoted in the *Times*. "Faith, family, freedom, and peace centered on God." Like Trent Lott's speech about "God-centered families," the phrase riffed on Moon-ese.

The ACLC posed as a grassroots group of black ministers, though its Web site is dominated by nonblacks praising Moon. The week before, the group's Rev. Lonnie McLeod challenged President Bush to stand behind the ACLC. McLeod is also the president of Exodus Transitional Community, a Harlem ministry for ex-cons, which has received $1 million under Bush's Faith-Based Initiative, and whose director, a contrite former New York drug gang leader named Julio Medina, sat with the First Lady at the January 2004 State of the Union Speech as a poster child for "compassion in action."

That wasn't enough for McLeod. A former Democrat who had voted for Bush, McLeod penned a cheeky piece for the *Times* promising to support W. if he'd put his money where his mouth is and stand behind the upcoming ACLC seminar. It would settle the question of whether his "family values" talk was "for real, or just for the camera."

During that several-day seminar, the hosts held yet another well-photographed crowning for the reverend. Moon told the crowd that "God's heart is under confinement," waiting to be freed by the True Father from limbo. This cause also occasioned a letter of congratulations from George W. Bush, a president who had snubbed the NAACP but thanked this other group for rallying the "armies of compassion," as the *Times* reported. Shortly thereafter, a Moon-owned company, the Washington Television Center, dumped $250,000 into the fund for the second inauguration of Bush.

Late into the summer, the NPR producers finally got back to me, unaware that during their vacation the crowning had become a small Washington controversy. Exasperated with the aggressive tone of my piece, and

bewildered as to why I thought Danny Davis's behavior warranted attention, a semiretired producer told me, in a world-weary voice, "Politicians
are whores, my dear."

• • •

In footage taken in 2002—apparently at the anniversary party for the
Washington Times—the Rev. Sun Myung Moon swung his arm in ax-han-
dle blows while he demanded that all Christian churches abandon the
symbol of the cross.

"Revolution! Revolutionary movement! All the crosses down. Take
them down."

God, the church said, had told the Reverend Moon to ensure the cross
no longer hindered our appreciation of him. "On June 11, 2001," reported
his church, "lightning struck down the cross decorating the front of the
Unification Theological Seminary"—an idyllic former Catholic monastery
along the Hudson River in upstate New York. "In view of this act of God,
our True Father initiated the 'taking down the cross' movement. Unificationist leaders and diverse theologians have presented many profound
reasons for the taking down of the cross."

It was left to Moon's American ministers to invent a palatable reason
for a war on the symbol of traditional Christianity. It was decided that
"Trade Your Cross for a Crown," a reference to a beloved American Protestant hymn, would fit nicely into tradition.

I will cling to that old rugged cross
And trade it some day for a crown

The bespectacled composer of "The Old Rugged Cross," a Methodist
minister from an Ohio coal-mining town, would probably have been surprised by what the Rev. Sun Myung Moon did with his message. When
George Bennard wrote the song in 1912, he meant no slight to the cross—in

fact, his life was memorialized in small-town Reed City, Michigan, by one three stories tall. The crown, he meant to say, is your heavenly reward.

But Moon openly jeers at the notion that "Jesus is coming in the clouds"—his official description of Christian belief—on the basis that it doesn't fit the Old Testament. Instead, he has claimed for some time that the kingdom has already arrived, here, in swampy, corrupt Washington, D.C.

Which means the time to ditch the cross is now. It is his obstacle. "The fact that the cross is a symbol of division, shame, suffering and bloodshed prove that it is not of God but Satan," said pastor John Kingara in the *Unification News*, who is photographed hoisting a cross into the Dumpster.

Lonnie McLeod, the preacher whose halfway house is funded by tax dollars to the tune of a million dollars, defended the campaign to erase the Christian cross. "I do not want to spend a lot of time explaining how the cross was insinuated into Christianity by a pagan emperor," he sighs in a Mar. 27, 2005, message sent out on a Moon preacher's e-mail list, apparently authentic. "I reverence Rev. Moon with the title of Father. I do so because he welcomes the stranger, feeds the hungry, clothes the naked, and comforts the sick and those in prison," he said. "We believe in 'Redemptive Suffering' but chose to move from the theology of suffering into God's promised Crown of Glory."

To bury the cross six feet deep, the original plan, according to volume 22, number 6 of the *Unification News*, came from Moon's lips. "Bury the cross in Golgotha where Jesus was crucified," he told his pilgrims. But they got there and a cathedral was in the way. "[T]he floor is all made of marble," the report said. So they settled for leaving a little cross there, hung with the blue and yellow flag of the Unification Church, and headed in the predawn to a funeral a mile away, on May 18, 2003—Easter.

Some of the same folks from the Dirksen ritual tagged along, interfaith clerics drawn to Moon's message of peace and perks. According to the *Jerusalem Post*, Arabs and Jews in the Holy Land had not been overwhelmed by the peace marches Moon directed past the ancient buildings of

Jerusalem. A retinue of mostly ministers and imams (there has long been a rabbi shortage) sang and carried banners reading "Heart to Heart" or "A Mother's Heart for Peace" that some local Jews rejected as meaningless.

One notable in the procession was Haitham Bundakji of the Orange County Islamic Society, who was once punched in the face by the "American Al Qaeda," Adam Gadahn, for embracing Jews. Nevertheless, the IIF-WP struggled to draw rabbis, who remained wary of Moon's anti-Semitic teachings. The paraders sang peace songs as they walked, one cowritten by Sen. Orrin Hatch (see chapter 6).

Unimpressed, Arab children pointed toy Uzis at nearby police officers, the Israeli reporter noted. It was summer 2004, after the coronation. Rabbi Aaron Rubin, director of an anticonversion group, complained that Moon's campaigners had fooled non-English-speaking rebbes into signing group confessions for the murder of Jesus. "These people don't have a peace plan; they have a theological agenda," Rubin said. "Their tactic is different from most cults, since they don't try to convert people directly, but instead try to gain legitimacy through different public conferences and festivals."

New Jersey minister William Whitehead has said that a "scary" attempt to win his loyalty came from a fellow Baptist who "invited me on a free trip to the Holy Land paid for by the Unification Church. Yes, Sun Myung Moon wanted me to visit Jerusalem on his dime, no strings attached—except for the meeting I had to attend to get to know people in the organization. Just spend some time in fellowship and friendship with fellow believers in Jesus." Had Whitehead joined the pilgrims, he would have gathered around a shallow grave, cut into the clay earth of Potter's Field, the two-thousand-year-old burial ground traditionally believed to have been purchased with the silver Judas earned by betraying Jesus.

At bottom lay a four-foot-long cross. While holy men looked on, undertakers draped it under the blue and yellow flag of the Unification Church and posted photographs on the Web. "After the prayer," the report said, "the participants put soil on the cross one by one, repenting for the false faith for 1700 years."

After breakfast, according to the *Unification News*, they held a 10 A.M. conference and heard that a Palestinian suicide bomber struck Jerusalem right after sunrise—a sign, said the church journalist, that "Satan attempted to stop this historical conference desperately." The travelers then discussed the next command from the Reverend for reuniting the religions. "Have Jewish people repent for the sin of killing Jesus," Moon had said. After a difficult discussion, a rabbi, unnamed, agreed to apologize for the crime of the Jews, and the guests raised a glass of Holy Wine.

··

FIVE

THE REVEREND MOON AND THE CONSERVATIVE REVOLUTIONARIES

*After realizing that God is the parent of humankind, I was sitting, and feeling
ecstatic about the Divine Principle, when suddenly some blinking lights
approached me and covered my entire body. . . . You must follow Rev. Sun
Myung Moon, who has revealed the Divine Principle and Unification Thought.
I hope that everyone will consider this most seriously.*

—PRESIDENT JAMES GARFIELD
(ACCORDING TO THE REVEREND MOON)

*I think the conservative movement is where it is today because of a handful of
people. Take away an Adams, a Jefferson or a Washington, and you wouldn't
have had that first revolution.*

—RICHARD VIGUERIE, 1981

William McKenzie, now a columnist with the *Dallas Morning News*, can
still see Grover Norquist's January 5, 1983, temper tantrum as if it happened yesterday, with George W. Bush's future economic "field marshal"
hurling papers to the ground in fury, he remembers, after a congressman
accused Norquist of selling his soul to the Reverend Moon.

Norquist, twenty-six, and his friend Jack Abramoff, twenty-four, had
been accused by Rep. Jim Leach (R-IA) of having "solicited and received
funds" for the College Republicans from an inappropriate source: the Lord
of the Second Advent, whose malnourished fund-raisers chanted "Smash
Satan" as they drove through the night to their next flower sale; who that
very week, defiant over a conviction of felony tax evasion, had summoned
a worshipful audience to New York to joke that he had broken free of
the American melting pot ("instead of America melting Reverend Moon,
America is being melted by him!") and proclaim himself "the elder statesman in the land of darkness . . . emerging in the new morning light."

In 1983, it would not do for a young conservative to be tied to this man. Norquist arrived at Leach's press conference and started a shouting match during Q&A time. "Those are lies," Norquist said. "You're saying we took money and we didn't. . . . That is not just a lie, it's charging us with a federal crime."

McKenzie, then a researcher for the moderate Ripon Society, believes Norquist's fit was all show. "He was throwing us off our game," he says in a wry southern drawl. "He knew full well what he was doing." He was showing his tooth-and-nail style, says the columnist: a guy who will "fight you at every turn."

Today Norquist, the fifty-two-year-old president of Americans For Tax Reform, is a key conservative advisor, a compact, serious, fair-haired man whose brows knit together in owlish sorrow when he talks about the capital gains tax. Having brooded on the IRS from boyhood, he has likened the estate tax to "the morality of the Holocaust." His homicidal view of government (he wants to "drown it in a bathtub") is often held up by critics as proof he's a bearded radical, out to disassemble the New Deal. And Abramoff has earned infamy as the ultralobbyist who corrupted huge swaths of Washington in the 1990s before being linked to a web of casinos, murder, and bribery. But in his salad days, Abramoff was a Brandeis University student with big dreams of driving liberals from Washington. He disliked the music of David Bowie, loved to blare "We Are the Champions," and let a young man named Ralph Reed sleep on his couch.

In 1983, Norquist and Abramoff were part of a new wave of Republicans—the "movement conservatives"—struggling for control of the GOP. Figures of the old guard, including Rep. Jim Leach and his think tank, the Ripon Society, urged caution at the new politics of God, gays, abortion, and trickle-down economics. They warned that the new faction was ripping up the pre-1964 roots of the party. And Norquist and Abramoff were not the only revolutionaries accused by Leach of befriending "the elder statesman."

"Jack Abramoff is an Orthodox Jew and I am a Christian," Norquist shot back. "We do not take this very kindly."

Leach was gracious to such criticism—maybe excessively. After some-one in the Norquist camp called the piece "a bunch of ridiculous malar-key," Leach courteously confessed to his audience that the work might well suffer from "less-than-perfect research, and less-than-perfect facts." *Jim!* thought McKenzie in consternation.

. . .

But no one had accused the duo of being Moon Children, as the press called Moonies then—at least not literally. Over six months, McKenzie and fellow investigator Ken Ruberg had painstakingly researched what they saw as a cynical symbiosis forming during Reagan's Morning in America. A number of deals had been made between right activists, who raked in more money than ever by claiming to defend American tradition, and Moon, who was hostile to it. "Our position," McKenzie says, "was, 'Do you want to have Republicans lined up with a group that has these values?'"

What could the two groups have in common? Crude fearmongering, Leach argued. "Appealing to the lowest instinct rather than the highest in the America psyche," he wrote, conservatives had "inundated the country with fundraising appeals that tear apart the ethic of tolerance which binds our society together. . . . Just as Moon attempts to influence the young by offering simplistic allegiance to himself, the 'Father,' as a palliative to the anxiety endemic to modern society." What was on the line, he said, was "whether the Republican Party returns to its traditions, re-establishing it-self as a party of rights and pragmatism, or adopts an agenda catalyzed by Moon and Richard Viguerie, becoming instead a party of anger and social-ized values."

Viguerie, whose direct-mail empire had funded the rise of Reagan, was the most intriguing of all Leach's targets. Besides the *Times* itself, he'd also singled out Gary Jarmin of Christian Voice, a religious right lobbyist of indistinct faith who used his influence for the peculiar purpose of attack-ing anticult groups; and Warren Richardson, a friend of Sen. Orrin Hatch's who had been rejected as Reagan's health czar for ties to anti-Semites and who had just accepted a formal position within the Unification Church anti-Communist group CAUSA.

Wrote Leach, "A party basing its appeal on old-fashioned patriotism and family values simply cannot justify an alliance with a cult that preys on the disintegration of the American family and advocates allegiance to an international social order operating with cell-like secrecy."

But Leach's assertions died and lost steam. The way the press conference went, says McKenzie, it "blew up in our faces." The *Washington Times* called his claims "flummeries." Richard Viguerie told the *Washington Post* that the attack on him was "silly" and that he'd "be hard put to name one or two people whom I know are Moonies."

• • •

The year 1982 had been one of bitter defeats and glorious inroads for Moon.

On February 13, President Reagan had screened—and liked!—the Reverend Moon's $46 million Korean War movie *Inchon!* He found *Inchon!* "brutal but gripping," and refreshing for making Americans the good guys. He had only a vague sense that the producers were Asian and might have missed that Sun Myung Moon is listed in the opening credits as "Special Advisor." The film, about a daring U.S.-led amphibious landing in the Korean War, is widely considered one of the worst war movies ever filmed. Miscast as middle-aged American general Douglas MacArthur is elderly Brit Sir Laurence Olivier, piteously caked in make-up. But the Hollywood press kit for *Inchon!* claims that the dead U.S. commander, deeply moved by Moon's portrayal of him as guided by God, gave special casting approval from the Spirit World: "I was very happy to see this picture made because it will express my heart during the Korean War. . . . I will make more than 100% effort to support this movie." At the box office, however, the film made just $5,200.

On May 17, the *Washington Times* had printed its first issue. The very next day, a jury convicted its publisher of tax fraud.

On July 1, Moon had married 2,075 couples at Madison Square Garden in his biggest wedding to date. The stadium was on the roaring 34th Street, just across from the forty-three-story New Yorker Hotel, which he had purchased and claimed as his World Mission Center.

. . .

In the early 1980s, activist Jack Abramoff was a "freebooting pirate," one associate recalled, hunting relentlessly for a cash channels that campus Republican groups could sail on to victory. He wanted no less, he told a colleague, than to "remove liberals from power permanently."

Part of his vision was making it as exciting to be a Young Republican as a sixties radical, staging outlandish events. But his pint-sized budget of $250,000 wasn't enough to work with, he complained. He blew through it into debt. Those around him worried that young Jack was bending laws to keep his ship going.

In the fall of 1983, the Soviet Union killed 269 people when it shot down a South Korean airliner. Abramoff took the opportunity to stage anti-U.S.S.R. protests coast-to-coast, calling on Reagan to take a harder line on the Communists. At a rally in Washington, one speaker was John T. "Terry" Dolan. The inventor of the "liberal media" attack ad, known for his practical jokes, he was a closeted gay man who had politicked against homosexuality. He wasn't the only one conflicted over the issue. Moon's parsons, having funded Dolan, later had to explain why they had helped a "dung-eating dog," Moon's term for homosexuals. "It was said he'd ceased acting gay," a Moon pastor claimed in a sermon, "when he directed his formidable talents towards the saving of America."

Joining Dolan in a separate protest down the road were two hundred members of the Rev. Sun Myung Moon's group Collegiate Association for the Research of Principles (CARP). CARP was Moon's recruitment arm— demonstrating for right causes but also luring credulous eighteen-year-olds into weekend getaways. On the sidewalk in front of the White House, the CARP Moonists burned Soviet premier Yuri Andropov in effigy.

CARP's Divine Principle conservatives didn't just cheer for conservative causes. An ex–FBI agent, Frank Varelli, told the *Boston Globe* that during that period, he'd habitually "go to SMU [Southern Methodist University] to pay the Moonies" in exchange for information on left-wing activists. Like critics of George W. Bush's presidency, demonstrators against Reagan policies found themselves in FBI files. Obtained by the *Globe*, the papers revealed spying on ten campuses by the church network over a period of five years.

The Reverend Moon's troops believed they were scourging communism in heaven as on Earth. When the Moonies burned Andropov before the White House gates, the real-life Soviet leader, a ruthless KGB operative, was in a hospital, dying of kidney failure. In 2002, the Unification Church released a "remarkable document" in which it claimed Andropov and 119 other Communists were telegramming home to warn what lay in store in hell. It is still available on the official Web site.

"Can you imagine what kind of punishment I endure here?" he said. "I live in a stable and eat nothing but dog intestines. . . . Friends! . . . I am revealing my cruel life to the public in order to be released from here. . . . [Y]ou must study Unification Thought and the Divine Principle and receive Reverend Moon's guidance on the Earth."

• • •

In 1983, the fund-raising efforts of Richard Viguerie were in full flower.

It is the stuff of Republican legend that in January 1965, an enterprising young fellow set out with no more than a vision, and the wreckage of November's failed Barry Goldwater campaign, and changed the world. Viguerie had seen the possibilities of postage stamp fund-raising appeals. He made $100,000 his first year, the beginnings of a behemoth that would send billions of letters and one day help sweep Ronald Reagan into office.

In 1964, Goldwater, the irascible Arizona small-government conservative, had just been trounced 486 electoral votes to 52 by the War on Poverty Democrat Lyndon Johnson. So much for conservatism, the media said. But Viguerie refused to quit. He collected the names of twelve thousand people driven to give $50 or more to Goldwater, many of them small-business owners who felt helpless to stop liberalism. They were the first recruits in his army, a targeted, direct-mail operation that would be sending millions per year to the more conservative candidates.

"Before Rush Limbaugh, there was Richard Viguerie," the *Washington Times* has said of Viguerie. "[His] mail was delivered over hill and dale, through rain, sleet and snow, to conservative donors and activists, prodding them to take action." One defeated California Democrat, Lt. Gov. Mervyn Dymally, blamed his defeat on "Ronald Reagan on the West Coast and Richard Viguerie on the East Coast."

People credited him with "creating the sound effects for the thunder on the Right," naming him one of the year's twenty-five most intriguing people in 1981. (The next year, the Reverend Moon would be on that list and boast of it in his end-of-year sermon.) Today Viguerie is frequently seen on television, threatening to withdraw support from George W. Bush for being too far left. "He's been working this hustle for over thirty years," says *Village Voice* journalist Rick Perlstein, author of a biography of Goldwater. Right after Reagan took office, Viguerie and his colleague, the *Washington Times* columnist and radical Reconstructionist John Lofton, began threatening to withdraw support from Reagan if he proved "not a true conservative."

The president seems to have been stung by the threats. On August 10, 1982, he wrote in his diary, "Rec'd letter from Richard Viguerie with a copy of *Conservative Digest*. He tried to write in sorrow, not anger about my betrayal of the conservative cause. He used crocodile tears for ink."

· With his bottle glasses, parted hair, and vest, Lofton, Viguerie's partner, was openly fuddy-duddy in the pre–Ann Coulter days, when social conservatives were rarely sex objects. The Reconstructionist movement, created by the American Dominionist philosopher R. J. Rushdoony, promoted a return to the ancient laws of Moses in Christian separatist communities where the wicked might even face stoning.

Lofton was "ever on the prowl for heresy," one colleague remembered, reprimanding an irreverent staffer, "Satan is real." He was also a considerably entertaining personality who had asked Beat poet Allen Ginsburg to his face if his mind had been "destroyed by madness," as per his famous poem. One night in 1986 on CNN's *Crossfire*, musician Frank Zappa looked incredulous when the nerdy little man from the Moon press earnestly pled for the cavalry of government censors to ride in and rescue Americans from Prince's dirty song "Sister." "Kiss my ass," Zappa told Lofton. The next year, Lofton accused a conservative writer of "silly, stupid, arrogant nonsense" for questioning the rightness of the Reverend Moon's help.

The February after receiving the Viguerie letter, Reagan fretted that he was "getting real hung up on the press." A few days earlier he had spoken to Lofton and Viguerie's group, the Conservative Union. It had gone fine, he thought, and yet (absurdly, he thought) Moon's *Times* had detected a certain coldness between the right and the president. The paper, Reagan wrote in his diary on February 21, 1983, "has become as R. Wing as the Post is L. Wing." Over the next twenty years, that "R. Wing" would become the mainstream of the Republican Party. But before conservatives could control the GOP and the nation, according to Viguerie in his recent book *America's Right Turn*, they had to set out on the industrious task of assembling their own "alternative media" and their own fund-raising machine.

What his index leaves out, under *M*, is any mention of a certain messianic Korean businessman who supplied the "alternative" newspaper, at staggering personal expense. Lately the Dominionist R. J. Rushdoony and his essays on "Biblical Law" have become a fixation among liberals explaining the rise of the Religious Right, with some justification. But if power can be measured in money and favors as well as ideas, then a figure deserving equal if not greater attention is the great Pontifex Maximus of the Unification Church, under whose grace even Viguerie himself, the cash genius of the right, was plucked from the flaming furnace of bankruptcy in a relationship dating to 1965.

• • •

[B]abies are being harvested and sold on the black market by Planned Parenthood Clinics!

Direct-mail fundraising appeals don't have to be true, except in a rough and poetic sense. The above baby-harvesting pitch reached worried citizens on behalf of the Traditional Values Coalition, a group of forty-three thousand churches that had paid Viguerie to send that one.

The point is not to inform but to bring new donors into politics—Americans who might have given up on making a difference, whose views aren't represented on TV, who have never considered giving. You discover silent majorities, the stuff of sleeping revolutions. The key is that your emotional appeal will tap a chord deep within, a feeling of lingering injustice.

Unnoticed by the mass media for years, the letters "allowed us to bypass the monopoly of [CBS anchorman] Walter Cronkite and the gatekeepers out there," Viguerie said in a C-SPAN interview, "and go right into people's homes. So that's what built the conservative movement in the '60s and '70s." On the dinosaur mainframe computers of the seventies at his center in Virginia, his software crunched the mailing lists and showered Red State Americans with direct-mail appeals. Besides appealing to their distaste for communism and taxes, he harnessed public unhappiness at gays in schools, dead fetuses, sex on television, gun control.

But by 1986 he was a victim of his own success. After Reagan's 1984 trouncing of Democratic Party candidate Walter Mondale, warnings that "the liberals are coming" were a harder sell. Funds dried up in his world. Carter Clews, a former communications director for the Senate Republican Conference Committee, was perhaps exaggerating the importance of the Unification Church, a former client of his, when he told the *Seattle Times*: "If it hadn't been for Rev. Moon and his dedicated cadre, the conservative movement would have dried up and blown away" during those lean years.

Having killed the golden goose, Viguerie found himself $4 million behind payment of debts to the creditors—from banks, to Western Union, to the client who had hired Viguerie to promote a Ron Paul–esque return to the gold standard. The gold people were upset that thousands of leaflets, instead of being sent, were allegedly sitting in a heap of garbage in Chicago. In dire straits, he'd even sold his ten-year-old *Conservative Digest* in 1985. (Shortly thereafter, the new *Digest* featured a flattering profile of Bo Hi Pak, written by Arnaud de Borchgrave's business partner, John Rees.)

Bo Hi Pak now came through for Viguerie. Not only did the fundraiser win a hefty contract from *Insight*, the *Times* sister magazine, but he also arranged a $10 million purchase of an office building in Fairfax, Virginia, by the Unification Church. It was a sweetheart deal, according to Sara Diamond, a sociologist who studied the right, because the place was only worth $9 million.

The bailout was only the latest postcard moment in the bizarre Viguerie-Moon relationship. In 1977, New York auditors punished Viguerie for sending out heartbreaking pitch letters for Sun Myung Moon's "Children's Relief Fund," administered by an obscure South Korean organization calling itself the Korean and Culture Freedom Foundation (KCFF).

The KCFF was raising as much as $1 million a year by 1973, "helped by unsuspecting people in the cause of anti-Communism," wrote government investigator Robert Boettcher. The Viguerie letters for the KCFF showed a child's shriveled body and said: "Thousands of little boys and girls are suffering from the terminal forms of malnutrition. . . . What better gift could you give than a gift to fight suffering and death?" Accordingly, $1,508,256 rolled in from Americans stumped by this question. But only six cents on the dollar fought suffering and death: $920,000 went to Viguerie. This enormous gift to himself led auditors to punish him, banning this proto-Limbaugh temporarily from soliciting in Connecticut and Ohio for children or anyone, according to the Ripon Society.

In another apparent con, the KCFF had invited conservatives to send money for "one of the most daring undertakings against the Communists on the mainland of Asia in the last 30 years": renting state radio towers to beam free-world propaganda over the "bamboo curtain." "Give as much as you can TODAY," the letters read, "and support freedom's vital stand in Asia." The con was that there was no fee for use of the towers, leading to suspicions that the KCFF was a slush fund for the Reverend Moon. In the spring of 1964, Bo Hi Pak told Bob Roland, a Presbyterian elder who was a KCFF board member, that the group "would be an avenue of charitable fundraising to finance the activities of the Moon organization in the United States," in Roland's words, and Roland protested "this obviously unethical, if not illegal, front activity." The investigation also turned up a December 14, 1970, State Department memo expressing "grave doubts about the competence and integrity" of the people behind it, saying there was a "question as to what [the radio group] does with the funds it raises."

How long had the King of America been in business with the direct-mail king and his company, whose opening in January 1965 was called among the one hundred defining moments of the American political century by *George* magazine? It turns out that by that first March, one of his clients was the Reverend Moon's KCFF, led by Bo Hi Pak, who was obsessed with building a base for Moon in America but was assiduously concealing the KCFF's connection to the Returning Lord.

So Viguerie was likely clueless as to his secret benefactor on May 25, 1965, when, after the first wave of seventy-eight thousand mailings brought in $12,147.50 in checks, he sat down to write a letter. "We have been especially pleased by the cooperation given us by Col. Bo Hi Pak," Viguerie wrote. "He has been most efficient in keeping records and fulfilling our every request. It is a distinct pleasure working with him." The letter was to U.S. Navy admiral Arleigh Burke, the first man to be conned into promoting the Reverend Moon.

• • •

You have every reason not to have heard of Koreagate. The bewildering 1976–1978 scandal is little known beyond the stack of manila-colored bound books, deep in the stacks of your local university, compiling the mimeographed government documents of the influence-peddling scandal that time forgot, misunderstood even in its own day. "Most people who followed the scandal did not even know Moon had anything to do with the Korean influence campaign," wrote Robert Boettcher, the boyish but graying staff leader of the investigation, a veteran foreign service officer. The focus was instead on Tongsun Park, a Washington socialite who had been involved in the relatively simple business of bribing congressmen and was exposed.

Unlike the free Seoul of the 1988 Olympics and today, the country was then under repressive control, with democracy years away. Leaders of the junta, installed in a 1961 coup, feared that opinion in Washington would turn against them. Upset by Nixon's decision to withdraw troops from Korea, the government allegedly set out to bribe more than one hundred congressmen.

Unlike Tongsun Park, wrote Boettcher, "Moon is still riding high." His book *Gifts of Deceit*, full of explosive details about Moon's dreams of American power, was named one of the best of 1980 by the *Washington Post* and *New York Times*. But the public ignored it. Boettcher left government service, moved to Manhattan, and died falling from his apartment in 1984.

• • •

There is a boast that is ludicrous, but not ludicrous enough for comfort. The Reverend Moon jubilated in 1986, according to the *Seattle Times*, that he had come to be "considered the mainstream leader of the conservative movement. Look at the facts," he said. "Father is not a citizen of the United States. Father is not even a citizen . . . [but] when he goes to Washington, they say, 'You are the No. 1 conservative leader in this country!'" Madness—but we are obliged to look at the facts.

The process by which the Grand Old Party became a vessel for the Religious Right is, of course, an enormously complex historical development, owing to tectonic changes across America after 1960. As scholar Sara Diamond has detailed, a coalition of businessmen, anti-Communists, and evangelical activists joined forces and tapped changing conditions in America, making the party what it is today. The work of "skilled New

Right organizers," she says, from Jerry Falwell to Phyllis Schlafly, gradually made churches across America less receptive to the born-again Christianity of President Jimmy Carter and more receptive to that of the hard new politics.

But follow the money to the pockets, and it is hard not to see that the Reverend Moon belongs not to the hippie world but the inner world of the Religious Right revolution. Imagine a portrait gallery of the conservative Declaration of Independence, Jerry Falwell and Pat Robertson sitting in for Benjamin Franklin and Samuel Adams. "When in the Course of human events it becomes necessary for one people to dissolve the wall between church and state. . . ." If Moon was not invited to the head of that table, he was, at least, a welcome signatory.

Consider, as a random sampling of key players in the takeover of 1980 onward, a list rattled off by Viguerie, who assigned himself, with justification, a place as an Alexander Hamilton or John Hancock in that gallery. "There were just a handful of us here in Washington," he said. "[Paul] Weyrich, Terry Dolan, Howard Phillips, Ed Feulner, myself, and then out-of-town people like Pat Robertson, Jerry Falwell." The Moon dollar surfaces a few times in this list.

- **Terry Dolan**'s organization took two checks in 1984, totaling $750,000, from the church and then spent the money on computers and polling. "The reason we took the money," he said, "is because I'm absolutely convinced that these are good, honorable people who have a funny theology that I simply don't agree with but who are generally well motivated and want to help this country. . . . In all their funding, there has never been a quid pro quo. All they've ever said is, 'Spend the money the way you're going to spend it.' I find that very refreshing."

- However, **Paul Weyrich**, cofounder of the Heritage Foundation, said early on that "all Americans should be concerned" by Moon, because he "opposes the constitutional system of government." The only major conservative outspoken about rejecting Moon's philanthropy, his daughter, a journalist, quit the *Washington Times* in 1991 after the editor rewrote a story of hers.

- **Jerry Falwell**, founder of the Moral Majority, celebrated Moon's release from prison in 1985. In 1997, his Liberty University was rescued by $3.5 million from Moon, who has called Falwell's top aide, Ron Godwin, a "heavenly locomotive pulling the train of America in the right direction." Godwin, a marketing Ph.D. who insists on being called "doctor," is former vice president of the *Washington Times*. A lawsuit by a former business associate accused Falwell and an aide of flying to South Korea on a January 9, 1994, "secret trip" to meet with Moon's men.

- **Pat Robertson**, founder of the Christian Broadcasting Network and Christian Coalition, has condemned Moon, but his long time deputy Billy McCormack—the "Jimmy Swaggart of Louisiana" and a founding board member of the Christian Coalition—was celebrated by the Unification Church on March 22, 2001, for joining the Reverend's "We Will Stand Tour," in which he shared a stage with the Returning Lord. McCormack also helped present Moon with an award for family values at a January 19, 2001, prayer meeting.

- **Ed Feulner**, cofounder of the Heritage Foundation, wrote for the Reverend Moon's 1970s newsletter, *Rising Tide*, when his own operation filled merely a small office. According to a House investigation, Feulner was introduced by the Unification Church's Dan Fefferman to South Korean officials who would soon direct funds his way: "In 1975, Ed Feulner . . . was introduced to KCIA [Korean Central Intelligence Agency] station chief Kim Yung Kwan by Neil Salonen and Dan Fefferman of the Freedom Leadership Foundation [a Moon group]." After Feulner's trip, $2.2 million in mysterious Seoul cash rolled into the mighty think tank.

The Heritage Foundation is an idea factory. It is housed in a glassy building in Washington that may as well be named a government ministry. Besides helping the Bush White House articulate its ideas, it also staffs TV shows with conservative talking heads.

Did the mystery millions come directly from the regime of Chun Doo Hwan, the last dictator of South Korea? That's what intelligence officer Chang Se Tong testified to his country's parliament on live television in 1988, the year his country became a democracy, putting behind them a tyranny that the *Washington Times* had supported so strongly that it outraged even anti-Communist conservatives (see chapter 3). Or were the funds merely *encouraged* by the KCIA, as Heritage protested in 1989? After the gift, in 1982, Heritage set up an Asian Studies Center pushing the policies of the givers. "Under U.S. law, groups receiving major funding or policy direction from a foreign entity must register with the Justice Department," note reporters David Corn and Morley Jefferson of *The Nation*. "Heritage has not done so."

The Heritage Foundation, that training dojo for the Republican right, forbade its personnel to attend Unification Church functions of the early 1980s. At one time its director of administration, Michael Warder, was himself a former church official and close associate of the Reverend Moon. According to *New Republic* editor John Judis, who observed in 1989 that its officers were freely hanging out at Moon functions, Heritage must have relaxed the ban.

Under George W. Bush, baby-faced Nile Gardiner, an English protégé of Margaret Thatcher who cowrote her book *Strategies for a Changing World*, became an expert at Heritage. He has advised the executive branch, according to his bio at www.Heritage.org. He has pronounced the United Nations "doomed to failure." He has also vowed that Al Qaeda connections and WMD will vindicate the Iraq war. According to a variety of other sources, he is a second-generation follower of the Reverend Moon who jokes that the religious workshops he attends are akin to Christian Bale's training in *Batman Begins*.

According to a 1995 article in Moon's *Unification News*, Gardiner, "one of the Unificationist graduate students in history," took part in a "spiritual battle" at Yale in advance of Mrs. Moon's visit to campus, wielding a mop and a bucket to erase progay chalk drawings. A gay professor, John Boswell of the English department, had died of AIDS, which *News* reporters David and Kathleen Burton saw as part of God's triumph.

• • •

How long has it been such an easy game to play Two Degrees of the Reverend Moon within the conservative world?

The answer lies in an old photograph, in the confusing clutter of documents left behind by the walk of the True Father. It's from 1965. It shows a retired man, frail and maybe bewildered, seated across from an unlikely visitor to his ranch, the Reverend Moon. What is jarring is that he is Dwight Eisenhower.

Moon's hair is jet black—he is forty-five, in the prime of life. He has set his fists in a sharp, rigid gesture, as if spinning a gyroscope to describe his view of the Cosmos, or showing how Eisenhower could purge the globe of Communists in a one-two punch.

Every such photo left in Moon's trail to 2004 has a story to tell, but each story is so odd, so removed from the Washington, D.C., we know from C-SPAN, that it demands a backstory, and then the backstory demands a backstory. The past offers some of the clearest views of Moon, with more indignation and fewer pacts of silence.

How long has this been going on? To understand the story behind that photograph, and the baffling history of Moon in Washington, means driving to Nevada to meet Robroy, as he calls himself on the Internet. Behind the scenes of the Eisenhower con, he was an insider, investigating Moon's world on a personal mission. Then he testified before Congress about what he found. He's a retired airline pilot and Presbyterian preacher who is terminally ill. His story starts near the beginning.

SIX

···

Origin Stories, 1920–1970

The year is 1967. A passenger plane skids to a stop, and Bob Roland, a forty-one-year-old preacher with a problem, walks off, changes from his United Airlines captain's uniform into street clothes, and heads for his secret meeting at a bar near Denver International Airport. Roland, who hails from a long line of Virginians, is a stubborn former World War II Marine who insists on his right to smoke in the cockpit. He hopes the man he's meeting with, a traveler he met whose final destination is Korea, can help him.

A man called Sun Myung Moon has become the bone of contention in Roland's troubled marriage. So when his passenger, a young American GI, mentioned being headed for duty north of Seoul, Roland chewed over a thought the rest of the flight. Then he asked if the GI could do some detective work.

At the watering hole they form a plan. To prevent discovery, the soldier's research will be mailed to Roland care of the airline. His wife can't be allowed to find out that he's digging up dirt on her spiritual hero, a smiling mystery guru who is behind some shenanigans at the South Korean embassy, whose world Roland has infiltrated.

The airline pilot is at wit's end. Here he is, a Presbyterian church elder who has preached the Gospel in the tropics, and he can't stop Moon from enchanting his own wife, Moon, who claims to be the one man on Earth who can unlock the identity of the Messiah.

None of it makes sense. *Who are these friends of hers?* Since Moon's grand arrival in America—for which his wife had waited with bated breath—the Korean has stayed at an apartment in the suburbs south of the Potomac. There his chief aide, Col. Bo Hi Pak, a diplomat at the embassy, hosts dinner parties to win friends for the Master, arranges for photo opportunities with politicians, and runs a questionable money-making scheme known as the Korean and Culture Freedom Foundation (KCFF), whose board of directors Roland has joined in hopes of exposing the truth.

There is even a throne room. In a spare bedroom Pak has set up a winged chair, brocaded with gold, positioned on a white shag carpet. There, Moon reposes with his slippered feet tucked underneath, disciples at his feet, and a silver pitcher of water brought in from time to time on a red lacquer tray.

Meanwhile, at the Rolands' home on Apple Tree Drive in Alexandria, Betty Roland, according to Bob, has been sprinkling Moon's "holy salt" in the four compass directions. Blessed by Moon's hand, the salt is believed to drive Satan out of the home, like a snail from a garden. One day after returning from a flight, Bob Roland came home early and saw his wife praying with Colonel Pak over the crib of his newborn son. "We dedicated him to the Lord," his wife explained to Bob, who was furious, convinced the "Lord" in question was Moon, not God.

Three months after the Denver meeting, Roland checks his airline mail, finds a letter postmarked Seoul, and opens it, hands shaking. The letter explains that the GI has asked around and discovered that Moon is considered a laughingstock in Korea, linked to some unnamed sex scandal. It feeds Roland's hunger for more.

• • •

Robert Roland waves dismissively at a Kinko's box, in 2006, on the rolling shelf beside his easy chair in Las Vegas, in a tract of ranch homes northeast of the Strip. Inside is the origin story I've been afraid to touch. It's hard enough to explain to people that the Reverend Moon owns the *Washington Times,* let alone that before he was a national phenomenon, he was let into the country by Sen. Strom Thurmond (R-SC)—let loose by unsuspecting politicians upon American youth.

From the opening of Roland's manuscript: "[T]he gathering and research of data and material spans the years since February 1963. It was then that I became directly involved with the organization and its leader who, with cunning deceit, would ultimately wreak havoc upon the lives of my family." A dog at his feet, Roland flips between cable news stations in the light of late afternoon. There are paintings on the wall, propeller planes from forgotten airlines, and a dominating painting of Charles Lindbergh and the *Spirit of St. Louis*. His helper, a husky ex-soldier in his forties named Ken Cross, ambles in with TV dinners.

In the 591 meticulously detailed pages are names of Japanese businessmen, duped U.S. diplomats, South Korean officials, dollar figures, and cloak-and-dagger high jinks. During the late 1970s, Roland supplied his research to American congressional investigators. While Bob Dole had narrowly focused on cult recruitment in his 1976 hearings, the follow-up probe from 1977 to 1978 had gone deeper—into manipulation of politics, not just people. If little is known about the Unification Church, most of it is from the huge dump of documents released during the Investigation of Korean-American Relations.

In sworn testimony before Congress in the Jimmy Carter years, Roland said his wife and daughter had been taken from him by a group with unhealthy political aims. In response, Col. Bo Hi Pak, formerly his close friend, testified that it was "sad that the U.S. Congress gave a man like Robert Roland credibility and a forum to pursue the obviously personal vendetta against our church, Reverend Moon and myself. He is filled with hatred and anger, and has a long history of trying anything to destroy the Unification Church."

Now Roland has a bad case of emphysema. What's on his mind is being reunited soon with a soldier buddy, gunned down sixty years ago by the Japanese on a beach in Saipan. "Marines don't cry in public," he told a historian. Then there is the woman he loved, who has been a member of the Unification Church for decades now. It's because of her that almost to his dying day he walks with difficulty into the front room of the house, logs onto the Usenet forum alt.religion.unification, and picks Internet fights under the name "Robroy."

"Stick your Moonie True Love where the sun don't shine," he types to them.

They write back. "I know that Robroy believes he is a hero for exposing the enemies of God in this forum. I for one pity him for I know what is in store for bigots."

"The sickest bunch of people I ever met in my life," Roland says.

"He is among whoremongers and drunkards," they write.

At the Las Vegas Rescue Mission, Roland drove up one day and hired a homeless man, Cross, to care for him, and he has also put up a single mom in one bedroom. Cross gets a look in his eye when he talks about Roland, whom he calls the Captain: both his pastor and drill sergeant. Cross swears that a dove that settled beside him the other day foretold the Captain's power to bring a tramp to Jesus.

"Aw, bull crap," retorts the Captain. He does not want to be a cult leader. Later he grumbles at the television: "Fox News can bring Bill Gertz on time after time and put him forth as an authority," he says of the *Washington Times* national security reporter. "And no one ever connects him to Moon."

As usual, Gertz's reporting has been supporting the White House's positions. One of the strangest reports he has written is that, yes, Saddam Hussein had WMDs—but they were spirited away, at the last minute, by Russians. The fable remains popular among the staff of the *National Review*. ("Thank *God* for Bill Gertz," one of Moon's parsons has preached. "We don't know where we would stand as a nation without him. . . . It didn't come from his own hard work. It came from True Parents.")

Soon the Captain is back thirty years in time and thousands of miles away, in Alexandria. That's where, according to the story he outlined before Congress, Robert W. Roland went undercover to keep his family together and expose the influence of Moon. It is a cloak-and-dagger story that is striking for how different it is from the college student captivity narratives that we associate with cult leaders.

"I had a way with them," he says. "I'm pretty cagey."

• • •

For years Roland kept an eye out for travelers who could answer his question: Who is the Reverend Moon? "He had moles everywhere," remembers his daughter, Linda Mattix. From the GI headed for Asia, to the eyes and ears who spotted Moon one day on the Vegas strip, the tips came in.

In 1976, Roland says, he paid a showgirl to try and photograph Moon. News had come to him that the Returning Lord, along with American church president Neil Salonen and others, were taking in an 8 P.M. show that day at the Riviera. Ostensibly Moon was here to scout for talent for one of his enterprises, a troupe of dancing little girls called the Little Angels. Moon also enjoyed blackjack. His daughter-in-law Nansook, confused one day as to why the True Father was placing wages, was told he went to the casino to be among sinners.

Years earlier, Roland was a whistle-blower, convincing a legendary Navy admiral that he'd been drawn into a con to support Moon's messianic dreams. Before that he had infiltrated the inner ring of Moon's Washington, D.C., world, and pretended to play along with his wife's guru. "I did things that would give him the sneaking suspicion that I was coming around," he says. He even invited Pak to speak at his church. Roland sat in the pews, watching Pak, letting him think that the group's latest fish was Bob Roland, president of the Men's Council of the Presbyterian Church of the Potomac, friend to top evangelicals in the area.

Around that time Pak was arranging meetings for Moon using an adorable facade, a gimmick whose simple brilliance he credited to the Master. Who could resist a traveling musical troupe of patriotic little girls?

•   •   •

In the twilight of Dwight Eisenhower's life, in the fall of 1965, he and his wife, Mamie, emerged from their white farmhouse in Gettysburg, Pennsylvania, where they kept a hundred Angus steers, to greet the little girls and their hosts. A photographer from the local *Gettysburg Times* covered the charming rendezvous: the old American general and the Korean moppets.

The Little Angels toured major American cities with little scrutiny. They even opened a number of shows for the performer Liberace, revealing a hidden link between the two most flamboyant men in American history.

One Little Angel saluted in a U.S. Navy admiral cap, like Shirley Temple. They performed the Sword Dance, the Drum Dance, and the Court Dance. Cameras flashed.

With their drums and silk dresses, their red bodices and fans, their streamers and ribbons, their celebration of golden harvests in an ancient land, the Angels left arts critics breathless across America. "Little fragile blooms," wrote a smitten newspaper arts critic in Maryland, "like a branch of a peach tree that had been brought in during winter. Back stage after the performance, with little angels scattering around like nervous little mice, giggling, helping, hindering, I had a chance to talk to the charming Colonel Bo Hi Pak . . . director of the Little Angels."

Bo Hi Pak stepped from the caravan of sedans. He had brought Eisenhower a guest: the Reverend Moon.

Pak had worked as an officer at the South Korean embassy in Washington. It was only in his spare time that he worked his diplomatic connections to find friends for Moon. But now that the patriarch had formally arrived, Pak resigned from government work to become a full-time promoter of the Lord of the Second Advent.

Having set foot in California early in the year, Moon consecrated "holy ground" in his name as his campaign marched east to the Potomac, starting with the Twin Peaks of San Francisco, which Moon had likened to a mother's breasts, overlooking the bay that reminded him of a womb. He had crossed the Grand Canyon and listened with interest to stories of the Dust Bowl, of the heartland he believed he was destined to rule. Now the procession had reached the East Coast, ready to cap off its victory with a photo op that could multiply Moon's perceived importance.

"Never seen anything like this before," the general said as he looked at a photograph of sixty-two couples, married at once, according to an account in *New Age Frontiers*, an early church newsletter.

Eisenhower had a right to be confused. The Korea group had shifted shape. It had been presented to him as somehow affiliated with the South Korean government, not a messianic religious leader. Equally in the dark were officials who had booked the meeting, who were under the misapprehension that Moon was merely some exotic Buddhist priest.

In internal documents, the director of the Little Angels warned churchmen not to say too much about the link between the girls, referred to as "Divine Principle Children," and Moon. "If we use the Little Angels to promote Our Master and the Church too extensively," read a memo that later turned up before Congress, "Satan will attack by saying that Reverend Moon is exploiting these children for his own glory." The Divine Principle Children were presented as orphans, though most were from middle-class families. They were also used as mules for unregulated foreign cash, stuffed into their socks. A single troupe once hauled $58,000 in Japanese yen to Pak's Virginia home.

Pak was savvy enough to know that no one in Washington would warm to Moon if he came on too strong as an incoming political ruler. Nor would a New World messiah be the kind of cause for which Americans would write big checks. So Pak surrounded the KCFF in a cloud of Cold War patriotism. Presenting it as a grand diplomatic project of enormous weight and respectability, he scouted out top names who would agree to be listed on his letterhead in the cause of standing up to communist North Korea. He succeeded in snagging Eisenhower as well as Adm. Arleigh Burke, a World War II hero with a class of warships named for him.

The Gettysburg visit surpassed expectations. In the Moon publication *New Age Frontiers*, a disciple raved, "Time originally allotted for our Leader's visit—5 minutes. Time spent with General Eisenhower—45 minutes! Truly a successful day!"

Moon, the forty-five-year-old Washington hustler, owed Eisenhower. But he saw it the other way around. Ike, Moon told his followers, had "paid his bill in full," and they smiled on this turn of luck. Pak confided to an American associate that the president had "opened all the doors for Sun Myung Moon." He went ahead and quoted Eisenhower in one of the fund-raising letters, likely distributed by the Richard A. Viguerie Company: "I urge my fellow Americans to study and support the objectives and programs of the KCFF."

• • •

The intertwining of Bob Roland's life with Moon's had begun in 1963, with a chance meeting at the Washington Golf and Country Club. There, on Tuesdays, businessmen and preachers mingled, prayed, and took turns speaking about the gospels. The luncheons were put on by a Protestant group with strong political connections, International Christian Leadership. One day Roland was standing before the table, giving off-the-cuff remarks, when he was surprised to see a balding, somewhat awkward-looking Asian military officer in uniform, hanging on every word.

Colonel Pak was taking copious notes. After the meeting broke up, he approached Bob with folded hands and introduced himself as assistant military attaché for his country's embassy. "Mr. Roland, never in all of my life have I met anyone with such wisdom as yours," the pilot recalls Pak saying. "Especially someone so young as you."

Embarrassed by his new fan, Roland could already picture the ribbing he was in for at next week's lunch. He wasn't Billy Graham, for Pete's sake. "But at least *someone* was listening this time," he thought dryly.

The pilot walked out into the cold, clear day and left Pak standing at the country club. He didn't think they'd meet again, but they did.

• • •

"A dragon emerges from a ditch," they say in Korea, of great men whose iron will has lifted them from poverty, war, and other hardships that have tested the Land of the Morning Calm for centuries.

As he put the pieces together in the Reverend Moon story, Robert Roland learned the basics. Born Yong Myung-Moon ("Shining Dragon") in 1920, Moon's parents were poor farmers who struggled to get by in northern Korea. Under the humiliating occupation of Imperial Japan, Koreans were forced to speak the colonizer's language and answer to Japanese names. In this misery, the story goes, Moon grew up weighed down by the suffering of the world, as if preternaturally knowing his destiny.

Yong-Myung Moon became Sun Myung Moon only after his vision of Jesus in 1935. During Easter, he went up a small hill, at the foot of the rocky peaks of Mount Myodu, to pray. Then God appeared to tell him, "You are the son I have been seeking, the one who can begin my eternal history."

When Moon's vision came, he balked at the impossible new mission. "God does not easily give the title 'Son of God,'" Moon recalled in 1977. What hurt wasn't just the crushing responsibility to save the world but intimate knowledge of the Fall of Man that even God found too agonizing to admit. "Even God said 'No' to Father three times when he presented the Divine Principle," according to a June 10, 2001, Unification sermon by Kevin McCarthy. "Father told God: 'Bullshit!' [God] knew he was right."

Moon learned that Jesus had failed in his mission—as Moon saw it, not to die but to marry, beget children, and build a tangible, thriving Peace Kingdom. Instead, Jesus had failed miserably. In 1978, Moon would explain, "by the imperfection of Jesus's dispensation, two thousand years ago . . . all previous work was nullified, no value." A softer version is presented to kids in *True Parents' History for Children*:

"I came to earth almost two thousand years ago to save the world from Satan. I was the Messiah. I wanted to make this world into a beautiful and loving place where everyone could be happy. But they killed me before I could finish my work. Now, another person must be the Messiah. . . ."

. . . Then Father began to feel achy and miserable all over. He began to cry. The tears came faster and faster. "Oh, it hurts so much," he cried to God. My heart is aching. I feel like I can never stop crying. Why is this?"

He bent over in pain. He was feeling the pain that had been in God's heart for so long.

But Moon mustered the strength to embrace his quest. Meanwhile, his rise had caught the attention of Lucifer. "'Hey, [Satan] snarled, 'if this guy learns about what happened in the Garden of Eden, I'm doomed,'" the children's account goes. "'I've gotta put a stop to this nonsense.'" The evil forces swooped in upon Moon, but like Robert Johnson, he tamed the devil—then beat the truth out of him. Under his interrogation techniques, Satan confessed to his "secret crime," omitted from the Bible: having sex with Eve.

• • •

After his vision, Moon went to Japan to study electrical engineering, a discipline that would lend a technician's logic to his holy book, the Divine Principle. But as the young man began to preach in prewar northern Korea, Christians angrily rejected his message. One explanation for Moon's cold reception was later given by U.S. embassy officials in the 1960s, who periodically passed along rumors that his church performed X-rated rites to drive Satan from women. But the Unification Church calls this a libel. "I have lived a chaste life," Bo Hi Pak would tell Congress, sobbing, in 1977, telling a congressman the claim—which had made the American press— "will haunt you to your grave."

But the Reverend Moon, by his own admission, was surrounded by female admirers. He recalled years later that "all the women around me, from age eighteen to eighty, wanted to be my spouse. . . . I would kick them out but they would climb the fence to come back. Husbands would confine them to the house, take away their clothes, and underwear, and tie them up. . . . Many rumors began. Husbands wanted to kill me."

In 1948, the Japanese driven from Korea, and the Communist guerilla Kim Il Sung took power in the north. According to official history, Moon was sentenced to a miserable work camp in the northeast, the notorious Hungnam Prison. In camps like that, dissidents were worked to death, while guards told them the Great Leader's benevolent mercy kept them alive. They grabbed fistfuls from mountains of old fertilizer, stuffed it into straw bags headed on trains to Kim's farm collectives, ate rice from dead men's lips, and suffered beatings.

There, fellow inmates came to see Moon, Prisoner 596, as a man of miracles. He often debated points in the Bible with his work leader, Pak Chung Hwa (no relation to Colonel Pak), Prisoner 919. At first he scoffed at Moon's unusual teachings—especially the idea that John the Baptist, Jesus's disciple, had been no hero, but the weak link in God's failed plan.

"He could not fulfill his responsibility," Moon insisted. "That was the reason why God could not prevent King Herod from cutting off his head." It was the same reasoning he would later use to explain the Holocaust: those who bungled Jesus's mission must suffer.

As the story goes, Prisoner 919 found this line of reasoning questionable until one morning when he woke from a dream of an old man, telling him that Moon was the Second Coming. And once he started thinking about it, it seemed to explain why the reverend was such a physical dynamo. Where others died all around him, three years of hell hadn't reduced Moon's electric vigor. Amid that suffering, the church teaches, Moon became the perfect human being.

The official account of his escape is right out of a movie. The two men, and a third friend, were facing certain execution when they heard the thunderbolt of American warplanes over the nearby city. The forces of the United Nations, which would occupy so much of Moon's spiritual imagination, were liberating the death camp while Moon and his friends fled the bombardment. It was all part of Korea's divine providence as the Father Nation—so destined, Moon has said, because of the peninsula's resemblance to a penis. Japan, the Mother Nation, "yearns for male-like peninsular Korea on the mainland."

The children's version explains:

During this time, the war continued between the communists and the United Nations troops. The communists were led by two men. One was a Chinese man named Mao Tse Tung, and the other was a Korean named Kim Il Sung. Satan was using these two men to build the Satanic Kingdom on earth. God was using Father to build the Heavenly Kingdom on earth.

There were three men headed south through the devastation. Pak Chung Hwa was wounded, and it's said he begged to be left to die. But Moon told him, "If we die, we die together; and if we survive, we survive together."

A ramshackle church of the new faith was set up in Pusan, southern Korea, in 1951, built from U.S. Army ration packets and other war debris. Soon the faith grew to number thousands of followers. At first the South didn't look on Moon any more kindly than the North had. But then, in 1961, the government collapsed, stunning the Kennedy administration, which didn't know what to make of new generalissimo Park Chung Hee but opened friendly relations with him.

In the name of fighting communist subversion, the military regime cracked down on most Christian churches and outlawed a wide range of groups, but for some reason it smiled upon Moon and his fanatically anti-Communist religion. The Reverend Moon now had congregations in thirty cities. Four Korean Army officers close to the new junta were also friendly with Moon's group. They included Col. Bo Hi Pak, the young embassy liaison. The most powerful early ally was a politician and later prime minister named Kim Jong-Pil, who established the new regime's Korean Central Intelligence Agency, an instrument of political repression that modern South Korea has since scrapped.

In a February 26, 1963, report, a CIA analyst wrote in an intelligence cable that it was Jong-Pil who "organized the Unification Church while he was director of the ROK [Republic of Korea] Central Intelligence Agency." Eager to build a mutually beneficial relationship with Moon, this chief of the secret police met with Moon's proselytizers at the St. Francis Hotel in downtown San Francisco, according to congressional investigators, and promised support. Another U.S. intelligence agency memorandum, dated December 18, 1964, said that Pak's money-making scheme, the KCFF, was "the first step towards organizing a Tong-Il [Korean for *Unification* group] in Washington."

Roland, though an anti-Communist, was horrified as he read about the KCIA's reign of terror. Its torture practices included waterboarding, as well as the KCIA "barbecue," the practice of stringing citizens spread-eagled over a flame to elicit confessions. By 1967, South Korean agents were kidnapping Korean exiles and sending death threats ("you will be killed Sunday") to the editor of a reformist Korean newspaper editor in California.

But it was in Japan that Moon had made perhaps the most impressive strides. Seeing potential in him, the right-wing tycoon Ryoichi Sasakawa, who presided over an empire of motorboat gambling, convened a meeting near a lake in Yamanashi Prefacture, where he invited Moon to meet with him and Shirai Tameo, a youth training leader for the *yakuza*, the Japanese Mafia. Their discussions would lead to the formation by 1970 of a joint project combining the muscle of the Mob with the feverish devotion of the Unification Church. The name was Shokyo Rengo, "Victory over Communism." It became Japan's official chapter of the World Anti-Communist League, an international coalition also affiliated with neo-Nazis, terrorists, and various other extremists across the globe.

• • •

Prisoner 919, the man said to have been carried hundreds of miles on the Reverend Moon's back, later accused him of running a sex club.

In postwar South Korea, the government had accused Moon of luring girls into a life of sin. For refusing to abandon the Rev. Sun Myung Moon, fourteen girls were dismissed from Ehwa Women's University, and two professors were fired. Moon called this "the climax of persecution." In 1955, he was arrested, on charges that vary depending on whom you ask: draft dodging or bringing a woman who was not his wife to a "love hotel." He was acquitted.

In 1993, Prisoner 919 wrote an inflammatory tract, *The Tragedy of the Six Marys*, claiming inside knowledge that it was all true. The early sales pitch to young men, said original Moon follower Chung Hwa Pak, had been that membership brought access to a harem.

The charge echoed earlier U.S. intelligence reports on Moon, long rejected by the church as slander by Christian missionaries with axes to grind. Moon's defender, journalist Carlton Sherwood, quotes this Defense Intelligence Agency (DIA) report: "Directly under Founder/Sect leader MUN [sic], are his six main disciples, all females, who are called 'Marys' in the UC. In spreading the religion, each of the 'Marys' first recruited three males." An FBI file had furthermore speculated that the rites involved "having a nude women in a darkened room with MUN while he recited a long prayer and caressed their bodies. . . . At these meetings, MUN prepared special food and drink, and gathered his nude congregation into a darkened room where they all prayed for twenty-four hours." Now Prisoner 919 claimed that sex with the six had been an initiation rite, a "blood exchange" that freed women from the stain of Eve by infusing them with God's bloodline.

. According to Prisoner 919, Moon hadn't been content with just six but sixty, and pregnant women were not guaranteed child support. "He violated mothers, their daughters, their sisters," wrote Moon's ex-comrade. One woman, Yu Shin Hee, said she was ruined after being discarded as a woman that the men had tired of transmogrifying into a Mary.

But in November 1995, as Moon was touring with George Bush, Prisoner 919 recanted his attack on Moon, saying it had been made in bitterness. "I've always wondered what the price was of that retraction," Moon's daughter-in-law, Nansook, wrote.

For his part, the aging veteran of the North Korean death camp insisted he was retracting the story in response to his conscience. After their great escape, he had wrongly held a grudge against Moon, blaming him for his own hardships as a refugee in shattered, postwar South Korea. Hadn't Moon promised to look after him? "Just the thought of Reverend Moon, even at night when I was asleep, would make me jump up and want to take an ax and smash his head open," he said.

Now he saw his error and recognized Moon as the Messiah. Part of this, he said, was seeing tremendous works in America: the East Garden palace, the New Yorker Hotel.

"I was glad, too, to see the *Washington Times*," he said. "It made me understand how Reverend Moon's work is being accomplished all over the world. I saw where God has appeared to us in the form of Reverend Moon and is accomplishing His will in our midst."

• • •

"I must lay a firm foundation for Master by making influential political and social contacts," Pak explained one night over dinner to Bob and Betty Roland, whom he had finally won over as friends despite repeated rejections. They dined at Pak's house in a middle-class neighborhood on Utah Street in Arlington, which by evenings were awhirl with guests—not just Pak's fellow Moonies but new potential friends—other figures in the northern Virginia suburbs drawn, like the Rolands, to his hospitality.

Pak hadn't mentioned Moon until months after their first dinner. He was combing Washington for anti-Communists and Christians with whom he could find common goals, while presenting a mainstream image. The country club luncheon had been a good lead. Started in the Depression, the cozy atmosphere of men's fellowship was intended by Republican founders of the International Christian Leadership (ICL) to combat labor unions with the new fusion of Jesus and American enterprise. ICL soon found friends on Capitol Hill, and from 1953 onward, it hosted the presidential National Prayer Breakfast. The Senate chaplain hailed the new tradition as a sign of a "Return-to-God movement" in America.

• • •

The topic of Moon wasn't brought up until months after the Rolands had been dining with Bo Hi Pak. Over dinner one night, the ice melted, and Bob asked about Pak's diplomatic title. What did an "assistant military attaché" do, exactly?

Pak told him it meant ferrying secret information back and forth between the Kennedy administration and the Korean regime.

It was months before Pak revealed his other purpose in Washington. That night Mr. and Mrs. Roland were surprised to find themselves the only guests. Pak said something in a thick accent that Roland didn't understand. It sounded like "The Lord is back on Earth." His wife's eyes flashed with what looked to Roland like excitement.

"What did you say?" they said.

"The Lord of the Second Advent is back on Earth," Pak said, and he told them about a man named Sun Myung Moon who, through his work, had identified the savior.

"I think your friend Bo Hi has flipped his lid," Roland told his wife after they left. His wife wasn't so sure.

Out of curiosity, according to Roland, Betty pored over the dense passages from Moon's leather tome, the *Divine Principle*, an intricate anatomy of the universe. It begins:

Everyone, without exception, is struggling to gain happiness. The first step in attaining this goal is to overcome present unhappiness. From small individual affairs to history-making global events, everything is an expression of human lives, which are constantly striving to become happier. How, then, can happiness be attained?

The Principles would not come into focus, the church taught, unless the student read them dozens of times for understanding.

Through origin-division-union action, the dual characteristics of God are projected to form two distinct and substantial object partners, which interact with each other as subject partner and object partner. The object partner responds to the subject partner to form a common base and begins give and take action around the subject partner. As they are held in balance by the force of giving (centrifugal) and the force of receiving (centripetal), the object partner revolves around the subject partner in a circular motion, and thus they become harmonious and unified.

By the end of the book, the clouds have parted, and the language has become simpler.

> Therefore, the nation of the East where Christ will come again would be none other than Korea.

· · ·

One day in 1965, Adm. Arleigh Burke—who had pushed destroyers to boiler-busting limits and survived kamikaze plane attacks—opened an envelope to read some typed passages that had been mailed to him, using unfamiliar language. "We today are now the Third Israel. We are those who come under the protection of the body and blood of the Divine Principles."

From a newsletter called *New Age Frontiers*, published by a church he'd never heard of, the excerpts described a "Throne Room" where Moon sat in a "magnificent wing-chair." And this Third Israel, whatever it was, was somehow linked to a meeting with Burke's old commanding officer, Dwight Eisenhower.

The letter had come from Robert Roland, one of the names on the KCFF letterhead. Roland claimed the group to which Burke had lent his name was a secret front "for the financial support and propagation of the ideology of the Holy Spirit Association and its leader, Mr. Sun Myung Moon of Seoul, Korea."

"It jolted me," Burke wrote in a letter describing how he'd misunderstood the group's nature.

> I had never heard of the Unification Church or Mr. Moon, and I knew nothing at all about either. I had previously known that Col. Pak was quite religious and an ardent Buddhist. . . .
>
> I called Mr. Roland, who was with United Air Lines, but he could not add more than was in his letter. He was sure he was correct. I checked

with a few people who knew Mr. Roland and they said he was a man of good judgment.

The admiral resigned from the board but appears to have gone out of his way to avoid embarrassing Eisenhower, giving only the most polite explanation for his resignation. Eisenhower, whose name remained on the KCFF letterhead, wrote back to Burke that he sympathized with the admiral for not having the energy to devote to the project.

"Time takes its toll," Eisenhower wrote. "On top of this, you and I are not blessed with the large and comprehensive staff of aides and assistants that we once had."

Burke phoned Bo Hi Pak, who promised to explain his complicated relationship with Bob Roland.

• • •

While Roland tried to hold his marriage together, the divide over the Returning Lord sometimes became too much. One night after he flew into a rage—"I am asking that you choose whether you want this family, or whether you want Moon," he said—he drove Betty over to Bo Hi Pak's house, suitcases and all, feeling shot through with pain.

He peeked into Moon's small throne room, where servants came in from time to time, wearing white linen. The door opened to a long coffee table and, at the end of it, Moon on his American throne.

Sometimes Roland had tried to communicate with Moon, speaking in simple English, with no luck. He'd wondered if Moon would behave the way he did the first time they saw him, when he gave a welcome speech that built up to a tenor of flailing arms and a contorted face. Instead, he just smiled peacefully.

Today, as usual, there were guests at the Pak home. "The least I can do is to warn those innocent participants downstairs," Roland told his wife. "Please don't persecute my master," she told him. "He's suffered enough already." He pulled away and went downstairs to talk to the arriving dinner crowd.

Moon had emerged from his room amid the fuss. As Roland began accusing Moon of a secret agenda, one of Moon's new American followers screamed at him to stop. The airline pilot found himself face to face with Moon, right in front of all these people. The reverend didn't understand a word of his English but looked on, beatifically, while the airline pilot shouted that he was a liar and a fraud. People started flowing out the doors. Roland went home and wept.

Bob Roland, Moon's sworn enemy, continued to surface at events around the country, trying to stop the church's campus recruitment. Later his daughter Linda briefly joined the movement, to Roland's grief and rage, but left on her own accord—freaked out, she says, by the pagan rituals at Unification Theological Seminar. At meetings of CARP, Roland would appear with a trench coat and a sign, trying to warn people, as he had that day at Bo Hi Pak's basement, that everything was not as it appeared.

His wife, now Betty Lancaster, became a spokesperson for the church. In 1969, she traveled with Moon to George Washington's plantation, with its veranda view of the Potomac. The first president, she wrote, "surely must have been there . . . to receive True Parents. Father has often spoken of the faithful prayers of President Washington." Looking out on the Potomac, she told Moon, was "like the 'Kingdom of Heaven.' Father just looked at me with a smile. But he did ask us to check on possible property nearby." But there was no available land for Moon's own Mount Vernon.

In 1976, she attended the Yankee Stadium rally, and "Satan was furious that day," she remembered. A youth gang had attacked a well-dressed churchman, and hoodlums threw bottles at Lancaster and a line of believers on the way to the parking lot. "Our brothers and sisters who were kidnapped in earlier times had far more drama. . . . But we wouldn't trade one moment of our life for any other. To live during the lifetime of the Messiah, the King of Kings, True Parents, is worth every good and challenging moment."

She made the news in 1979 after a trigger-happy young churchman fired rifle shots at fleeing exit counselors. The visitors had brought two ex-members by the dorm in Norfolk, Virginia, to collect their belongings.

Lancaster told the *Washington Post* that the visitors were "criminals" who made off with church property—including an anticommunism film featuring Ronald Reagan.

As the van lurched into gear, young Unification Church member Mark Boitano, twenty-six, was ordered by another sect member to shoot a rifle at the fleeing ex-members. One bullet punctured the front tire. Another pierced a door on the passenger side, but no one was hurt. In an unlikely twist of fate, Boitano stayed with the church and is now a GOP state senator in New Mexico.

Roland died in 2007 and was buried that summer at Arlington National Cemetery. Decades after he had met Moon, a church testimony was posted on the Web under his wife's name—saying that every follower had in some way obeyed "the voice from Heaven, that same voice that said to Abraham, 'Pack up your family and all your belongings and leave your homeland and move to a new land to which I am sending you.'"

• • •

Congressional investigator Robert Boettcher wrote in 1980 that Moon

> is skillful at transforming the illusion of power into real power. [He] seized every opportunity to be seen with influential persons and especially to be photographed with them. This technique helped increase their power in Korea by convincing government leaders that they were close to the most important people in Korea. Likewise, in the United States they exaggerated their actual importance in Korea, which opened more doors to American influence.

In 1987, one of Eisenhower's most respected aides, U.S. Navy and later Treasury Secretary Robert B. Anderson was on a downward spiral of alcoholism and corruption, worsened by hiding donations from the Unification Church. He had been hiding half of the $500,000 paid to him from 1983 to 1984 by the organization, for the service of endearing Moon—just convicted of tax evasion himself—to high officials, including Vice President George Bush, asking them to commute Moon's prison sentence. The pardon has never come. Stripping him of his law license, New York judges said it was a "sad but we think necessary end to the legal career of one who has in times less beclouded by poor and corrupt judgment served his country in high office." Anderson died two years later.

The Returning Lord was not humbled by his audience with the old president who had welcomed him to Gettysburg or the Ike aide who had come to ruin. A decade later, Moon bought full-page advertisements in major newspapers, claiming that Eisenhower, among the other presidents, had vouched for him from heaven.

"Life on earth appears like that of the satanic city of Sodom," the church has Eisenhower saying, having died four years after his meeting with Moon but then, allegedly, attending a "Divine Principle Seminar" in 2003, conducted entirely in the afterlife and chaired by Richard Nixon. "Today, the United Nations and America are confronted with the situation where they absolutely need the ideology of the True Parents," he says.

"Every time God sees his true son fighting alone," says Eisenhower's ghost, "his distressed face is covered by dark clouds of worry."

And Nixon adds the cry for ten thousand years of victory: "Mansei."

SEVEN

GOD FORGIVES RICHARD NIXON

January 25, 1974: With a frozen, hideous grin and a bulbous nose, the giant papier-mâché idol coasts down a busy street in Tokyo to the American embassy, escorted by hundreds of worshippers. It's a crude likeness of Richard Nixon, a president in peril, a man who could use a friend. "God has chosen Nixon through the will of the people," the Reverend Moon has explained via a flier handed out at the event by his legions. "It is the people's duty to support him."

In Washington, D.C., the Returning Lord is similarly putting on large demonstrations intended to prove that he is an important ally who loves Nixon and his collapsing administration unconditionally. He deploys his young believers on the Capitol Steps to wave signs reading, "Forgive, Love, Unite." He is hoping to stun the White House with kindness, so that Republicans will owe him for his kindness. In paid announcements across the country, Moon showcases himself as a humble outsider who, seeing that "no great American spiritual leader or evangelist would rally America around God above the Watergate at this stormy and depressing time," has stepped into the role himself, selflessly ordering his followers around the world to fast for forty days in support of Nixon, who is struggling to explain an eighteen minute gap in his secret tapes. The pro-Nixon extravaganza is calling itself the Freedom Leadership Foundation (FLF).

Garry Wills, the historian and journalist, is tickled when Nixon comes out to greet the young FLF stalwarts, and they kneel before Nixon like subjects of a Roman emperor who has declared himself a god. "When a man has sacrificed all honor, he must settle for adoration," Wills writes. Pathetic, he opines, that the president's admirers have dwindled to "a corrupt Korean regime's least honorable extension." To Moon, the phenomenon of Moon is a mirror image of crass values exported to Asia by Western colonialism. "We taught him that God loves a succeeder," Wills quips, "not like that prodigal Son of his who went off and got crucified and had to be disowned. . . . That is the religion we taught our subject colonies, and Moon comes innocently to remind us of it, and get paid. Make a buck for God."

On June 10, 1974, as the storm worsens, a young political wunderkind named Karl Rove writes to George Bush, head of the Republican National Committee (RNC), reporting happy progress. At twenty-four, he is already a man committed to total victory.

Rove, in his position as head of the College Republicans National Committee, has been hammering home the need to galvanize support for Richard Nixon among young people, by training a cadre of dedicated volunteers. As part of his mission to claim college campuses for the GOP, he is reporting to Bush that young Democrats have just been voted out of the U.S. Youth Council, a fifteen-member nonpartisan group for college students, backed by the State Department. Their seven replacements, he brags, are from conservative youth groups. He ticks these groups' names off: the College Republicans, the Young Republicans, and something called the Freedom Leadership Foundation. He doesn't mention that the FLF is an arm of the Unification Church.

Replying to Rove, Bush has scribbled on the letter—reprinted on colorful Republican National Committee stationary—"Thanks for this. Glad you are involved—keep up the good work."

● ● ●

Did Bush know Rove was referring to the Reverend Moon's youth cadre? Did Rove?

"Based on twenty years of covering Karl close-up," says *Bush's Brain* coauthor Wayne Slater, "my sense is that it's impossible he did not know about the Moonies and Rabbi Korff"—Sun Myung Moon's ally in the sunset of Nixon's presidency, an eccentric Jewish cleric who forgave Nixon his anti-Semitism and joined the Moonies at prayer rallies. "It would have been in keeping with the way [Rove] has always operated—a remarkable ability to survey the field of opportunity and to use every tool available to advance the cause. That's Karl."

A look through Rove's collected papers, kept at Stanford University, summons up what it must have been like to peruse his desk clutter in 1974. In a folder are letters of thanks from politicians for "bringing home the bacon" and first drafts of Rove's fawning notes back to them. Here's a flyer for Rove's fake grassroots pro-Nixon group, Americans for the Presidency. Here's a flirty note from a girl, and here's an apology to Rove from a Gino's fast-food manager who ruined his dinner on Pennsylvania Avenue.

And here's a September issue of *Rising Tide*, the newsletter of Moon's Freedom Leadership Foundation. It profiles Dan Fefferman, the Moon disciple, one of the right-wing Youth Council (YC) appointees that Rove is so happy about. Besides leading the "Save Nixon" campaign, he would, as part of the USYC, help introduce the Heritage Foundation to its patrons in the South Korean government, according to the 1978 congressional investigation. The issue features, as usual, a profile of the publisher: "FLF Founder Sun Myung Moon: One Man's Struggle for Truth."

• • •

No revolutionary campus movement is complete without a paranoid weekly newspaper that you hand out to passing freshmen, filled with headlines of violent confrontation and imminent doom, and hinting that history has prepared just one man to fix America—typically the publisher—whether it's Lyndon LaRouche, a conspiracy theorist who wants to become the American Il Duce, or Bob Avakian of the Revolutionary Communist Party USA, who wants to be the American Mao.

And the clean-cut Moon youth had their *Rising Tide*. In its pages, its liberal enemies are "under Soviet control" . . . Jimmy Carter is making secret deals with North Korea . . . Communists and the ACLU are teaming up to tie the CIA's hands behind its back . . . Communism "is the true antichrist of this age," Moon reveals . . . "Will America Self Destruct?" . . . Karl Marx may have been a Satanist . . . Gary Jarmin proposes a "moral revolution in politics" . . . East German thugs are disrupting Moon events . . . an elite squad of clean-cut young men, posing in Washington, have been selected to take part in a "Victory over Communism" thought seminar . . . Josette Sheeran (now a Bush UN appointee) says the public dislikes Carter's missile treaty . . . Bill Gertz (now a star investigative reporter for the *Washington Times*) is saying that "the true solution to Communism then is a God-centered ideology, emphasizing man's responsibility before God . . . one world under God."

The not-entirely-forthcoming ads for Moon in *Rising Tide* invite the reader to order a "New Home Study Course" in arguing with Commies. "You are against Communism, but do you know why Communism is wrong? Do you know what you stand for?" Look closer and the book is *Unification Thought as a Critique and Counterproposal to Communism*. Then there is an upcoming event called "Cybernetic Warfare: The Battle for Men's Minds," held by something called CARP, which turns out to be the recruitment arm of the church.

Occasionally there is a huge spread on Moon. In one, he plays the God of science, speaking at a conference featuring real professors, under a bizarre sign with an arrow running a circle into itself: "The Centrality of Science and Absolute Values," it says. Another: "Reverend Moon Gives 'God's Plan for U.S.' in 'Sermon on the Hill"—a headline for a 1975 speech before congressmen, his second.

And then there are the other voices, surprising to find here: regular contributions from Accuracy in Media (AIM), the conservative watchdog group, and Ed Feulner, the Heritage Foundation cofounder. Arnaud de Borchgrave and Michael Ledeen, the neoconservative, put in appearances, too.

It is jarring to find one of the minds behind the Heritage powerhouse sharing page space with invitations to join a cult. In 1977, Feulner was an outsider trying to change Washington from a small office. In *Rising Tide*, conservatives like him play up Communist atrocities, while Moon seizes on such reports in sermons promoting an America "armed with Godism," his term for the theocracy that must prevail. "She [America] must free the Communist world, and, at last, build the kingdom of God here on Earth," he writes in the *Tide*. Ideology, ideology, ideology . . . there's even an "Ideology" column on the back of every issue, with the writer debating the fine points of Marx. An April 1975 issue declares that "Three Hundred FLF Trainees Teach Ideological Victory," a "120-day national leadership program" at the Barrytown, New York, monastery in upstate New York.

The training dorm is no ordinary Young Republicans retreat. The smiles of the True Parents hang in the entrance hall of the old Catholic monastery. The saints, the cross, and the Virgin Mary have been removed. A banner proclaims the 21-Day Blessed Wives Workshop. A large pack of Asian young women in training marches past us, ignoring greetings. "Let's get out of here before they cut the brake lines on my car," my friend says, rattled. Outside, a meadow path, "Father's Trail," winds to a pond with a bench, specially designated because Moon has sat there. And a rickety-looking old barn, as if built to substandard specifications by the long-ago labor of grinning eighteen-year-olds, bears the red-sun-and-interlocking-arrows sign of the Unification Church.

•   •   •

A reliable way for the Peace King to make friends in Washington was to rally youth for the unpopular Vietnam War. On October 12, 1969, with a colossal antiwar march coming in three days, Moon assigned his American leader, Neil Salonen, to lead something unheard-of: a fast for war. The young cadre lived off pumpkin soup and pig fat, and they entreated Washington to keep troops in Vietnam.

Though only forty students fasted for war, a pittance next to the two million who would march on October 15, Moon's ploy for attention paid off. The event drew national attention from the AP and UPI news services, and an NBC crew covered it, Salonen reported. A telegram came from Nixon: "I have noticed your three-day fast for freedom in Vietnam, and I am grateful for your understanding and support of our patient efforts."

In March 1970, a bushy-haired young man named Allen Tate Wood was installed as new head of the peace group for war, American Youth for a Just Peace. Recently he had undergone an astonishing change in perspective. Just two years earlier, Wood had been a war *protester*. Now he found himself a born-again war hawk on Capitol Hill, fighting for Nixon. CBS filmed Wood with a shovel, digging a trench and saying he was part of a group of young Americans on a "fact-finding mission." They handed out leaflets and even flew to South Vietnam to meet the U.S.-backed president, Thieu. A few years later, Wood's astonishing story would be entered into the public record as he testified during the Koreagate scandal.

As a teen, Wood felt unhappy and lost, raised in a Tennessee family of poets and writers. His father, drinking martinis one night, told him, "You always *have* been a failure." His parents pointed to the C's and D's he had earned at a small liberal arts college, where he cut class but devoured books on Eastern philosophy. He was proudest of his extracurricular passions—as a leader in Students for a Democratic Society, the antiwar group.

But in the catastrophic year 1968—riots at the Democratic Convention, the failure to change U.S. policy, the assassinations of movement heroes Bobby Kennedy and Martin Luther King Jr.—the movement melted down.

Badly shaken but still chasing down the dream of a new way of life, Wood drifted in 1969 to the Bay Area, hotbed of the flower children. He navigated the marijuana smoke of the University of California campus at Berkeley. Near Sproul Plaza, where the free speech movement had roared under the big arch, he found a bulletin board listing places to live. He decided to post on it.

He sat on the steps and asked to borrow a pen from the young man sitting next to him—who had the look of a long-haired creature of the counterculture. The bearded dude gave him a yellow ballpoint and took an interest as Wood scribbled his situation on a piece of paper.

"I know a place," the bearded boy told him. "It's called the Unified Family. Come, I'll show you."

On the way to the boarding house in Berkeley, the two really seemed to hit it off. "Sort of a religious community" was how his friend described the destination. The longhair, who mentioned he'd recently kicked heroin, said it wasn't a coincidence that they met. "It was prophetic," he said.

Wood walked into a household full of people ready to feed and care for him. They also invited him to seminars they held on "The Principle of Creation." The gist was that sex is that root of all sin, though it was unclear just who had invented these ideas. The lessons boiled down history to a formula that was intricate and simple at the same time. All situations in history, he was taught, could be seen as the story of the Garden of Eden and its aftermath, in eternal recurrence. Take World War I, for example: it came down to a war of Cain Nations and Abel Nations, not so unlike the Bible's first murderer and victim.

One day he opened up a closet and was surprised to see a photograph of a man he'd never seen before. The smiling guru looked on benevolently from his perch on the wall photo.

Fasting followed dinner. Soon he attended lectures on the Principle. It wasn't until weeks later his friend told him the Messiah was here on Earth, the man Wood had seen in the closet. The way Wood remembers it, they were on the UC campus and could smell tear gas in the distance and hear shouts from People's Park. But unlike in Chicago, it no longer seemed to matter. He was finally insulated in the peace of the True Father.

• • •

"Serve 'em to death," Wood tells me, is the philosophy of Moon's church: "We will make ourselves useful and serviceable to people in power," he puts it. "And then eventually, when we understand where they're at, we'll help them get what they want. And once we start helping them achieve their goals, they will become dependent on us."

What Moon could offer in help was bodies who could create the illusion of support for unpopular policies. Today they call it "Astroturf," a play on the idea of "grassroots" where there are none.

In 1970, when the actual substance Astroturf was invented, Moon was already hard at work on the political practice.

According to Wood's later sworn testimony before Congress, the FLF drew attention from prominent conservatives in Washington, who recognized that student support for the war was in short supply and sent veteran organizers to train them in political mobilization. Wood has also said he and another disciple scored a meeting with members of Richard Nixon's Committee to Re-Elect the President (CREEP), a few years before it became infamous for its role in the Watergate scandal.

Chuck Colson and Jeb Stuart Magruder, he says, were under the impression that Wood was a perfectly ordinary college Republican when they met. Colson, adds Wood, offered a $3,000 check from "friends of the president" to help take out full-page newspaper ads in May 1970 in the *Los Angeles Times* and *Washington Star*, defending the presidency against two bills under consideration, in which Nixon's foes sought to rein in his war powers.

The Peace King's group opposed two pieces of legislation: the Cooper-Church Amendment to restrict bombing in Cambodia; and the McGovern-Hatfield Amendment, the equivalent of the modern-day timetable bill to end the Iraq war, setting a date of December 31, 1970, to stop the Vietnam War. In the end, only the Cambodia bill passed, stripped of key provisions.

Magruder, who started a Christian ministry after leaving prison, told me the meeting with Wood's group "doesn't ring a bell" but said it was entirely possible that CREEP members met with the group, not knowing its ties to Moon. "Any group that wanted to support our efforts in Vietnam would certainly be a positive situation," he said.

But Bruce Herschensohn, a Nixon aide and prominent California conservative, told me it was entirely likely. "Their support of staying the course in Vietnam," he said of the Moon youth, "was one of the things that attracted me in terms of having a kinship with them." In an old photograph, he and Rabbi Korff are sitting at the Prayer and Fast.

•   •   •

That Christmas, Moon's children in Washington raised money,

according to one account, by selling "pixie chimes, popcorn plastic plaques, and holiday sachets."

The Master was pleased with Wood's progress and eyed him as one of his most promising leaders in America. The young disciple was summoned to a tour of Asia to familiarize himself with the church's other achievements, including the enterprises that had given Moon control over millions of dollars: factories in Asia producing paint, soda, ginseng, weapons, stoneworks, machine parts. There also hung in the air the dazzling prospect of meeting Moon himself, who was then working through some visa problems reentering the United States.

First stop was Japan. At a rally of twenty-five thousand fervent adherents in Tokyo, they saw that the Moon church was already much bigger here than it was in the United States, more fiercely disciplined, and ahead of the American movement in forming strong ties with that country's right. They lived on rice and breadcrumbs, Wood recalls, and had the discipline of a kamikaze army.

Next, Wood and nine other followers flew to the Republic of Korea, where they were taken to a wartime-era barracks in the lush countryside thirty miles outside Seoul. At Moon's dormitory and factory, the industrial sheds had tin roofs. Outside was a makeshift athletic field.

The next day, it was like the arrival of a movie star at the Oscars. From a black sedan emerged a man in a Mexican *guayabera* shirt and his wife. The True Parents crossed the field and came into the dorm to meet the American delegation. "This is the most important person on the planet," Wood remembers thinking. And from all the faces in the crowd, Wood and a small number had been chosen to attend to this man and help build his kingdom. But the Master was informal, joking, and gentle.

They were taken on a tour of Moon's gun factory, which had a contract with the South Korean government to manufacture M16s, shotguns, and other armaments. The church, responding to criticism that the King of Peace profited from military-grade arms, rejoined that under the Korean *jaebol* system of centralized economic planning, Moon, as a factory owner, was conscripted against his will into making such equipment. (Editor

Arnaud de Borchgrave toured one of these factories and was told, "You are seeing the logistical tail of the Washington Times.")

"Would you like to see more of me?" he asked them.

"Oh, yes, yes," they begged. They speculated: who would get to meet the Master first?

During dessert at the dorms, Moon sent for Wood.

Wood met privately with Moon in his office, where a table was inlaid with dragons swirling in figure 8s.

"What do you wish me to do, Father?" he said.

"We need support on university campuses," Moon said through a translator. "We must unify the students, the faculty, and bring them with us. The faculties hold the reins of certification to all professions. If we make gains there we can shape the thinking of all America. . . . *We must serve them until heaven gives them to us.*"

A few years after the meeting, Wood broke with the church during a long road trip. He had remembered moments when the Korean, who liked to hit Wood on the shoulder, had singled him out before the congregation, kicked him in the rear, and challenged the crowd: "Would you still follow me if I treated you like *this?*" (They would.) He wasn't going back.

"If we can turn three states of the United States around, or if we can turn seven states of the United States to our side, then the whole United States of America will turn," Moon told follower Chris Elkins, a former fraternity president at the University of Arizona. "Let's say there are five hundred sons and daughters like you in each state. Then we could control the government. You could determine who became senators, and who the congressmen would be." Elkins had been told that "every cell of your body" must be part of Moon. "That's the only way," Moon had said. "This is the secret of our movement."

•   •   •

Training for the war on Satan, Moon's soldiers did calisthenics, chanted "Out Satan" at all hours, and went without essentials. The recruit grew haggard, took on a faraway gaze, smiled more. Every recruit was assigned a Central Figure, a minder to be obeyed. There were reports of Hitler Youth videos screened for the more central of Central Figures, so they could study how to whip a youth corps into shape.

Here's one account of the discipline they reached:

MOON: Would you prefer to sleep for seven hours or five hours?

GROUP: Five!

MOON: Would you prefer to sleep five hours or four hours?

GROUP: Four!

MOON: Would you prefer to go to work without sleeping or sleeping?

GROUP: Without sleeping!

MOON: I don't want you to die, so I will let you sleep barely enough to sustain your life. What I'm thinking is that although you get thin like ghosts, with big eyeballs, skinny all over and stooped down like *this* in walking, stuttering—but if by your doing that, by your being like that, we are successful in God's providence, I would prefer to have you do that.

Around the corner was the prophetic year 1981, when Satan, Moon taught, could be exiled forever. Steve Hassan, a former leader in the program, told the *Boston Globe* that he was "programmed to believe that Armageddon would take place in 1977, that Satan loved democracy, and that we were going to be the future rulers of the new kingdom of heaven on earth." Later, explaining how John Walker Lindh became an American Taliban, he compared Lindh's path with his own experience.

In the meantime, to test the power of his movement, Moon waded into politics. By his calculation, it would only take victories in three states.

His soldiers' tireless volunteering would, he hoped, put Washington hopelessly in debt to him. An early effort at influencing state races was a failure. But, said Moon, "Someday, in the near future, when I walk into the Congressman's or the Senator's offices without notice or appointment, the aides will jump out of their seats, and go to get the senator . . . saying he must see Reverend Moon."

• • •

"God Has Given an Answer to Watergate," proclaimed a church press release, as the church campaigned for Nixon with advertisements taken out in twelve major newspapers, encouraging love and forgiveness.

"Mr. President, I love you very much," Moon wrote in a November 29, 1973, letter to the White House, postmarked Omaha, Nebraska.

"We were told we had to hold a series of five rallies over five days, that would look like popular rallies," says former church leader Richard Barlow. They would load into vans and drive all night, sometimes through winter rain and treacherous ice, like the night a deadly accident almost happened on the way to Little Rock. "The whole thing was to show that, all over America, there was a swelling of support for the president.

"And everyone converged. Moon could do that . . . the most efficient mobilization process you've ever seen . . . everyone was like a soldier."

• • •

If only the Reverend Moon could somehow arrange for Nixon to be seen on camera as a beloved figure, the president would be in his debt. The church concocted a scheme to hoist Nixon on their shoulders, a flawed but forgiven hero.

"We are right on the edge of influencing people," an excited church leader wrote. "Master wants to give an address to a joint session of Congress."

Everything was in place for the operation to take place at the White House Christmas tree lighting on December 14, 1973. They'd rehearsed the plan in a warehouse at the National Armory, near RFK Stadium. "We practiced singing and lining up to make the procession look orderly," church leader Dan Fefferman said in congressional testimony.

One of Moon's people stood in for the beleaguered president. Unification Church president Neil Salonen had split a group of 1,200 Moon soldiers into a dozen "tribes," who'd lunge for Nixon at the appropriate moment and create a photo op for the ages.

The day came, and the Moon children, wearing armbands reading "Project Unity," crushed against a fence that separated them and the White House lawn, hoisting "God Needs Richard Nixon" signs. Excitement mounted. Just when the button was pressed to light up the tree, the fence collapsed under the weight of Moon's youth.

They blitzed Nixon, whose aides hastened him away. Presidential aide John Nedicker later testified that turning Christmas into a Nixon rally infuriated Nixon. But he did stop by later that night to thank a group of Moon followers who were holding a candlelight vigil for him across from the White House.

After that, the movement took out full-page newspaper ads promoting Moon as the man working to save the president and heal the nation's wounds, and it held pro-Nixon marches of young people across America. Just as Moon had deployed his people for the unpopular cause of the Vietnam War, he now gave their bodies to the fight for the president with the 27 percent approval rating.

• • •

On February 1, 1974, a Nixon aide, Bruce Herschensohn, led Moon into the Oval Office. Other staffers might not have thought much of the Korean evangelist. But Herschensohn, today an elder figure in California conservatism, was touched by the young devotees who demonstrated in the cold.

They were supporting the president "during a time in our history," Herschensohn told me, "when young people were going on dope, and it was awfully refreshing to see people well-dressed, who spoke well—and not use obscenities or dope or any of those things."

He led the evangelist through the White House for a photo opportunity with the Archangel himself. The church's account of the meeting is that Moon asked the president to maintain his steely resolve in the Vietnam War—then cautioned Nixon he was about to share a revelation from God. "You may find my words somewhat shocking and abrupt," he said. "Can I ask you to listen to me with an open mind?"

"Yes, of course, Reverend Moon," the president allegedly said. (His aide, Herschensohn, won't vouch for the church's version of the events, saying the use of a translator made things confusing.)

Now the unearthly visitor to Nixon explained that the divide over Watergate was the Civil War all over again. "Mr. President, more than one hundred years later, America has come to a similar juncture of history. You must do something extraordinary. . . . May I suggest that you declare a week of repentance of fasting. . . .

"The hearts of the American people will be moved, and millions will follow your example," Moon said.

If one week wasn't enough, Moon said, the president should fast for forty days, following in the example of Moses. Nixon, according to Moon, said he would certainly consider it.

The Master now began a long prayer in Korean that Nixon and Herschensohn couldn't understand but bowed their heads for. Patiently, the president clasped his hands over his desk. The prayer went on and on until Herschensohn thought, "Oh, God, I really messed up." But he looked to Nixon, whose wink back at him signaled it was OK to have brought the spiritual visitor, he says. The church gushes in its account that Moon spoke with the power of a Bible prophet confronting a king, but it chastises Nixon for ultimately repudiating God's direct orders.

Like Eisenhower, however, Nixon got the last word—as published in full-page newspaper ads long after his death. On July 31, 2003, according to the Unification Church, Nixon spoke for all dead U.S. presidents when he said, "We resolve and proclaim that Rev. Sun Myung Moon is the Lord of the Second Advent, the Messiah, the Savior and the True Parent." He may have been the only president to resign in disgrace, but to Moon he was worthy enough to preside over all.

• • •

In a metaphysical sense, leaders of his American church saw themselves as destined to "bring new life to the archangel, Nixon—hence to make him aware of our significance," as official instructions for Project Watergate explained. But church leader Dan Fefferman, placed in charge of the project, also brought cutting-edge public relations savvy to the effort to showcase Moon.

"Play Him up as the leader and initiator," a church director wrote, "but don't make Him the central focus." The goal was "to show Nixon and Congress both our own power and the outer support that we can generate." Churchmen issued instructions for keeping their agenda elusive and for "small, intimate, personal things" that, caught on camera, might swing national opinion—suggesting that activists emulate the Moonie who was seen "crying as she prayed."

And they warned that the church's victory chants of "Mansei!" would be off-putting, "inappropriate to this project." As would petitioning God in the "Smash Satan" style. "On camera, medium strong prayer looks good. Very strong prayer doesn't. It looks strange. Don't clench your fists when you are singing."

For now, the church said, members should "be American." Chris Elkins has written about chanting "God Needs Nixon" over and over again, with a group of six hundred, each wearing a giant sandwich board-sized image of a particular member of Congress, under the words "I Am Praying for . . . ."

As the scandal of 1974 progressed, and God decreasingly seemed able to save the presidency, the Messiah was still dead set on succeeding through Nixon. In a June 29, 1974, Q&A session, Moon described the usefulness of the fading president. Moon was using his resources to lobby against a vote to censure the president.

He spoke to followers at the church's new training center, the sleepy former Catholic monastery along the Hudson.

"Father, what do you think will happen with president Nixon?" someone asked him.

Moon's answer was less sentimental and more strategic than his Oval Office appearance. "Even if many people label somebody as dying, not all of them will die," Moon said. "If this dying person, Nixon, is revived, then Reverend Moon's name will be more popular and famous, right?"

In July, Neil Salonen, president of the U.S. branch of the Unification Church, told the press, "We should take note that both Hitler and Stalin took power on the heels of leaders made impotent by constraints."

• • •

It was a lost cause, but a successful campaign, in that the Reverend Moon was now in with people who could help him, even after the fall of Nixon. Things were shaping up. He was only beginning to show up in the news. With the KCFF raking in donations and the FLF making contacts—and church president Salonen reporting yearly church profits had risen from $100,000 to $8 million—he was well on his way to constructing a labyrinth of forking paths that would eventually lead to a thousand American front groups.

And then there was the good news of his residency. He had some visa troubles, but a U.S. senator, Strom Thurmond, intervened on Moon's behalf, allowing him to stay. The Unification Church and Thurmond had met at a meeting of the World Anti-Communist League (WACL), that international confederation of hard rightists known for extending a hand to unsavory groups (see chapter 6).

Moon's church in Japan was closely affiliated with WACL, having formed the regional chapter of the group itself: Shokyo Rengo, or Victory over Communism. There were ties to the Japanese mob. Two supporters were former prime minister Nobosuke Kishi, a war criminal, and Ryoichi Sasakawa, a gambling tycoon and yakuza boss who had atoned for his sins with vast humanitarian gifts for world hunger but also referred to himself, in a jocular spirit, as "the world's richest fascist."

Moon's Japanese sponsors had seen his success in staging feverish South Korean rallies that made anticommunism into a fanatical religion. The reverend's hope was to make anticommunism a force synonymous with the Divine Principle. That way, when the Soviet empire collapsed, his philosophy, and not democracy, would become the replacement philosophy. By the time Moon returned from Asia to America to see what Bo Hi Pak had made of the movement, he was expressing disappointment. The American Moonies had not attained the tenacity of their overseas brothers. They had to be fiercer.

• • •

Over the next four tumultuous years, war broke out between families and the Unification Church.

Ex-recruits told the press of being lured to countryside weekend retreats like Booneville in northern California where, as one young woman said at a press conference, "my mind was totally coerced into leaving home, into leaving my parents, into dropping out of school . . . thinking that I was working for God." Hundreds of parents had thrown themselves into fighting the church. "Our daughter is not our daughter anymore," the mother of Wendy Helander, eighteen, told a Connecticut judge, having had her kidnapped, the legality of which was rejected by the courts.

The desperation of the times gave rise to a new job title, the "deprogrammer," and a varied industry in cult departure services. At one end were consultants hired to deliver aggressive chats on the evils of cults. At the other were vigilantes, hired to retake a mind, no questions asked. Even many ex-Moonies detest the kidnappers; others still praise them. But psychologist Steve Hassan, today the leader in the field, himself kidnapped out of the Moonies, rejects forced seizure as terrifying treatment that no one deserves.

Ted Patrick coined the term *deprogramming,* and, in 1973, decades before *Dog the Bounty Hunter,* CBS followed him on a mission to snatch a girl from the mushroom-eating, child-abusing Love Israel sect. It was "the first and only time in history," Patrick said, "that a kidnapping was televised live in front of millions of people." A black San Diego activist born in a Chattanooga red light district, he was a fundamentalist Christian and a Republican who had won acclaim from Governor Ronald Reagan for preventing rioting in his city. He took an interest after his own son was drawn into the Children of God cult. He likened the new prophets to ghetto hucksters but came to see them as Communist indoctrination in American colors: a "totalitarian conspiracy."

The CBS show was a fiasco. The cameras seemed to encourage Kathy, and Patrick threatened to wreck them if the crew kept shooting. She later escaped to press charges, the incentive for the bounty hunter not to lose his case. Patrick was frequently broke, a condition worsened by the lawsuits he incurred. Deprogramming could cost $1,500. "I hit them with things that they haven't been programmed to respond to," he said of his method. Within the tightly controlled world of the Unification Church and other groups, there were whispers of Patrick as "Black Lightning," a kidnapper lying in wait, a sinister captor who would talk you into rejoining the satanic outside world, "a nigger-thug rapist, some hallucination of an interior lineman for the L.A. Rams, a raw meat eater," Patrick himself said. "The cults tell them that I rape the women and beat them," he told writer Flo Conway. "They say I lock them in closets and stuff bones down their throats."

• • •

In the multimillion-dollar public relations drive to improve the image of the Unification Church in the 1980s and 1990s and to shield its allies from criticism, a major part of the mission was painting the anticult movement as dominated by monsters. Thus could the church shift attention from its Achilles' heel: images of weeping parents, their children lost to the True Family. Even after apologists had proved violations of First Amendment rights of adult believers, a mother's hurt and desperation would never, ever be a PR asset.

So the church called on Carlton Sherwood. He was a down-on-his-luck Pulitzer winner and decorated Marine. In happier times, Sherwood had admirably exposed Vatican corruption. Then he busted. "Reporter's Project Ruins His Career," read the headline in the *New York Times*. In 1983, he had produced a libelous series of TV reports, accusing a Vietnam memorial fund group of misusing money. He was arrested for illegal tape recording, and his D.C. station, WDMV, agreed to pay $50,000 to the target of its false story, which the victims called "conjecture, smoke and mirrors."

In 1991, Sherwood published the canonical defense of Moon, *Inquisition: The Prosecution and Persecution of the Reverend Sun Myung Moon*.

Today, having drifted far from the news world, Sherwood is a well-connected Homeland Security consultant. In 2004, he produced a film, *Stolen Honor: The Wounds That Never Heal*, attacking Democratic Party candidate John Kerry. Sherwood argues in the film that by calling the Vietnam War a mistake in 1971, Kerry had betrayed American soldiers who were captives of the Viet Cong. If Kerry's positions made him heinous to Sherwood, the Rev. Sun Myung Moon's were ones he felt the need to defend in a 644-page book. Maybe. His book is an angry text whose schizophrenic shifts in tone raise questions about its authorship. Its premise is that Sherwood went undercover when he joined the *Times*, hoping to dig up dirt on the owners—only to *come up empty*. Now, the marketing material explains, Sherwood is ready to expose "the worst kind of religious prejudice and racial bigotry this country has witnessed in over a century." On the book jacket, he resembles comedian Will Ferrell's creation, Ron Burgundy: a journalist with almost too much social conscience.

But PBS's *Frontline* discovered that before publication, one of Moon's top aides had reviewed the manuscript and made edits. Maybe it wasn't so independent. Moreover, the church had promised Regnery, one of the top conservative publishing companies, that it would buy one hundred thousand copies. "When all of our suggestions have been incorporated," Moon public relations expert James Gavin wrote in a letter leaked to PBS, "the book will be complete and in my opinion will make a significant impact . . . in addition to silencing our critics now, the book should be invaluable in persuading others of our legitimacy for years to come."

In patches, *Inquisition* is clearly the work of a journalist, a cool-headed discussion of jury conduct in Moon's 1982 tax case. But then, for long spells, the text shifts gears, and the angry, single-sentence paragraphs become unreadable. The smoke and mirrors include telling the reader not to worry his layman's head with the mountain of U.S. intelligence cables about Moon, on the basis that only experts are qualified to analyze them. And like most of Moon's defenders, Sherwood assiduously avoids quoting Moon himself, whose theocratic tirades have always been a vulnerability.

Sometimes the journalist voice creeps back, with its hoary newspaperman jokes (ever hear the one about the reporter who says, "There's no story—the governor's plane crashed on the way to the press conference"?). Then it fades and *Inquisition* reads like the voice of Col. Bo Hi Pak, indignant to find himself in the time of the Pharisees.

> [I]t was as though I had been strapped in a time machine and shot back to Nero's Rome, or seventeenth century New England, or Hitler's Germany.
>
> To be sure, we don't feed people with odd religious beliefs to the lions, . . . After all, we're civilized. . . . We just harass, intimidate, and ridicule them and their families and occasionally throw their leaders in jail.

Sherwood goes after the news media for pillorying "friends of Richard Nixon [who] can expect no quarter and no mercy." He complains about cruel, "ultra-hip," "gonzo" writers who attend Moon events "and whack away," and he cites the *Chicago Tribune*'s removal of a flag from its masthead as a sign of hating America.

He finds little sympathy for parents of the lost—"none of those who joined the church were kids," he says of Moon's eighteen-year-old recruits, and he is fond of putting *child* in quotes. In a forty-page stretch, he attacks the parents' groups who oppose Moon, finding their hired counselors to comprise an evil-hearted "cult" with no redeeming value. And then, in page after page, he also goes after Ted Patrick the deprogrammer as if assailing Vatican corruption.

The complex "Black Lightning" was no saint. He was a kind of conservative vigilante who felt the world was going mad, driving him to take on causes both heroic (battling the totalitarian LaRouche Youth) and misguided ("rescuing" children from lesbianism and Mormonism). And he has been behind bars a few times, largely because of a legal onslaught by Scientology. Jail is proof of martyrdom, in Moon's case, but prison for Patrick is, in *Inquisition*'s logic, proof of a stereotypical black beast. In a racist flourish that one hopes belongs to the ghostwriter, Sherwood claims that Patrick's only conceivable motive is "the brutality of lording it over hapless, white, mostly female victims."

"He was cool, man," remembers one ex-Moonie. Patrick himself proudly admitted force in the name of good. "Sit your ass down," he yelled at a boy hurled onto a bed, "and if you so much as move a muscle, I'm going to knock the shit out of you." But Patrick maintained that the actual sessions relied mostly on providing cult members with information that has been kept from them in a tightly controlled universe. That is also the approach recommended by an American Psychological Association report on the subject, which condemns all violent rendition of young people but advocates delivering them the information that totalitarian groups hide. That is a gray area unaccounted for in Sherwood's world of First Amendment martyrs and brutes.

Ironically, a day was coming when the royal court of the 36 Families would produce, as if sprung fully formed from the well of the Moonies' collective fears, a confessor many degrees more intimidating than Ted Patrick: Cleopas the Inquisitor, the Black Heung Jin (see chapter 8).

● ● ●

Patrick, for his part, asserted in his autobiography that his ultimate weapon was a damning NBC report.

A boy named Bernie Weber, carrying a book by Dr. Lee on Unification principles, finding himself in a car with deprogrammers, has agreed to come home peacefully. He is frog-marched into his parents' basement, hears footsteps, fears the worst. But the man who comes down the cast-iron railings of the stairway is a plump, short, ordinary man with glasses and a speech impediment who talks to him for hours about the Bible, asks why he is giving up his mind and cheating old ladies, and scribbles a mustache on a photo of Sun Myung Moon, which he then rips apart and tosses into the boy's lap. "You're not doing the Lord's work," Patrick says. "You worship this son of a bitch."

A videotape is dropped into the VCR: an NBC news piece on Moon. Suddenly the man from the photo is on television, speaking at Madison Square Garden, 1974. It is a notorious debacle that the church stopped showing members. Moon had miscalculated the appeal to curious New Yorkers of a long, ferocious rant in Korean about what a loser John the Baptist was, leading him to subsequently tone it down.

"Unattractive, monotonous," remembers ex-leader Richard Barlow, saying Moon's karate chops of the air with his hand, locked in spiritual warfare with New York, must have reminded unfamiliar audiences of some Asian Hitler. "He was really over the top." A tape of the rally makes it hard to argue. It's not the words but that machine-gun cadence. Like a man imitating a bear or a lion, Moon snarls, screeches, and hisses. Korean is normally a soft-spoken language, but his delivery challenges the listener not to picture fluttering zeppelins and swastikas. His aide, the colonel, shouts the English translation in angry staccato:

> This world is under the rulership of Satan. . . . God, in order to protect his agents, must give a coded message. . . . I would like to give you a deeper meaning of the Bible. . . . America is running towards individualistic ideals. . . . America is becoming selfish . . . bring yourself as a sacrifice to the world, and bring the world back to God! . . . I want you to know, today

> America is in parallel position of Israel nation, 2000 years ago . . . we must
> serve as the landing site of the Messiah, when he returns, second time. . . .
> America is Rome of today! . . . Did you know that Satan is laughing at us?
> . . . [W]e must not be in same position to make mistake of 2,000 years ago.
> . . . [T]hey rejected [Jesus] because they did not know who he was.

At the Weber household, Ted Patrick, the family, and the boy watched the videotape of this unsuccessful sermon. "You are never going back to that bunch," the elder Weber tells his son, who by now is thinking he won't.

Richard Barlow was working security at that rally, under Michael Warder, the future whistle-blower and think tank director. It was Barlow's job to scan the crowd for left-wing and Christian rabble-rousers. After someone called out "blasphemer," he says, he remembers that Moon's accountant, Takeru Kamiyama, excused himself and rammed his fist into the disbeliever's stomach, then had him ejected.

• • •

The dream of addressing both houses of Congress in session never happened. But on December 18, 1975, apparently thanks to the work of Strom Thurmond and other anti-Communists happy to let Moon promote himself as the Solzhenitsyn of the Far East, Moon was inexplicably invited to speak at the House Caucus Room. The appearance was reported in the *New York Times* the next day, and his campus newspaper, *Rising Tide,* ran the speech in full.

> The focal point of controversy with the media is the claim that I am brain-
> washing American youth. In view of this, may I ask one question to this
> audience of distinguished American ladies and gentlemen?
>
> Are Americans really that foolish? Can they really be brainwashed
> by Rev. Moon, a Korean? I know your answer is no. My answer is no,
> too. No American is so foolish. I respect Americans very much, and I am
> surprised at such accusations.

Today, however, I did not come here to defend myself. I came to speak what God has asked me to speak. As for the rest, I will let history be the judge. I would like to share with you the topic, "God's Plan for America."

The gasoline had been poured for the firestorm of Congress mixing it up with the Unification Church—not over religion but over influence. The church would call it an inquisition in which the devil himself was working through Rep. Don Fraser (D-MN), an uncharacteristically shy congressman, who would rather be at home tinkering with motors than being accused of torturing God's only gladiator in Washington.

· · ·

In 1978, Moon's chief aide, Pak, went head-to-head with the plainspoken Fraser with a ferocity on the witness stand and a gift for escalating the proceedings into an opera of persecution and *han*, stunning everyone. "If Congress were to make a list of the ten all-time most difficult hearing witnesses," wrote staffer Robert Boettcher, "Bo Hi Pak's name would probably be on it."

Koreagate was the name of the affair—back when the idea of nicknaming scandals in imitation of Watergate ("Zippergate," "Prosecutorgate") was still fresh. A number of factors had led to the conflagration. For one thing, in 1976 it had been revealed that the Unification Church had bought half the ownership of the Diplomat National Bank, at a time when Moon himself was telling his church about plans so that "currency will be freely coming back and forth" within the movement. But in an SEC probe, Pak had been charged with gaining control in violation of antifraud limits. (The charges were later settled.)

The United States had intercepted a South Korean government plan to influence members of Congress, and a handful were caught. One prong of the influence campaign involved Korean socialite Tongsun Park, the self-described "Asian Great Gatsby." The Fraser Committee hoped to find a link to the lobbying of the Rev. Sun Myung Moon, who traveled in some of the same circles and had similar but distinct goals. Moon, the investigation revealed, had staged demonstrations for the South Korean government. (The narrow focus on Korea kept the government from exploring the scope of Moon's backing by Japanese nationalists.)

Moon's girls had become a common presence. *Newsweek* had reported that "attractive young Moonie women prowl the halls of Congress daily, chatting with Congressional staffers and carrying flowers, cookies and tea to the congressmen." For what end? In 1976, the blue-eyed beauty Susan Bergman followed around Democratic House Speaker Carl Albert and presented him with a copy of *The Divine Principle*. After Albert retired, she won a position in the office of Rep. John Hammerschmidt (R-AR).

On one of the hearing's most dramatic days in 1978, Fraser hoped Pak could explain why $3,000 in hundred-dollar bills, along with a six-page letter, had been allegedly brought to his house by an agent of the KCIA. Pak's reply, as was his style, was to change the subject to worldwide cruelties being perpetrated by one Donald Fraser. "Millions of innocents around the world, known as 'Moonies,' are practically looked upon today as KCIA dogs as they try to bring witness to the world of our religious faith," Col. Bo Hi Pak said as part of a long statement. "Oftentimes people call to them in the streets: 'Hey, Moonie, you KCIA dog? How much do they pay you?'"

He also held up a November 6, 1970, letter from Sen. Strom Thurmond assuring him that it was OK to lobby in Washington.

On April 11, 1978, Pak said he'd misunderstood some of the questions due to his limited English. "While they were learning the 'master tricks' of interrogation at Harvard or Yale," he said in a prepared statement, "I was busy fighting a war against Communist aggression to defend my country and the free world," adding that he didn't want to "match wits with this subcommittee in some kind of 'game.'"

The committee asked if he were almost through. Only six more pages, he said, on the "suffering of UC members around the world." "Mr. Chairman," he said, "I must give you hell." The last straw for him is a news report of a cable from Thomas Chung of the Korean Students' Association in Washington, alleging that Pak had tried to induct the spouse of a South Korean government minister into a sex ritual.

"When I read this article, my mind and body were consumed with anger," Pak said. He demanded the congressmen pick up the phone and phone Chung, whom he promised would retract the slander. "The subject of sexual immorality is one subject which no one can rightfully harass me about."

"Have you ever been interested in the truth?" Pak asked Fraser, rather than answer questions about the $3,000. "I may have become the most investigated man under the sun but I have turned out to be a 'Mr. Clean,'" referring to the detergent mascot. "Now this 'Mr. Clean' has come to clean the dirt from your house, Mr. Chairman. . . . I have read the growing desperation on your faces."

What the intense man meant was that they were afraid of being unmasked as KGB spies. "What if you are an agent of influence for Moscow here on the Hill?" Pak said. "If these things are true, then the government of the United States itself is in grave danger."

Rep. Ed Derwinski (R-IL) interjected after his long speech: "Colonel, let me say that I don't know who advises you in your public relations, but I don't believe this statement you just read helps your cause."

At one point in the hearings, Pak reached a crescendo of tears and rage. "You are being used as an instrument of the devil," Pak told Fraser, laying out his ultimate *j'accuse* at Fraser in piercing staccato. "You—yes, you—an instrument of the devil. I said it. Who else would want to destroy man of God but the devil?" On film, the members of the panel are unsure how to react to the man who says the Lord's Prayer as he collapses into tears on the table behind his pitcher of water, sobbing for two minutes.

The allegation that the quiet Fraser was an ambitious agent of evil didn't end there. In a preview of the Moon press's modern-day power to push stories, Moon's *News World* printed story after story on Fraser, accusing him of communist ties. (*Rising Tide,* the campus newsletter, was apoplectic: "Fraser's Korea Witch Hunt," read the cover of the August 15, 1977, issue.)

The attack on Fraser's patriotism spread to his home district. Despite the presence of Derwinski and others, the panel was castigated as a leftist attack on South Korea policy, and an investigation of Fraser for ethics violations was demanded June 30, 1978, in a letter from conservative activist John T. "Terry" Dolan, who was subsequently paid by the church.

The congressman lost his reelection primary, which he had been expected to win, by just a few votes. God, Moon said, had punished the lawmaker for defying the will of heaven. The issue of investigating Moon lost steam. Within the week of Fraser's defeat, someone tried to burn down his house. The fire department, which put it out in time, said an unknown arsonist had poured solvent on the floor.

• • •

In the so-called Fraser Report of October 31, 1978, congressmen recommended that the U.S. government take further action to curb the Rev. Sun Myung Moon's growing influence in America and apparent access to military hardware in South Korea.

"Although many of the goals and activities of the Moon Organization were legitimate and lawful," the report said, "there was evidence that it had systematically violated U.S. tax, immigration, banking, currency and Foreign Agents Registration Act laws," all for the sake of power. The report concluded the following:

- Moon's religious and secular organizations were part of one complex network, its parts moving in tandem—a machine that "depends heavily upon the interchangeability of its components and upon its ability to move personnel and financial assets freely across international boundaries"
- Among its goals was something like a Moon caliphate—a "worldwide government in which the separation of church and state would be abolished"

- The group "extensively used the names of senators, members of Congress, U.S. presidents, and other prominent Americans to raise funds and to create political influence for itself and the Republic of Korea government"
- The group was a major defense contractor for the South Korean government, producing M16 rifles, antiaircraft guns, and other weapons.

Fraser hoped a government arms control board would take a closer look at the latter issue, keeping in mind that Moon had once called for a "Unification Crusade Army." With Moon's access to the guns of his corporation, Tong-il, he apparently had the means to win a small African civil war. (The church strenuously denied the report. It defended Moon's manufacture of armaments as something mandated for all industrialists by the South Korean regime: service against North Korea.)

According to the report:

Moon's speeches foresee an apocalyptic confrontation involving the United States, Russia, China, Japan and North and South Korea, in which the Moon Organization would play a key role. Under these circumstances, the subcommittee believes it is in the interest of the United States to know what control Moon and his followers have over instruments of war and to what extent they are in a position to influence [South] Korean defense policies.

And all of this before the famous 1982 wedding.

EIGHT

RONALD REAGAN AND THE AFRICAN INQUISITOR

POTENTIAL PROBLEMS

Current Moonie involvement with government officials, contractors and grantees could create a major scandal. If their activities and role become public knowledge, it will unite both the left and the right in attacking the administration. . . .

If efforts are not taken to stop their growing influence and weed out current Moonie involvement in government, the president stands a good chance of being portrayed in the media as a poor, naive incompetent who is strong on ideology and weak on common sense. . . . The likelihood of a reporter or a Democratic staff member piecing the total picture together is too great to be neglected. Any thought that this festering problem will go away if ignored is foolish.

—*PENTAGON MEMO OBTAINED BY THE WASHINGTON POST,
REPORTED AUGUST 16, 1984*

Christmas Eve, 1984: Another president—another era. *Saturday Night Live* has done another zombie spoof, this time with the alien pods from *Invasion of the Body Snatchers* turning Bill Murray's hippie friends into Republicans. And the Korean messiah parodied in the show's old "Night of the Moonies" skit has now been sentenced to federal prison in Connecticut, capping off his eight-year clash with Sen. Bob Dole, Rep. Donald Fraser, the SEC, the IRS and the Justice Department.

It is a traumatic period for the Moon faithful—and not only because their master is incarcerated at the Federal Correctional Institution, and they have turned to portents from the afterlife to light the way out. His seventeen-year-old son Heung Jin, known as the sweetest-tempered of Moon's thirteen children, is dead after a December 1983 collision on a freezing highway in upstate New York. The accident came before his planned wedding to Julia Pak, the ballerina daughter of Moon's first officer, Bo Hi Pak. As it turns out, the dead boy's wedding will go on, but a terrible logic has been unleashed that will claim Pak's coveted leadership position. After the Moonies excitedly report signs that Heung Jin is speaking from beyond the grave—a glass breaking by itself and other supposed signals from heaven—a rival within the inner circle, on the pretense that he has discovered a reincarnation of Moon's son, will support bloodcurdling beatings of church leaders.

A bright sign here on Earth is that the church's newspaper is delivered every morning to Ronald Reagan, who reads and quotes the *Washington Times* more than any other, according to chief of staff Don Regan. "And you were worried about the influence of astrology on the White House?" *Daily News* columnist Lars-Erik Nelson quips, referring to the First Lady's reliance on horoscopes.

Reagan is nevertheless ill at ease when, after his landslide second election, some Republicans ask him to pardon the man behind the paper. "Senator Hatch is after me to grant clemency to the Rev. Moon," Reagan writes in his diary that night. "I've explored it & I find I just can't." It was embarrassing enough when Jack Anderson, the *Washington Post's* muckraking bulldog, had exposed an August government memo cautioning that the administration would look absurd were it known how closely it had worked with the Unification Church in Latin America.

Orrin Hatch has begun a long friendship with Mr. and Mrs. Moon. He will remain commander of the pardoning task force through 1988, by which time $50,000 is flowing into the law firm of Reagan's close friend, Sen. Paul Laxalt (R-NV), to lobby for forgiveness. In the 1990s, Hatch will appear in a Unification Church video, introducing Mrs. Moon as "my friend," before she takes the podium and declares the "Completed Testament Age." And in 2004, Hatch, a composer in his spare time, will receive a songwriting credit for a "Jerusalem Peace Song" on a music CD honoring Moon's world peace tour.

By 1988, the pardon team will include Ralph Abernathy (a civil rights legend who has gone to the right) and William Rusher (*Times* columnist and publisher of the conservative *National Review*). Defending a trip to Korea on the church's dime, Rusher has said, "I suspect the Unification Church's real crime, in many eyes, has been the pro-Americanism, anti-Communism, basic neatness and rather old-fashioned morality of many of its members."

But an attorney at Laxalt's law firm, Paul Perito, will grow uneasy at the apparent use of the conservative newspaper to lobby for its own publisher's pardon. When editor Arnaud de Borchgrave pleads Moon's case, it's as if Moon runs the place, Perito suggests. That could "materially damage our prodigious efforts."

Reagan sees fit in 1984 to give the Returning Lord a vacation, writing, "I have, however, taken action to see if I can grant him a furlough over New Year's. It seems that day is holiest in that religion."

· · ·

A week after Christmas—as God's Day, or New Year's, approached—the *Washington Times* publisher left Danbury, Connecticut, and headed for world headquarters in New York City to address the flock. Less than a year remained in the eighteen-month term for tax fraud.

Considering all the forces had arrayed against him, the Reverend Moon had emerged in a surprisingly strong position. Between 1977 and 1982, there'd been talk of deporting him for fraud or challenging his foreign agent status. Instead, Moon would be free to go about his business after leaving Danbury.

It could conceivably have been curtains for his ambitions after the *New York Times* front-paged no less a critic than Kim Hyung Wook, former director of the KCIA. Kim said in 1977 that Moon and Bo Hi Pak had been on his agency's payroll as propagandists. "I had extremely extensive powers at my disposal," Wook had testified before Congress on June 22, "more power than you can imagine, covering virtually every aspect of my country." According to him, the Korean dictatorship had outsourced some of its promotional work in Washington to the Unification Church and its fanatical rallies in support of South Korea. But even then, the preacher with the farming accent had been a mystery to him, Kim said—a figure "isolated from Korean intellectual circles." He'd heard Moon criticized in Korea as a "phony evangelist." Moreover, Kim was at a loss to explain how such a man "could mobilize allegedly thousands of young Americans."

Rep. Donald Fraser's committee had recommended U.S. government action be taken to check Moon's influence peddling. In the end there had only been a conviction, in 1982, for conspiring to avoid income tax on $150,000 in personal income. On the day of the jury verdict, his followers streamed out of the courthouse, weeping. "Anybody who stands up for God in a world like this is going to get it," a supporter told ABC News, "and Reverend Moon just happens to be the most significant figure of the twentieth century as a religious leader."

He had faced up to fourteen years in prison but, in the end, received a sentence somewhere between Martha Stewart's (five months) and Leona Helmsley's (nineteen months.) William Martin, of the anticult Christian Research Institute, remarked that the sentence "shows the mercy of the jurors, not persecution."

In 1984, the Supreme Court had rejected his final appeal. Now that he was behind bars, his prelates considered Moon to be undergoing a sacrifice like the passion of Christ, or possibly worse. "Even Jesus did not have to deal with the *New York Times*," Bo Hi Pak had said on March 22, 1978, during the congressional hearings. A newspaper article claiming that the church "interprets the Bible in sexual terms," he said, had already "crucified Reverend Moon on a worldwide level," and that was before the Internal Revenue Service pierced Moon's side. In prison, Moon had completed an ominously titled tract, *God's Warning to the World*, that included long discussions of racial unity. "If you have hated black people in the past," he wrote, "you should invite the ugliest fattest Black man or grandmother to go out for lunch to a Chinese restaurant . . . when you beg her with tears to eat the dinner you buy, you will have indemnified your hate in the past."

White people, he observed, were the coldest and least trusting race, and their power at the "top of the mountain" would eventually wash away.

• • •

On God's Day, 1985, Moon gave that first sermon since prison at the New Yorker Hotel, at 481 8th Avenue in Manhattan, which he had purchased and renamed the World Mission Center. His worshippers awaited their new marching orders. Their mission for 1985, he announced, was the same as last year's: The Building and the Creation of the Fatherland.

Today that old headquarters is a Ramada Plaza and Inn, open for business again to the tourists and businesspeople who stream through the lobby, big band music playing as they head to the forty-two floors above, traveling through crooked, underlit hallways that could use recarpeting. In 2007, a young woman sued the hotel over "itchy, disgusting bites" inflicted by bed bugs in a room upstairs. Down on 8th Avenue, an exhibit plays up the radio-days nostalgia value of the New Yorker. The famous Hammerstein Ballroom is here, and Will Rogers and Walter Winchell were regulars.

In the ballroom is a striking exception to the Jazz Age décor. Inlaid in white plaster of Paris on the far wall are the interlocking arrows and Imperial sunburst of the Unification Church, whose chief has reportedly kept a penthouse on the top floor. The hotel also houses a studio of Moon's television postproduction giant, the church-owned firm Atlantic Video. (Its $20 million headquarters in Washington, D.C., link Moon to such clients as ESPN, HBO, CNBC, Bloomberg, The Koppel Group, XM Satellite Radio, and others.)

The bed bugs are not the only reason the heights above are unsettling. Between 1976 and 1979, during the tensest days of Moon's clash with Washington, three members plummeted to their deaths: Allen Staggs, twenty stories down the shaft, on June 6, 1976 (an accident, the church said); Kiyomi Ogata, who fell from the twenty-second floor, August 23, 1976 (reasons unknown); and Junette Bayne, exactly three years later, from the twenty-first—"If she wasn't pushed physically," said her husband, who was angry she had joined Moon, "she was pushed psychologically out that window." The plunges were tallied by congressional aide Robert Boettcher, who, six years after leading the Moon investigation, fell to his own death, at age forty-four, from his apartment.

"Who owns this place?" I ask the busy hotel clerk.

"Reverend Moon," she says as if it's something she gets asked all the time.

· · ·

According to church Web sites, Moon's speeches here reminded the faithful of his power to unlock Bible mysteries—and challenged them to make themselves worthy of his sacrifice behind bars: a result, they believed, of their weakness. At Danbury, he lived in an 8 × 8 room, worked the kitchen, and befriended inmates. Moon was pleased to report that America was shedding hippie decadence and might yet align itself with the sexual purity of his coming kingdom.

"We have seen many evil things coming and going here on the earth," he said. "For example, when I first came to the United States, I heard a great deal about 'streaking,' or naked men and women running around in public places." But young people, he said, are "turning very conservative and idealistic. They are saying, 'We young people don't accept that. We don't buy your sins.'" He also warned that Satan was encouraging people to be gay: "an evil love culture." (In a widely quoted anecdote, a group leader asked the Reverend Moon one day for advice in dealing with homosexual disciples. Moon said to laughter, "Cut it off, barbecue it, put it in a shoe box, and send it to me.")

Hanging over the talks was the loss of Heung Jin. The boy's two passengers that rainy night on State Route 9 swore that he saved their lives, swinging the wheel to take the brunt of the impact from the tractor-trailer. Heung Jin fell into a fatal coma and passed away a few days later, on January 2, 1984, named henceforth the "Day of the Victory of Love."

Moon preached at the New Yorker that his son had been a sacrifice at the altar—a karmic balancing of the scales, his priests would say later, that might even have prevented Moon himself from being assassinated. Now Heung Jin had been promoted higher than Jesus in heaven. "We have to give enough that Satan is satisfied," Moon said. "Thus the books will be closed."

During this hardship, he said, influential Americans were coming to see the good in him. "It is almost like Reverend Moon has shed one layer of his skin," he said, "the way a snake does . . . people are coming to me and taking off that old skin, trying to see for themselves what is really inside." The persecution, he said, would soon end.

"This process should have been completed in Jesus's time," he said. "He was supposed to have entered the Roman Empire and walked the same steps that I have gone through." Instead, of course, he had been crucified.

Unlike the first son of God, Moon was a succeeder ready to move beyond lepers. Now he had built the basis of his army and could reliably look to high places for allies. "No longer do we have to deal with 'street people,' vagrants, and spiritually strange people," he said. "Now we are going to be working with ministers, lawyers, leaders of government, professors, and university presidents."

And because he often spoke in terms of the numinous number 120, he challenged them to find him 120 allied Christian ministers. Jesus, he said, would have been unstoppable had he boasted 120 disciples instead of a paltry 12.

• • •

In just a few months Moon would be a free man, he and his newspaper here to stay, and cash continuing to roll from overseas into the Washington political arena.

Would he be a new man as well as a free man? Conservatives like Dinesh D'Souza, a bright young Heritage Foundation fellow, wrestled with the question of whether the experience had humbled Moon, changing him into someone the movement could openly work with. In 1985, D'Souza wrote a six-page essay for the think tank's journal, *Policy Review*, titled "On Moon's Planet: The Theology and Politics of the Unification Church," in which he interviewed a variety of right-wing activists who had taken Moon money. "Others," he said, "keep their distance but are not willing to say so publicly. One reason is a reluctance to embarrass friends at the *Washington Times*." D'Souza asked whether Moon's demand for a "socialistic society centering on God" might "cause discomfort for conservatives primarily concerned with individual liberty."

"What I can't figure out," he told *The Nation*'s Eric Alterman at the time, "is whether Moon is trying to purchase respectability for his theology or whether he wants to jettison the theology in order to purchase respectability for himself."

By 2007, D'Souza had stopped asking the question, at least in public. That summer he was on tour promoting his headline-grabbing book, *The Enemy at Home*, which charged that "the cultural left in this country is responsible for 9/11." Our pop culture, including Britney Spears and *Brokeback Mountain* are, the book says, the fruit of "an aggressive global campaign to undermine the traditional patriarchal family and to promote secular values in non-Western cultures," arousing fury in the Muslim world.

This message, which he was delivering for $10,000 to $15,000 an appearance, was welcomed May 16, 2007, at a Washington, D.C., gathering of the Universal Peace Federation, the Reverend Moon's newest initiative. D'Souza told me the Moon connection was news to him. The event, "The Culture Wars in Global Perspective," was "sponsored by them [the UPF] and the Washington Times Foundation," he told me.

"I know almost nothing about Reverend Moon," D'Souza, author of a five-page article on the Returning Lord, said in an e-mail. Had he heard of the coronation? "This is the first I've heard of this one too. Seems harmless enough to me, although I'm not sure what the monarchial reference means. As a Catholic I consider Christ the prince of peace."

• • •

In the beauty of the lilies, Christ was born across the sea
With a glory in his bosom that transfigures you and me
As he died to make men holy, let us live to make men free
While God is marching on!

In October 1981, a crowd of five thousand at Foley Square in Lower Manhattan sang the "Battle Hymn of the Republic" in support of their liege, just hit with a surprise indictment. Moon's minister Mose Durst stood and said that the IRS couldn't stand Moon because he was "the most moral man in America." Moon, too, spoke. To him, the Empire State Building and all the towers of Fifth Avenue were part of Satan's empire, closing in on God's son. "I would not be standing here today," he told the crowd, "if my skin were white and my religion were Presbyterian."

All summer the buzz had been that the onslaught, when it came, would be on Moon's green card, not his taxes. Questions had lingered since 1976, when an Immigration and Naturalization Service (INS) official complained that hundreds of Japanese had been brought into the United States from Asia on the pretext of "religious education and training." "As nearly as we can determine," the official said, "their 'training' consists of soliciting funds and selling some items."

Instead, federal tax attorneys turned a wrecking ball on Moon's $10 million-plus tax exemption. On October 16, the *New York Times* reported that he was being indicted for filing false tax returns over a three-year period. The story was that in March 1973, Moon had walked into Chase Manhattan Bank, deposited $1.6 million, made withdrawals for personal use, and failed to report $106,000 in interest. He'd also neglected to declare $50,000 in securities income. There were twelve counts, some directed at his Japanese accountant, Takeru Kamiyama.

Six days later came the first hearing. Moon, the *New York Times*'s Arnold Lubasch reported, wore a light gray suit and maroon tie as he entered that morning with his defense lawyer, Charles Stillman. Charming, he shook hands with prosecutor Martin Flumenbaum, catching him off guard. Moon, Lubasch said, "waved a finger at him, as if admonishing a naughty child." Then Moon said "good morning" in English to the press. His defense would rely on portraying the sophisticated businessman as an innocent abroad, who had misunderstood the laws of his host country.

"Mr. Stillman is a Jewish lawyer, and Marty Flumenbaum is a Jewish prosecutor," Col. Bo Hi Pak observed of the adversaries. Perceiving a yin-yang dynamic at work in the universe, he said, "So they are Abel Jew and Cain Jew." In this sermon he also called on followers to resist Satan's inevitable attacks on Moon's new daily paper. "We in the *Washington Times* need to conduct ourselves as it says in the Bible," he said, "wise as serpents and pure as doves. . . . We have to deal with the wicked world out there. Wolves are out there. Hungry wolves . . . ready to attack at the first opportunity. . . . The *Washington Times* is such an incredible project for God's side that all of Satan's side will hate for us to succeed."

•   •   •

The trial was set for March 22. The sky darkened, Pak said, just as Flumenbaum, the "Cain Jew," got up to give the prosecution's opening statement, the electricity flickering. But when Stillman, the "Abel Jew," got up to speak, "the wind totally died down . . . [he was] speaking so powerfully in a low, emotional voice . . . the drop of a needle could be heard." (*New York Times* accounts are silent on whether air pressure changed depending on the righteousness of the lawyer.)

While the church faced testimony against it by Michael Warder, the Heritage Foundation official and apostate Moonist, it was battling New York tax officials in a separate fight over whether its expensive real estate in Manhattan and Queens qualified as tax exempt. The Unification empire, the tax commissioners said, was a "complicated and interlocking corporate conglomerate," a "primarily politico-messianic organization," out to "influence public policy, engage in commerce and recruit cadres of believers."

In the fraud case, Moon's defense team argued that he didn't need to report his income because the cash wasn't technically his but held for the Unification Church. Dramatically, the tax case came down to two pieces of paper. In hopes of stopping this trial from coming to pass, churchmen had earlier provided Justice Department investigators with mitigating paperwork from 1973. To get Moon off the hook, the church had presented the Department of Justice with paperwork from 1973, showing a series of loans from Europe and donations from Japan that proved the cash flow was part of church operations, and therefore tax-exempt. "Every single penny went to the Unification Church," said priest Mose Durst.

The prosecution called Mrs. Pearl Tytell, a Lower Manhattan typewriting scholar. So trained was she in the fine points of paper that she could name the mill where pulp had been turned into any particular sheet, if not the forest. The "1973" documents, she revealed in a bombshell moment, were on paper printed in 1974—a "slam dunk," she said years later. A watermark expert made similar discoveries. The documents were phony.

On May 2, 1982, the defense rested. Prosecutors had presented thirty witnesses and one thousand documents. In his final instructions to the jury, Judge Goettel said they should reach a conclusion about Moon and his accountant without race or religious prejudice. Jurors were on a "holy quest," he said, "the search for justice."

The guilty verdict came down May 19. "Because he's a yellow man and he comes from another country, he was on trial," said Mose Durst, who also warned the New York diocese of the Roman Catholics: "If Rev. Moon gets it, watch out Cardinal Cody; watch out Cardinal Cooke."

On July 23, 1982, Moon was handed his prison term. Judge Goettel rejected the argument from Moon's lawyer Stillman that the trial was motivated by religious "blood lust." To reduce Moon's sentence, he said, would signal that in America "the rich and powerful go free." Prosecutor Jo Ann Harris, assistant U.S. attorney, said Moon had been dealt with like "any other high-ranking businessman and his chief financial aide" who avoided income tax.

By now, liberal giant Laurence Tribe, a Harvard University constitutional scholar, had been brought in to fight for Moon as a test case for the First Amendment. "I don't know that I have ever had a more skillful opponent," said a U.S. solicitor. For Tribe, it was a matter of principle and publicity—among a slew of high-profile church-and-state cases he had taken on. In 1981, he'd argued before the Supreme Court (unsuccessfully) that the Minnesota State Fair was infringing on the rights of Hare Krishnas to pass out religious literature. In 1982, he argued (successfully) before the Supremes the case of *Larkin v. Grendel's Den*, a landmark case overturning laws in nine states that forbade liquor stores to operate near churches. He said of Moon that it was "exactly the people who are hated who ought to have the protection of the courts against mass hysteria."

Now, in August 1982, when immigration officials came for the Moons the month after the sentencing—saying Mrs. Moon had turned in papers misrepresenting herself as a mere cook and chaperone for a dance troupe—Tribe persuaded the judge it would be heaping insult on injury to deport them. Citing the reverend's "extraordinary personal investment in this country," Tribe said it would be a "sharper, more stinging rebuke than any prison could ever inflict." (By this he meant more than politics. On a smaller scale, the church had paid for an America the Beautiful Cleanup Campaign, using unpaid or underpaid church labor; a War on Pornography program; and a track team for inner-city Washington youth, the D.C. Striders.)

On August 11, 1982, Judge Goettel allowed Moon to remain Stateside. Here, protected by the American institutions he hoped to unravel in his Peace Kingdom, he could would continue to invest. (For in his ideal world, according to his speech at the *Washington Times* anniversary in 2007, "people [would] govern themselves by the heavenly way and heavenly laws, with no need for lawyers, prosecutors or even judges.")

Over the next two years, *U.S. v. Sun Myung Moon* worked its way to the appeals stage. There, in a 2–1 decision, a majority rejected Tribe's argument that Moon had been singled out while mainstream Christians got a free ride. In an intriguing dissent, however, Justice James L. Oakes saw a worldly messiah's investments as potentially tax-exempt:

> [B]ecause Moon was the spiritual leader of the church, the issue whether
> he or the church beneficially owned funds in his name was not as crystal-
> clear as might seem at first glance to be the case. It appears that the assets
> in question came to Moon largely from members of his faith, and there
> was some evidence that the donors intended their contributions to be
> used by him for religious purposes.

After all, the goal of the movement was for Master Moon to prosper as
founder of a worldwide kingdom. "Heaven gave me this house," Moon
had said in 1972, after young Americans—living off chicken soup and
peanut butter and jelly sandwiches, remembers former leader Allen Tate
Wood—hit the streets to bankroll the $294,000 down payment on his home
along the Hudson River, in Tarrytown.

• • •

On May 14, 1984, the Supreme Court declined to review the case, in spite
of the close call. Meanwhile, the church set to work on an extraordinary
$30 million project to rebrand the Reverend Moon, convicted felon, as an
important martyr. It would include cash payments to civil rights leaders
and evangelicals, and rallies across the country with Christian ministers
posing in cages.

While "Mr. Moon's tax fraud raises no serious issue of religious or
ethic persecution," wrote former Supreme Court correspondent John P.
MacKenzie in the *New York Times*, a "public relations firm worked hard to
create the impression that the case had ominous significance."

A few weeks before Moon was to enter prison, ally Orrin Hatch held
a panel to confront what he saw as persecution darkening America's door.
During the meeting, Moon himself spoke of pouring "several hundred
million dollars" from overseas sources into the United States to change
history. He also told Hatch that "a dark spirit of atheism and religious
intolerance is found today, and this time there is not another New World
to receive us as refugees." The church made much of the *amicus curiae*, or
"friend of the court" briefs, that had been filed on behalf of Moon by mem-

bers of dozens of groups, including the National Council of Churches and the New York chapter of the ACLU.

Hatch agreed with them. "We accused a newcomer to our shores of criminal and intentional wrongdoing," he said, "for conduct commonly engaged in by a large percentage of our own religious leaders." Forging documents? No, "namely, the holding of church funds in bank accounts in their own names," Hatch said. "Catholic priests do it. Baptist ministers do it, and so did Sun Myung Moon. The Moon case sends a strong signal that if one's views are unpopular enough, this country will find a way not to tolerate, but to convict."

Journalist Fred Clarkson, who covered Moon for the *Washington City Paper*, disagrees. "For all of the histrionics about the terrible precedent and how poor churches would be persecuted by the feds, it just hasn't panned out," he says. Now a crusader against the Religious Right, Clarkson credits the episode with teaching Christian evangelicals to play the victim card. "The Moon tax case was used to help establish the frame that religion is somehow persecuted in America," he says. "He was prosecuted not because of his race, or because of his religion, but because he is a crook."

In 1982, Moon had protested ignorance of the law. But daughter-in-law Nansook Hong recalled in her 1998 memoir, *In the Shadow of the Moons*, that in the nineties, after the trial had impressed on Moon the requirements of the IRS, she was part of a continuing effort to stiff tax and customs officers. Into her makeup case went $20,000 in bills for the trek from Asia to Seattle. "I knew that smuggling was illegal," Hong said, "but I believed the followers of Sun Myung Moon answered to higher laws." Other members, she said, brought in paper bags of tax-free cash that went into a safe in Mrs. Moon's wall at East Garden, the church's gated Hudson Valley headquarters. And in 1994, $1 million arrived from Moon for her husband in cash, she wrote, $600,000 of which he delivered to a church business in a Bloomingdale's bag. Journalist Robert Parry was told by former officials of Moon's Manhattan Center complex that the cash was then laundered through various church properties.

"I watched Japanese church leaders arrive at regular intervals at East Garden with paper bags full of money," Hong said, "which the Reverend

Moon would either pocket or distribute to the head of various church-owned business enterprises at his breakfast table." She believed it was "doing God's will'," she told the BBC, to shield Moon from the indignities of the IRS.

Other cash questions have more recently been raised by Latin American politicians concerned about Moon's nineties purchases of land in the Southern Hemisphere. In 1996, there were widespread reports that a parade of 4,200 Japanese women followers lined up to deposit $80 million in cash at the Banco de Credito, a bank in Uruguay owned by the movement. Two years later, the Uruguayan government seized control of the *banco*, the country's third-largest, claiming that Moon's church had "cratered it," sucking out funds beyond the legal limit to use it as an ATM.

In a connection discovered by Parry, around the time deposit slips were being filled out for the mystery $80 million, retired president George H. W. Bush was touring the area on Moon's behalf. "[P]raise in Father's presence was more than we expected," a church account said of Bush. "It was vindication. We could just hear a sigh of relief from Heaven."

Newspapers reported on November 25, 1996, that Bush "traveled with Moon [from Argentina] to neighboring Uruguay Sunday to help him inaugurate a seminary in the capital, Montevideo, to train 4,200 young Japanese women to spread the word of his Church of Unification across Latin America." One could very easily imagine them to be the same 4,200.

• • •

First Amendment hero—that was a novel enough role for the Lord of the Second Advent. But in 1985, as millions of dollars began to change hands between the Unification Church and the Religious Right, his reinvention snowballed.

Was Moon the test case for the First Amendment, whose creed liberals and Christian evangelicals might find horrible, while duty bound to defend his freedoms? Or was he more than that? Was he a martyr? And not just a martyr, but a patriot whose words had been misunderstood, who had been by our side all this time, fighting for bedrock American principles? (This was the view that Bo Hi Pak, Moon's loyal aide, bade Jerry Falwell and others to consider.)

Yes, the stranger had spoken of building an "automatic theocracy to rule the world," humiliated his followers, and been accused of enslaving teenagers. But now the church was spending $4 million on a public relations campaign to introduce Christian evangelicals to the other side of Moon: the Moon who saluted us all in 1976 at the Bicentennial God Bless America Festival, who was funding Cold Warriors in Latin America, who was willing to go behind bars for everyone, everywhere.

That was the message of the "The New Birth Project," the lunar codename for a drive to romance preachers, civil rights veterans, and opinion makers. In a "goodwill blitz," three hundred thousand ministers received five-pound packages marked "A Gift for You from Some Folks Who Care," as *Time* reported. Inside were videotapes and books spotlighting Moon as a misunderstood figure, asking for a second chance. If his religious freedom was under attack, wasn't theirs?

Some returned the boxes, full of ashes. Others bought in. During his prison term, Moon received an honorary doctorate of divinity by the Shaw Divinity School in North Carolina, which had coincidentally accepted $30,000 from him. "In one year," said follower Mose Durst, "we moved from being a pariah to being part of the mainstream."

The prison sentence also brought a media reassessment. As if the *New York Times* were apologizing for its past, aggressive coverage, the paper presented readers with the friendliest treatment yet. The Divine Principle was "basically a form of evangelical Protestantism," one reporter explained in 1984. Complaints of brainwashing and lost children, according to the paper, were rarely ever heard anymore. Church spokesperson Joy Garratt admitted that "maybe some of [the early disciples] had been overzealous. They overlooked writing to their parents."

• • •

Two who rushed early to embrace the new, OK-to-work-with Reverend Moon Mark II were Jerry Falwell and Tim LaHaye, founders of the Moral

Majority. At a rally the week of July 27, 1984, at Washington's Hyatt Regency, LaHaye blamed "secular humanists" for Moon's confinement. Another speaker was a white supremacist preacher named Everett Sileven, whose church had been padlocked by the State of Nevada in a dispute over running an unlicensed day school. Sileven demanded "an amnesty, not to illegal aliens, not to draft dodgers," but to preachers "persecuted for their religious beliefs.

Another guest was In Jin Moon, the *Times* owner's daughter, a new bride in the royal family's marriages to the living and the dead. In the double wedding of February 20, she had been the wife who got a husband who was alive. The other woman was matched to a dead boy, Heung Jin.' "What is most painful to my father," she told the crowd, "is that the nation my father dearly loves has imprisoned him."

With help from $500,000 in Moon's cash, LaHaye had convened a new group, the Coalition for Religious Freedom, that focused on defending Moon. Its board members included televangelists James Robison, D. James Kennedy, Jimmy Swaggart, and others.

Jerry Falwell, who had in 1978 denounced Moon as a devil preying on American children, had a change of heart in these years. He spoke at an August 1985 "God and Freedom Banquet." Attended by about 1,800 guests, it was held under the banner of the Confederation of the Associations for Unity of the Society of the Americas (CAUSA), a church-run umbrella organization for anti-Communists whose aim was to enthrone the Reverend Moon in the guiding light of the Cold War in Latin America.

Leftist Catholics in Latin America, influenced by Marx, had developed "liberation theology" to support their causes. The idea here was that the Reverend Moon had devised a counterphilosophy so powerful, it could crush such ideas forever—just as his seminars in the Spirit World had the power to turn the soul of Stalin himself.

•   •   •

Sit a congressman down to listen to Moon, the church believed, and the

Divine Principle would win out. But whatever the church might have believed about the irresistible lure of Moon's teachings, in the next ten years of winning over the Christian right, it seemed to be his cash that spoke loudest.

In 1996, Ralph Reed, Beverly LaHaye, and Gary Bauer, major figures of the Religious Right, were filmed looking bored at a gala conference held by the church from July 30 to August 1 in Washington, D.C. The occasion: commemorating Moon's retirement of the name "Unification Church" and the inauguration of his Family Federation for World Peace. There, one theologian marveled, Moon had made a "a bomb-like proclamation" in which "all the secrets of heaven had revealed." During the festivities, Moon took the stage and gave a barking speech in which he chopped the air and posed the question "Who is the owner of love?" He angrily reminded the convention-goers of the arcane dance of horizontal and vertical forces in the universe, demonstrating with his hands.

Former president Gerald Ford attended one portion of the event, joylessly. So did vice presidential candidate Jack Kemp and George H. W. Bush. Singer Pat Boone is seen sauntering on stage with considerable enthusiasm, even asking Mrs. Moon if she has ever heard his song "April Love." And he gets a cackle from Moon when he wisecracks, "It's good for Mr. *Boone* to meet *Mr. Moon!*"

By 1996, politician after politician was dropping by these bizarre gettogethers, only to tell the press afterward, as Ford did, that they "didn't know" the reverend would be involved. Some seemed legitimately duped; others were repeat visitors. Comedian Bill Cosby discovered to his horror that the "Family Federation" he'd agreed to address was vastly different from what he expected.

"When I look down the list and see Gerald Ford," Cosby said, "you say, well, gee whiz, that's fine, so you go ahead and sign up." He tried to give the money back after learning he'd agreed to tell jokes for the Reverend Moon but couldn't escape his contract. He gave an "unsmiling perfunctory performance of sixteen minutes" to the two thousand followers of the Unification Church. "We'll have famous people come to events, and we'll advertise that it's completely different," one dishearted young church member told me. "Once they find it's Moonie related, they all run away."

• • •

In the early years, as they tiptoed into the new relationship with Moon, leaders who professed belief in Jesus still faced the threat of humiliation if they were seen cavorting with a man who claimed to be his replacement. That year, an amusing series of events were touched off when Carolyn Weaver, a writer for *Mother Jones*, interviewed Beverly LaHaye, fifty-six, of the powerful conservative group Concerned Women for America. Founded in 1979 to advance "biblical principles" in American politics, it has opposed gay rights, abortion, emergency contraception, pornography, stem cell research, and the theory of evolution.

Weaver hadn't brought enough audiotape to record the interview. Bev LaHaye generously gave her another cassette, an old one that had been lying around the office.

Tim LaHaye, Bev's influential husband, had forgotten to tape over it. Later, when Weaver popped it into a player, she heard the Moral Majority leader, dictating a fond letter to the head of the Unification Church.

"Dear Bo Hi," LaHaye's voice said.

Today, LaHaye has achieved new fame for cowriting the *Left Behind* novels about an antichrist UN secretary who transforms the UN into a "Global Family." Given his past intimacy with the Reverend Moon, it seems hard not to imagine that LaHaye was partly inspired by Moon's own fantasies of ruling the UN. In 1986, LaHaye was known principally not as an author of science fiction but as the powerful pastor of Family Life Seminars and Jerry Falwell's partner in founding the Moral Majority. And now he was caught on tape, discussing a Falwell for President campaign he envisioned for 1988, with help from the Reverend Moon, who had called Christianity his enemy.

"This letter is being written at thirty-seven thousand feet," LaHaye continued, "out of Chicago en route to San Francisco." He described how Washington, D.C., was becoming a comfortable place to live. "As soon as we get our radio [show] time changed from 7:00 to 8:00 each night to 1:00 to 2:00 P.M. daily," he said, "we want to have you and your wife over for dinner.

> Bo Hi, I am encouraged! Amid the bad signs I see today, I also detect a lot of good signs. The secretary of education [conservative Bill Bennett], Don Regan, Ed Meese, [*Washington Times* commentator] Pat Buchanan, and many others. Even physical ailments to three of the 76[-year-old] flaming liberal Supreme Court justices. . . . Bev was invited to the White House yesterday and was introduced to over 300 conservative leaders as "the president of the largest women's organization in America—over twice as large as NOW!" [referring to the liberal National Organization for Women].
>
> On this trip, I will be going to the Holy Land with Jerry Falwell. . . . Confidentially, during that time I am going to talk to him about 1988 and my strategy for winning the primary. I am convinced he can beat Teddy [Kennedy] in the general election if we could get him through the primary. . . . I think Jerry will like my plan to recruit 435 activists, one in each congressional district, to work under our [American Coalition for Family Traditional Values, or ACFTV] chairman.
>
> I'll let you know what he says.

Though LaHaye would protest that he had taken no more than $100 from Pak, he gave thanks for "your generous help to our work," as he put it, saying the work of ACFTV—which included well-known evangelists Jimmy Swaggart and Falwell—had been "extremely expensive." And here LaHaye, the defender of traditional values, gave lip service to Sun Myung Moon's title of Master. "I see daylight down the road," he said, "and feel it is part of the Master's plan."

He concluded with a little conservative-to-conservative humor.

Let's plan to sit together at the first CBS shareholder's meeting when
[conservative senator] Jesse Helms makes his move to take it over.

Your friend,
Tim

LaHaye paid Moon a tearful visit in prison, according to Bo Hi Pak. "Reverend Moon, I apologize on behalf of my government," LaHaye had said, holding the hands of the man who was a newly minted Reverend Doctor Moon. The colonel recalled that LaHaye told Moon, "Your suffering will cleanse the sins of America." The *Left Behind* author's "eyes were red and he was crying. What a beautiful union, a union of brothers, like Esau and Jacob" in the Bible. When the *Mother Jones* piece came out, LaHaye called the magazine "sleazy" and said the letter to Pak was only a "first draft."

• • •

And Jacob just kept giving huge infusions of cash to Esau, of unclear origin. "I'll tell you one thing," an inscrutable LaHaye had told Weaver, "it doesn't come from selling flowers." Conservatives, says ex-*Times* editorialist John Seiler, "were in the wilderness for years. Then all of a sudden Reagan is in power giving people jobs, the media are taking notice, and all this money is flowing around, much of it from Moon. It proved too tempting for too many."

In a 1987 that included a mass walkout from the *Washington Times*, the downfall of former treasury secretary Robert B. Anderson over hiding Moon dollars, hot debate on the right, and revelations of violence within the church, the wedding between conservatives and Moon seemed headed for a reckoning. William F. Buckley, the elder statesman of conservatism, had already voted other heresies off the conservative island, none of them as extreme as Moon's. Buckley had considered it his "unpleasant business" to "excrete unwholesome bodies," including the John Birchers (too paranoid), the Ayn Randians (too hung up on *Atlas Shrugged*), and paleo-cons (over charges of anti-Semitism.)

But as the storm gathered over the *Times*, conservative campaigner Bob Grant pressed ahead. He and the Unification Church hammered out an agreement that resulted in the American Freedom Coalition (AFC) with an eye on the next year's elections. He revealed that $5,252,475 of his $15 million budget came from "business interests of the Unification Church." Others continued to fret about the Reverend Moon's fishing for souls. One cited a campaign to send ten million letters on behalf of accused Lt. Col. Oliver North. "Only Moonies could do that," an anonymous conservative leader said darkly to the *National Journal*.

After Congress forbade funding for the Contra death squads of Latin America, North had envisioned a private "Nicaraguan Freedom Fund." It was announced on the front page of the *Washington Times* the week of May 9, 1985, with Col. Bo Hi Pak contributing the first $100,000. (Just that fall, according to the *New York Times*, Pak had been held for random in Orange County by kidnappers who tortured him with electric shocks until he agreed to pay $1 million to a Swiss bank, in a bizarre account he gave to the FBI.)

With the marriage tightening, conservative leader Paul Weyrich stood practically alone in announcing that "blasphemy" was being promoted. But defiant Richard Viguerie, a board member of the AFC, told reporters, "I won't let liberals define who we should associate with or not." Also associating with Moon was board member L. Brent Bozell III. The AFC furnished the 1988 GOP campaigns with thirty million Candidate Scorecards and other political literature, for free. They "had an enormous effect," Doug Wead told *Frontline*, "the slickest and the finest produced material." He added, "When that doesn't cost you anything, and it is not charged against the campaign and is widely distributed to mailing lists across the country, that has a very important impact."

Another favor for the Bush campaign in 1988 came when the *Washington Times* reported that Democratic opponent Michael Dukakis might

be mentally ill. The *Times* had picked up the storyline from the fliers being passed out by followers of conspiracy theory cult leader Lyndon La-
Rouche, who also asserts that Dick Cheney is a satanic "beastman" and
the Beatles were a CIA plot. The Dukakis story relied on a doctored quote
from the Massachusetts governor's sister-in-law and ran under the headline "Dukakis Kin Hints at Session." The story, which two reporters quit
over, helped make "mental health rumors" an issue. It received play on
CBS and NBC, and it is widely credited with inspiring Reagan to joke,
"Look, I'm not going to pick on an invalid."

Complained editor Arnaud de Borchgrave later, "It's just one boo-boo
that we are faulted for every time somebody comes to interview us." Michael Dukakis, now teaching at USC, doesn't remember any of this. "I do
know that I didn't do a very good job in the final campaign," he says, "and
no Democratic candidate will ever make the mistake again of remaining
silent in the face of attacks by his opponent."

• • •

While the church's dollars coursed across the land to Washington, basking
in a new aura, and some congratulated themselves for working with a civil
rights hero, Moon's most trusted servant, Col. Bo Hi Pak of the *Washington
Times*, was being pummeled until a blood vessel burst in his head.

It was late November 1987, and Moon had appointed a church inquisitor, a touring confessor with a baby's face, who would slap around
senior church figures until they owned up to having evil sex or mishan-
dling the collection plate. His name was Cleopas Kundiona, though officially he was only to be known as "the second self." He was a miracle man
discovered by missionaries in Zimbabwe, who believed they'd found in
the African a magical channel to heaven and Moon's son.

Suddenly church leaders were seen with black eyes, and there were
reports of especially harsh beatings of Unification Church members in
Japan. Arnaud de Borchgrave of the *Times* suspected a Communist plot
behind it all. Others said Moon approved of the violence. He "seemed to

take pleasure in the reports that filtered back to East Garden of the beatings being administered," remembered his daughter-in-law. "He would laugh raucously if someone out of favor had been dealt an especially hard blow."

After the 1984 car accident that killed Heung Jin, there had first been scattered reports of members channeling parts of his soul. Then, on September 6, 1987, high priest Chung Hwan Kwak, Pak's bitter rival, proclaimed in Belvedere, New York, that Heung Jin was communicating twenty-four hours a day through Cleopas.

Cleopas was brought before Moon, who quizzed the black African to see for himself whether this was truly his son in a new body. Not everyone was impressed. A former hotel waiter, Cleopas lacked Heung Jin's schooling, and he didn't even speak Korean. But Moon was satisfied. It wasn't long before the black version of Heung Jin—who answered directly to Kwak, the ambitious "Cardinal"—announced that he wanted to make some changes around here. Kwak gave the Zimbabwean a green light for a punishment tour of the world. He grilled church leaders in Washington, D.C., as well as Japan, Africa, and South America, allegedly to convince them to eliminate waste in church spending. "He discovered that a lot of savings were possible," one member, impressed, told *Newsweek*.

One woman remembers being terrified to meet him when she was seventeen. But when she refused to be servile, Cleopas, like any bully, saved his slaps for riper targets. Cleopas wasn't a big man, but stories of violence followed him around the world. Wearing a traditional Korean man's gown, he held court. He would "tie people to radiators," the woman says, "made them crawl around on their hands and knees." According to ex-member Graham Lester, many Japanese leaders met with him, including a priest and a wife who were beaten unconscious. Cleopas then shaved their heads and summoned their fifty followers for more of the same. He handcuffed and hit a woman for defending the practice of oral sex. Moon's aide Peter Kim confessed to misusing funds and was hit with a rope.

One day leader Richard Barlow received a communiqué summoning him to Colombia, of all places, where Cleopas was reviewing the performance of the local church mission. When Barlow got there, he says, Cleopas bade the Colombian hotel staff to scram. Cleopas shot a handgun into the pool. He made a church member strip and dive for the bullet. The confessions went on all night. "I'm disgusted for ever having bought into it," Barlow says. "At the time you're thinking, 'Yes, it's very physical, but it's your eternal life, and you probably *do* have a few things in your cupboard.'" He got away with a slap on the cheek.

But *Washington Times* president Col. Bo Hi Pak, according to numerous reports, spent a week in Georgetown University Hospital in Washington, D.C., where he needed brain surgery. Even Damian Anderson, a passionate apologist for the church, became dismayed when his pregnant wife risked being walloped by the Black Heung Jin. "With my own eyes," he said in a testimonial posted at www.tparents.org, "I saw this man in the Washington, D.C. church knock people's heads together, hit them viciously with a baseball bat, smack them around the head, punch them, and handcuff them with golden handcuffs." Church members, he said, were "preventing people by force from leaving. . . . The fact that Dr. Pak was almost murdered by this brute indicates to me that I was on the mark."

Pak forgave the inquisitor. He reemerged from his trials at the 1987 *Times* office Christmas party, barely able to walk without a guide. Today Moon's most loyal aide is described as a "broken man" by ex-members. He has been stripped of many leadership duties. In 2005, he was jailed in South Korea for being unable to make good on a real estate deal—having committed to pay millions of dollars that he had lost to con artists. (Pak's foundation listed, in 2001, $2,553,497 under "Loss from Nigerian Fraud Scam.") Because the Reverend Moon would not bail Pak out, his children had to put up a Web page, www.SaveBoHiPak.org, appealing for donations beyond the 36 Families.

Loyalists have defended Reverend Moon's involvement by saying the messiah was ignorant of just how badly his best friend was being battered. First, says Dan Fefferman, Moon "instruc[ted] Clophas [*sic*] to tone down the beatings." Then, when "he saw Pak for himself (in Korea a few weeks later), he began to realize that something was seriously wrong." There was also talk of the tireless Cleopas wearing down his body with preaching, causing interference in the signals from heaven.

In 1988, it was agreed that the spirit had departed from Cleopas. The African was quietly packed off to Zimbabwe, where he apparently reinvented himself as a candidate in his home country's bloody politics. A human rights group reported that he was charged, in 2000, with arranging the murder of a rival campaign manager, but he was apparently cleared of charges.

• • •

"The Pak beating smacks strongly of Jonestown," ex–*Washington Times* opinion editor Bill Cheshire wrote in 1989. "And with Moon lavishing hundreds of millions of dollars a year on newspapers, magazines and political action groups in this country and abroad. . . . If the 'reincarnation' doesn't rock those conservative shops that have been taking money from Moon, not even fire-breathing dragons would disturb them."

They weren't rocked. The fights became only more muffled over whether it was right for American Christians to continue accepting millions from a figure who'd said, "My enemies are America and Christianity." One of the few who spoke out was David Racer, an evangelical Christian who chaired Republican Alan Keyes's run for president.

In his book *Not for Sale: The Rev. Sun Myung Moon and One American's Freedom*, Racer tells of sumptuous, all-expenses-paid seminars attended by his erstwhile conservative allies, put on under the banner of Moon's American Freedom Coalition. Such was the AFC's influence that Doug Wead, a friend to the Bush family, told *Frontline* in 1992 that "I'd say right now there are probably two groups among conservative organizations that really have an infrastructure, that have grassroots clouts—Concerned Women of America would, and the American Freedom Coalition would."

But when Racer went to an AFC get-together, he was uncomfortable with a segment advancing what seemed less akin to freedom than to a "theological form of communism":

> An ideology called Godism. . . . The root teaching of Godism was that all god-receiving religions could unite around at least one cause and that cause was to oppose the spread of international atheistic Communism. . . .
>
> Godism, it occurred to me, was simply replacing one form of tyranny with another, the latter based on religious fervor . . . it seemed logical to me that Godism meant a system in which Moon ultimately would play a pivotal, if not leading, role. . . .
>
> Conservatives would rather not have this information made public, fearing that it will "damage the movement." I suggest that no one needs to fear the truth. If the conservative movement is based on fraud and deception, which it would be if this truth is stifled, then it deserves to be damaged.

The book outraged Bob Grant, head of Moon's AFC, who accused Racer of rank treachery. The Minnesotan struck back in a November 13, 1989, letter:

> Not only did you allow the Moonists to decide who would sit on the board, you even allowed them to control or heavily influence the hiring of CV [Christian Voice] state directors. . . . You suggested that I opposed the use of a Unificationist as regional liaison because of power. You are exactly right! But not my power; their power! . . .
>
> Since we both know that Moonist theology is as off base and offensive as any other cult, why then do you agree to accept their millions and their best volunteers to build the political machine they have lacked up until now? . . .
>
> You and Gary Jarmin have created the perfect model to bring together American patriots who otherwise have no financial resources with which to fight. With day-to-day directions and functions handled

by a full-time, theologically dedicated Moonist in each state . . . you have resolved the two major problems of the conservative movement: money and staff . . . .

P.P.S. Read Jude 4, II Timothy 4:3–4 and I John 4:1–3 before you go to prayer. As a theologian, explain to me how they might or might not apply to this question of Moon and his agenda.

In the Epistle of Jude, the author cautions early Christians that "certain men whose condemnation was written about long ago have secretly slipped in among you."

•   •   •

By 1989, *U.S. News & World* Report, edited by Mortimer Zuckerman, was declaring that Moon's empire had connections to almost every major conservative group, including Heritage. The magazine was set upon by Moon's church, which prepared an ad asking, "Who's next, Mr. Zuckerman . . . Kikes, Niggers, Papists, Gooks, Holy Rollers?" and by Arnaud de Borchgrave, who accused writer John Judis (now editor of the centrist *New Republic*) of being from the "far left." (At the last minute, the Unification Church decided not to stand behind its own "kikes" ad, instead running it under the name of a "National Committee against Religious Bigotry and Racism" that no one had heard of.)

In 1994, in a little-noticed report by a Christian apologetics ministry in California, it was claimed that strife had descended on cable presence Trinity Broadcasting Network (TBN)—which beams faith-healing and fund-raising pleas into the living rooms of tens of millions of Americans and audiences in 190 countries. The fight was over Moon's lucre, which much of the Christian audience would consider ill gotten.

It all started when David Balsiger, the producer of *The Quest for Noah's Ark* TV special as well as a Republican activist in his own right, went off the reservation. He had campaigned to keep the Soviets out of the 1984 Olympics and worked to defend apartheid South Africa. He had been in the world of Christian Voice and would have known Moon strategist Gary Jarmin through a joint project to send out "moral report cards." But now he was accusing TBN of broadcasting "Moon TV." He was alluding to the delicate issue of *The Washington Report*, a biweekly show put on by the American Freedom Coalition.

Reacting indignantly to the "Moon TV" claim, Paul Crouch—the host of *Praise the Lord*, famous for his "prosperity gospel," which promises wealth to viewers who donate enough to TBN, and the enormous hair of his lachrymose wife, Jan—called Balsiger a liar on TV. "But Balsiger had done his homework on the Moon-AFC connection," reported Christian journalist William Alnor.

Crouch and Balsiger threatened to sue one another but finally reached an agreement to formally apologize to one another on TV—and to broadcast a special "exposing Moon funding to ministries," blowing the lid off the connections. But the agreement collapsed in another round of squabbling. No exposé was ever broadcast. Balsiger's "conduct has forever foreclosed any possibility of Trinity participating in the television program we discussed," said a lawyer for the network.

Nothing less than a new theology of cash had been created to explain the scale of Moon's philanthropy to the right, which by now included at least $1 billion for the *Washington Times*. After reporter Bob Parry discovered that Jerry Falwell had concealed a $3.5 million money trail to Moon, the televangelist was quoted in *Christianity Today* as saying that if "Saddam Hussein himself ever sent an unrestricted gift to my ministries," he would "operate on Billy Sunday's philosophy. The Devil's had it long enough," referring to the 1920s revivalist.

"I think silence is what Moon was buying," writes Gary North, the son-in-law of Christian Reconstructionist fringe theocrat R. J. Rushdoony, in 2002, rejecting the charge that the Korean pontiff's ideas had seeped into the movement along with his funds. "That the American Religious Right has taken money from Moon is an old story, and not an illustrious one." Any minister, he says, faces that moment of decision, when the bearer of tainted cash comes to his door. He advises: *Don't take it.* "A lot of prominent conservatives took Moon's money. I opposed this at the time, and I still do."

•   •   •

"The whole thing is a snow job," said ex-*Times* staff writer Edmond Jacoby in the old days. "In the guise of the religion, the Unification Church has built a pervasive, Washington-centered political machine that buys and debauches political figures in surprising numbers, and has underwritten its political activities with some truly world-class influence peddling."

Besides the cruelty, just what on earth had been happening during this multimillion-dollar orgy of public relations?

"CIA, Moonies Cooperate in Sandinista War," the *Post*'s Jack Anderson reported in 1984. "In the Central American hinterlands," he wrote, "it is sometimes difficult to distinguish CIA operatives from the Rev. Sun Myung Moon's disciples." The messiah had a "solid presence in the region."

Years before George W. Bush outsourced much of the Iraq war to contractors, there was speculation the government had privatized a forbidden war, by giving part of it to the Moonies. There were photographs of Honduran children in CAUSA T-shirts and a Moon base in Tegucigalpa, the capital, where the church apparently handed out cash and supplies, not just to refugees but to Contra guerrillas.

CAUSA. Someone in Oliver North's office scribbled the mysterious name on a letter from secretary Fawn Hall, a nearly illegible diagram, perhaps a brainstorming chart of how help could be funneled to the Nicaraguan death squads. North had been pondering an end run around Congress, which had blacklisted the Contras from the foreign aid budget for their for tortures, rapes, and massacres in the name of fighting the Marxist regime of the Sandinistas.

For all the crimes of communism, CAUSA, the Reverend Moon's anti-Communist networking organization, consisted of an awfully motley bunch.

How motley? Here's an example: Remember the murderous Bolivian drug lords from *Scarface* (1983)? Screenwriter Oliver Stone may have been thinking of His Excellency Luis García Meza, installed in that nation in 1980 during what was widely called "The Cocaine Coup," with reports of CASA funding and of Bo Hi Pak being honored as a state guest before Meza was chased out in 1981. The coup was carried out with "consulting" services from Gestapo fugitive Klaus Barbie, who was months from being found hiding out there by a Nazi hunter. Liberal president Jimmy Carter refused to welcome the new anti-Communist government, citing its human rights record.

Pak's book, *Truth Is My Sword*, includes a friendly blurb from Meza—who is serving, as of 2007, a thirty-year sentence for drug trafficking and atrocities. "I consider the holding of this CAUSA seminar to be of great importance," the cocaine dictator writes, prior to his arrest, "because the ideology offers a solid basis for morality." (More recently Meza has been denounced in the *Times* for ruling "savagely.")

Other statements of support listed in the book are from U.S. senators Orrin Hatch ("I love you"), Richard Lugar ("a deep privilege"), Chuck Grassley ("I feel very much at home with the philosophy of this organization"), Jack Kemp ("thrilled that I can be with men and women who care deeply about the cause of freedom"); Department of Education secretary William J. Bennett ("Your efforts in support of freedom fighters around the world and the ideals of Western civilization command the respect and appreciation of all Americans").

There were other scattered reports in the press of the Unification Church getting involved in the Contra war. In Columbia, Missouri, the paper reported that Americans at a "quasi-military training camp" near Harrisburg had been boating material to Central America, with a Moon group providing logistical aid. Meanwhile, some mainstream American anti-Communists were trying to purge the cause of Moon, the fascists, and other extremists, while ex-Reagan National Security Council official Roger Fontaine remained close to CAUSA.

What little is known of the strange marriage of Latin American guerrillas, U.S. operators, and Moon priests comes largely from *New Yorker* correspondent Jon Lee Anderson (no relation to Jack) and his brother, Scott. "The Unification Church," the Andersons write, summing up their take on the Moon mystery, "made an alliance with the Japanese underworld and used vast amounts of money, funds of unknown origin, for influence peddling in the United States and South America through a variety of front groups."

One rebel leader they spoke to praised Moon's group for delivering $11,000 when he was struggling to pay bills. Another Contra accepted a trip to the United States on the church dime. One warrior, Fernando "El Negro" Chamorro—around whom conservatives in the Iran-Contra affair sought to build a united Southern Front—balked at an offer from the Moonies to "unite" the factions: the peasant militias, the Sandinista dissidents, and the displaced Indians of the Atlantic Coast. "I don't want them to give us money and then to turn this around into a Moonie thing," he said.

The Episcopal Conference of Honduras warned that a campaign there posed "serious dangers to the psychological, religious and civic integrity of anyone who yields to its influence." Another minister complained that CAUSA "could create a repressive extreme right that doesn't exist in Honduras right now." Today, Moon reportedly owns casinos and hotels in the country.

In San Francisco, meanwhile, a fake Catholic priest had emerged from the Reverend Moon's maze. Dressed in clerical robes, Father Thomas Dowling had testified before Congress in 1985 on the rightness of the Contra cause. He had claimed that it was the Sandinistas who were dressing up as Contras and framing the other side for the massacres. He'd learned this from visiting Nicaraguan rebel camps. As it turned out, he hadn't even been to Nicaragua. And the Catholic Church hadn't heard of him. Pressed, Dowling explained he was from *another* Catholic Church, a tiny splinter community that calls itself, confusingly, the Old Roman Catholic Church. Outraged, Rep. Sam Gejdenson (D-CT) called it a "phony church," and an FBI report speculated that Dowling's Celtic branch of the church had been inspired not by God but the IRS.

His expenses underwritten by both the Reverend Moon, through his salary from CAUSA, and Oliver North, from a secret $3.9 million bank account in the Cayman Islands, Dowling operated a "strategic studies" center in California that nobody ever visited, seemingly a front. His name appears repeatedly in a heavily redacted FBI report from February 27, 1987, in which it was said that the priest from the little church was involved with the big Unification Church's effort, through "a Moonie front [redacted.]" Shades of 2003, when the *Washington Times* would draw out of a hat the seemingly phony "Pastor Joseph" (see chapter 3), his cloudy religious affiliation, and his tales of Iraqis desperate for bombs to start falling.

In 1986, PBS screened a film, *Nicaragua Was Our Home*, playing up the plight of the Indians in a move to shift public opinion on the Contra wars. It had been produced by CAUSA and filmed by Lee Shapiro, a graduate of Moon's seminary and a gifted cinematographer. A *Minneapolis Star & Tribune* investigation suggested key events in the film "never happened," but the film was broadcast anyway by the U.S. Information Agency. Moon cheered his movement's media accomplishment.

"The U.S. government did not prepare that documentary," Moon said in an August 10, 1986, sermon. "They understand that our movement did it." In another speech, he proclaimed, "America will change its attitude towards Reverend Moon and will come to welcome me," he said. "The U.S. Congress is opposing the Nicaraguan aid bill, while the President is trying to get it passed. This means the President and Reverend Moon are both working for the same goal." A few months later, the filmmaker Shapiro was killed near Kabul, where he was filming a sequel promoting another group of rebel soldiers: Islamic jihadists fighting the Soviets in Afghanistan.

NINE

THE REVEREND MOON AND THE PIOUS PRESIDENT

A nation with the soul of a church.

—G. K. CHESTERTON

In early 2001, Dr. Morris Chapman, the fundamentalist CEO of the Southern Baptist Convention (SBC), complained to the *Baptist Press* of tricksters whose bait and switch had taken him entirely by surprise. On January 19—a day before the chief justice swore in George W. Bush—Chapman and other important Christian leaders had been lured to lunch with a guest they found intolerable. The experience, he said, "will serve to remind evangelical Christians that the world increasingly is filled with wolves in sheep's clothing," which was how Jesus described false prophets.

The Christians had agreed to attend a Friday gathering, something called the "Inaugural Prayer Luncheon for Unity and Renewal," under the impression they'd be there to bless the new presidency, which many evangelicals were claiming as their own. Bush slipped phrases from hymns into speeches and named Jesus Christ as his favorite philosopher, "because he changed my heart." They'd also heard that Billy Graham, the unstoppable man of God, would be receiving a lifetime achievement award at the affair, which featured TV evangelists Jerry Falwell, Paul Crouch, and Robert Schuller, as well as incoming attorney general John Ashcroft.

It was surprising, then, when the day of the lunch arrived and they found themselves listening to a rambling sermon from host Sun Myung Moon. Presented with a large trophy and treated as Graham's equal, Moon wanted to talk about being Messiah. There is no official transcript of his remarks, but that week he was pounding his chest after receiving a communiqué from, of all people, the original Buddha, who had recently caught up on the Divine Principle and been forced to admit that his own philosophy was a snafu. "My teaching is wrong," the Buddha told Moon. "It is so painful! . . . [M]an is born to have children and not live as a monk."

Remarked the Houston fundamentalist leader Paul Pressler, "I was not pleasantly surprised by the focus of the luncheon." The Christians reportedly left the affair fuming as women from the Unification Church handed them free booklets about the Divine Principle.

Strangely, the invitation to this lunar lunchtime had come directly from Douglas Wead. It was Wead who had taught George Bush Sr. how to appeal to evangelicals and who similarly helped Bush II tailor his message for the Christian base. Wead was such an intimate of the dynasty that the younger George, contemplating his future in 1998, confided to him in 1998 about the mistakes of his youth, and Wead recorded it.

What was the SBC doing in Washington, D.C., if not to counter rivals to Jesus? But over the years, the self-declared Second Coming and his cadre had become a more familiar presence than some would have liked to admit. In fact, according to the Nashville-based Baptist Center for Ethics (BCE), the "wolf in sheep's clothing" outrage of 2001 failed to stop a senior SBC official—the Southern California preacher Wiley Drake—from being listed in 2002 as part of the welcoming committee for Moon's April 27 wedding that year, the "Interreligious and International 144,000 Clergy Couples Blessing."

A founder of George W. Bush's Presidential Prayer Team, Drake had already apologized for spending time with the reverend by the time the IIFWP, Moon's world peace organization, freshly christened him an Ambassador for Peace and treated him to a gold watch. Drake is a pastor of evidently vengeful temperament who has called down the wrath of Psalm 109 ("May his children be vagrant beggars. . . . May no one treat him kindly or pity his fatherless children") on critics of his conservative politicking.

But Drake pooh-poohed protests by fellow Baptists who said they were shocked by the 2001 encounter with Moon. "[I]f [the Baptist leaders] didn't know that the *Washington Times* was tied to the Moonies," he told the BCE, "they just are, you know, not in the real world."

• • •

"Those who stray from the heavenly way," Moon admonished an audience in Taipei in December 2005, "will be punished." The "heavenly way," he explained, demanded a fifty-one-mile underwater highway spanning Alaska and Russia.

Sitting in the front row: Neil Bush, the recently divorced brother of the president of the United States. In 2003, he had claimed to be mystified by women who showed up at his hotel room in Asia and wanted to have sex with him. In 2005, he went into business with fugitive Russian tycoon Boris Berezovsky. Tonight he would be photographed with Mr. and Mrs. Moon, their deputy Chung Hwan Kwak, and others, all grinning in front of a gaudy "Universal Peace Federation" set, done up in a gaudy purple likeness of Earth and outer space.

The hundred-city speaking tour was to promote Moon's $200 billion proposal for a "Peace King Tunnel" construction project: both a monument to his magnificence and a totem to his prophecies. He also renewed his call to reinvent the UN to serve God's plans—part of what *The Hill* magazine called an "ambitious and diffuse" lobbying campaign directed at the international body on the East River.

The sheer range of guests revealed just how many Pacific Rim political leaders the *Times* monarch had won over, including Filipino and Taiwanese officials. One listener was Taiwan's vice president Annette Lu, described in a Taipei newspaper as "rapt" while Moon spoke. The head of the Arizona GOP was listed in the program for an event in San Francisco.

A brochure from Moon's Family Federation underscores that the tunnel was "God's fervent desire," dwarfing such past wonders as the English Channel Tunnel and heralding a "new era of automobile travel." And no bicycle lanes, for Moon, a creature of the right, is no stickler for carbon emissions. In fact, as environmentalists have pointed out, the influential Wise Use movement of the 1990s—a crusade against wetland protection, the Endangered Species Act, and other regulations—got its start in 1988 at a Reno convention attended by Moon officers. It turns out that yet another conservative direct-mail wizard is involved here: Alan Gottlieb. He and

Ron Arnold, the intellectual architect of Wise Use, were active board members of Moon's American Freedom Coalition, and for that reason some would-be allies kept a distance. "No one was aware that environmentalism was a problem until we came along," Gottlieb has said.

The thinkers behind Moon's Peace King Tunnel anticipated an antitunnel backlash by those who "demand the preservation of the polar region's ecosystem and the protection of polar bears and seals." An aggressive media strategy was called for. "[P]ublic opinion polls must be carried out all over the world . . . to educate environmental groups . . . and residents near the proposed construction sites." (Moon has said in the past that Caucasians are descended from polar bears.)

Shortly after the tunnel/UN soirée in Taiwan, Neil Bush next surfaced in the Manila press, whose accounts placed him at a similar dinner in the Philippines attended by *Washington Times* president Doug Joo and respected Filipino House Speaker Jose de Venecia. According to the *Manila Bulletin* piece, the elven-eared Venecia had proposed Moon's idea for the UN—to incorporate a "religious council"—to President George W. Bush in a 2003 meeting. Bush, according to Venecia's claim, said it was a "brilliant idea."

Not long after, according to *Business Week*, one of Moon's foundations donated $1 million to Ignite!, Neil Bush's educational software firm. Its trademark product, the Curriculum on Wheels, or COW, is a molded, purple CPU that teachers can roll to the head of the class, replacing books with wacky computer cartoons. Other investors have included a fugitive Russian businessman, junk bond crook Michael Milken, and Saudi prince Alwaleed Bin Talal. The COW appears to have received favorable treatment in Texas under the priorities of George W. Bush's No Child Left Behind Act.

• • •

"Free Sex: No!" "Extramarital Affair, You Are a Witch." On February 11, 2000, reported the Associated Press, a crowd of five hundred disciples rallied in Seoul with placards. These were the virginal shock troops of the Pure Love Alliance, an ambitious Moon push to relegate sex outside (his) marriages to the dustbin of human history. At a Berkeley, California, BART subway station, energetically smiling women from Asia stood at the top of the escalator, encouraging me to sign a pledge for a millennium of eternal sexual purity. It was the first time I had ever encountered the Unification Church. (I didn't sign it.)

The no-sex campaign also sprung up in Boulder, Colorado, where throngs of Moon worshippers cried out, "Absolute love, absolute life." In Chicago, they played "What's Going On?" by the band Four Non Blondes, and burned a Playboy bunny in effigy in front of Hugh Hefner's corporate headquarters. One of their signs admonished: "Do Your Homework, Not Yourself." They also protested outside the Kinsey Institute, on the grounds that its 1948 and 1953 studies of human sexuality had driven filthy Americans down the road to "free sex." They dressed in costume as sexually transmitted diseases and were invited by Chicago teachers to take part in the Windy City's school system—only to be driven out of the by civil rights leader Jesse Jackson. His Rainbow/PUSH coalition accused them of bringing "a message of fear and shame" to poor black youths.

At a May 15, 1999, meeting, leaders in Moon's church, pleased with their political prowess, eagerly discussed the prospect of official government approval for their "purity movement." One participant was David Caprara, a longtime Moonie who had been kidnapped at twenty-six by his parents in a failed deprogramming. George W. Bush would tap him to direct the old War on Poverty program Americorps VISTA, through his role as head of the federal government's Corporation for National and Community Service. According to notes from the meeting, Caprara "was working on an abstinence bill," likely for a state legislature, and was networking with black Democrats. "Now we need to develop curriculum material which can be shown in the school system," the notes read. "We could then take this a step further with the idea of betrothal and engagement and marriage."

·   ·   ·

When George W. Bush took office, one of the more controversial decisions of the White House was feeding $1 billion in taxpayer money to "abstinence-only education," in which federally funded experts tell teenagers they must overcome their horny natures. When you win a federal no-sex grant, strict conditions apply. You cannot, for example, teach that premarital sex is wrong but also recommend condoms; birth control must be presented as fatally flawed.

Who would apply? Not the State of California, which turned down all the money on the basis that the approach had proven useless. A number of religious crusades, however, bid and won millions in funds for such programs as "The Silver Ring Thing"—a Christian program that rewarded abstinent teens with rings inscribed with Bible verses.

The Unification Church received $1.28 million between 2003 and 2005 for Free Teens USA, a group that has promoted Moon's ideas about chastity to poor New Jersey youths. The leader was Martin Porter, a former Tongil Trading Company CEO from 1973 to 1983 whose face had appeared on promotional posters naming him "Moon's Man in Canada," according to a church history. In the summer 1987 issue of the church publication *Blessing Quarterly*, Porter testified to a series of supernatural visions that had led him to Moon. "I was sitting in my car, thinking about Father and what he may be doing," he wrote. "Suddenly, I saw little pink hearts appear in the car all around me." Program director Richard Panzer headed the Unification Church of Rhode Island in the 1980s—and was "special projects director" for the American Family Coalition, the family values successor to the American Freedom Coalition.

The Free Teens program boasts a "reality-centered" approach toward sex education. Its message is unmistakable: don't have sex before marriage, or you will die. Free Teens hosted a contest at Marshall High School, Wisconsin, in 1999, where teens were asked to compile a top ten list of reasons not to have sex. The winning entries were celebrated on a Moon Web site, including these:

3. If you don't want to kick the bucket, don't knock the boot.

1. Two words. Brighter future.

The specter of death similarly hovered over Free Teens' shambling Web site when it launched. Reminiscent of Moon's emphasis on the "blood lineage" that binds the biblical Adam to the True Father, Free Teens implores its subjects with the message "It's not just your body, it's your whole lineage forever." The site also heavily spun a 2001 study from the National Institutes of Health, claiming that the "U.S. Gov Now DOUBTS Condoms!" Under a link reading "Is Her Body Really Ready?" the federally funded site misleadingly reported a study on pelvic development and birth, making it look as if Harvard professor Rose Frisch endorsed the program. "I certainly do not support abstinence-only teaching for teens," Frisch said when contacted.

San Francisco Chronicle reporter Don Lattin, a longtime Moon watcher, discovered more ties between Bush social policy and the church. Under Bush's Healthy Marriage Initiative—in a $1.5 billion outlay of socialized values that Barry Goldwater was unlikely to have supported—a number of Moon's movement operatives won $366,179 in federal grants as "marriage specialists."

Meanwhile, the Centers for Disease Control (CDC) had briefly reached the conclusion on April 1, 2003, that there was only one group qualified for a no-bid contract for HIV/AIDS awareness training in Lagos, Nigeria: the Interreligious and International Federation for World Peace (IIFWP). The White House had earmarked at least a billion dollars for abstinence-only education in Africa. "In accordance with FAR part 6.302-1," the CDC announcement said—rules for government procurement—"IIFWP is the only responsible source and no other services will satisfy agency requirements." Encouraging Africans to become "heavenly citizens," the group had held twenty-one- and forty-day workshops to expose Africans to the Divine Principle.

Shortly thereafter, the agency did a U-turn. "Responses," the CDC's Kathy Harben told me, "showed that there were other organizations who could do what we were looking for."

TEN

KIM JONG-IL AND THE RETURNING LORD

The Messiah in this age is Rev. Sun Myung Moon. He was sent by God. Please never forget this point.

—PRESIDENT MARTIN VAN BUREN
(ACCORDING TO THE REVEREND MOON)

Not long ago, peasants in the bleak streets of Pyongyang, the North Korean capital, saw a new kind of billboard go up. Instead of the usual colorful advertisements for the state cult—the beaming faces of Dear Leader Kim Jong-Il alongside his guerilla general father, Kim Il Sung; a Godzilla version of a People's Army soldier, swinging a bayonet to smash the dome of the U.S. Capitol into rubble—the new signs were for a car company. They touted the compact sedans and SUVs of Pyeonghwa Motors, a car company founded by the fabulous expatriate tycoon, Sun Myung Moon, who had fled decades ago and returned in the 1990s as a demigod.

The faces in the automobile ads were well fed and healthy, unlike those of many North Koreans, most of whom couldn't afford automobiles, so that the streets are carless and ghostly quiet. But for wages of $120 a month, the proles could toil in the Reverend Moon's car plant—clanging away in a location several miles down a quiet highway, in nearby Nampo. That is where Moon, among a handful of South Korean entrepreneurs trusted to do business in this Orwellian state, has invested between $50 and $65 million for the car venture alone.

"We are bound to succeed," Unification Church officer Park Sang Kwon, head of the joint venture with state company Ryongbong, told *Los Angeles Times* reporter Barbara Demick in 2002, citing the advantages of the North Korean workplace. "There are no unions, low labor costs. The workers are very clever, very quick to learn, and they are harshly controlled by their superiors."

No stranger partner than Kim Jong-Il could be imagined for Moon, whose gospel of communism as hell on Earth allowed him to set up shop in conservative Washington in the first place. ("Some of us," writes *National Review Online* columnist Dave Shiflett, "will recall rallies of the Lunar Faithful during which thundering refrains of 'Victory over Communism' shook the very skies.") If international communism is the devil's kingdom, then North Korea, according to the rules of his Divine Principle, is the center of it all, testament to the continuing suffering of God's chosen country.

"We were taught to despise the regime as the ultimate Satanic example of dictatorship in the world," says former church leader Richard Barlow. His superiors in the Unification Church justified the partnership with North Korea—which also includes a fancy hotel in Pyongyang catering to foreigners, the Potongang—as a heroic feat, in which Moon had done the impossible, embracing his enemy, fusing together Cain and Abel, the yin and the yang, God and Satan. (He has also launched ventures in Vietnam and China.)

Yet to Barlow and other critics, there is something unseemly about the zeal with which the House of Moon has gone into business with North Korea. "You're supposed to love your enemy," says one apostate Moonie, "not join him." Another person who isn't pleased is Cliff Kincaid of conservative watchdog group Accuracy in Media, who has called for scrutiny of "an ominous turn in Moon's activities" since 1991.

When the Swift Boat scribe Carlton Sherwood had ridiculed the liberal media in 1991 for attacking Moon's ties to the South Korean CIA, he sneered, "One wonders if the *Post*'s reporters would have been equally disturbed if there had been church ties to communist North Korea." That year, a series of secret talks began between the House of Moon and the Kingdom of Kim.

Now those initial feelers have given way to a multimillion-dollar partnership, and no one's talking. The former editor of Moon's *Insight* magazine, neocon standard-bearer John Podhoretz, who paid early dues at the *Times*, declines to comment, telling me he "[makes] it a practice not to talk trash" about his former employers.

The *Washington Times*, that supposedly independent voice, has not criticized its owner's investments in the North. But its editors have cranked out pieces others attacking the previous administration for a "perverse policy of appeasement" that gives "enticements and sweetheart deals to North Korea." All the while, a church office on the third floor of the ineffably weird *Washington Times* building—housing Moon's personal foreign affairs office, the Summit Council for World Peace—has been handing out enticements and sweetheart deals of its own.

One way Moon can sweeten deals with potential partners around the world is by dangling before them his perceived power to reach U.S. politicians and to print the news. In the early 1990s, even as the *Times* purported to be separate from Moon and his goals, its editors were roped into a public relations campaign intended to impress Kim Il Sung into doing business with the Unification Church. While Moon offered his wealth to the cash-strapped dictator, a special present for the dictator rolled off the presses: a flattering edition of the *Washington Times* highlighting the warmth of that incomparable country, North Korea, and its far-sighted leader.

• • •

Opportunity knocked on Moon's door in 1991 with the collapse of Soviet communism and the ensuing financial crisis in Pyongyang.

Back then, South Korea hadn't yet begun its "sunshine policy" of thawing to the North. Sent to make the Communists an offer they couldn't refuse were two of Moon's most trusted officers: Col. Hi Pak, the loyal and bloodied servant, and Antonio Betancourt, a Colombian-born disciple who had headed the Latin American arm of CAUSA, the church's anti-Communist confederation, in the 1980s.

Striving to find a way into the Hermit Kingdom, Betancourt first approached the North Korean embassy in Beijing, China, presenting himself as head of the allegedly important new organization, the Summit Council. He was rebuffed again and again, according to church publications. He claims that he finally met with the North Koreans in April 1991, and he would go back and forth sixteen more times between then and 2003, winning personal audiences with Kim Senior and Junior.

By several accounts, it was through a mysterious woman named "Madam" Park Kyung Youhne—nicknamed "the gateway" for her contacts up North, such that Hyundai and other Seoul firms came to her for help—that the Reverend Moon himself finally won a meeting with the Great Leader Kim Il Sung. Involved in 1996 in food aid to the starving North, she was the subject of persistent rumors, according to the *Wall Street Journal*, that her cross-border deals were a front for espionage. By then, these enterprises included a joint bid with the Reverend Moon to develop resort facilities at Kumgansan, or "Diamond Mountain," a northern wilderness area prized for its sublime cliffs and waterfalls. (Moon eventually lost the costly bid to Hyundai.) Michael Breen, a witty *Times* foreign correspondent and former churchman who now runs a lucrative consulting business in Seoul, told me in 2005 that it was he who introduced the Moon men to the useful Madam Park.

In November 1991, Moon received the first of several invitations, just weeks before the red flag was hauled down at the Kremlin. The trips north are chronicled in U.S. government documents as well as Bo Hi Pak's book *Truth Is My Sword*. In a bittersweet homecoming, Moon paid a visit to the house of his childhood, specially refurbished for his visit. Behind the Bamboo Curtain, he brashly told his Communist hosts that "in a unified Korea, I will become supreme chairman of the unified Korean Peninsula. Kim Il-Sung will be the vice chairman, and the central ideology will be Godism." (He didn't mention whether the South Korean president would get in on the action.)

Kim (intrigued by Moon's insolence, according to the reverend's personal secretary) had the delegation flown to a guest house in Hungnam, near where the *Washington Times* owner had suffered in prison. The big man bear-hugged Moon and said, "Let us forget the past. Most important is now and the future." The men allegedly discussed reunification.

Declassified reports from the Defense Intelligence Agency (DIA) go still further, with Moon paying as many as "several tens of millions of dollars" into an overseas bank account as a down payment for doing business and promising to encourage millions in investment.

A U.S. diplomat in Seoul caught wind of Bo Hi Pak's sales pitch to a North Korean official, which the American quoted in a cable home to Washington. "I told him," Pak had said, "that North Korea has to make peace with the conservative ruling elite of the world."

• • •

The ongoing negotiations were not disclosed in the *Washington Times* on April 15, 1992, when the eleven-day visit to North Korea by a delegation of newsroom staff culminated in a special issue for Kim Il Sung's eightieth birthday. Editor Wesley Pruden's dispatches played up the schtick of a right-wing fish out of water. "The Koreans have a bent for this kind of mindless argument," he writes in a column about the dogmatic answers given him by his Pyongyang tour guides. "There must be something in the *kimchi*."

But Pruden didn't handle the paper's two-and-a-half-hour interview with Kim Il Sung, the first one he had granted to a Western media outlet in twenty years. That delicate task fell to managing editor Josette Sheeran, the highest-ranking Moon disciple in the newsroom at the time.

Her piece highlighted Kim's "robust appearance" (he died two years later) and his gift for positive thinking. "Even if the sky is falling down on us, there will always be a hole for me to rise up through," the dictator said—a sentence that Sheeran would later recall in a talk at Moon's theological institute as "this wonderful thing which I printed in the paper."

The sunny interview with Kim Il Sung was the page-one centerpiece of the April 15, 1992, issue of the *Washington Times*. It came out in the U.S. capital just as a national holiday erupted in Pyongyang: a week of birthday festivities for the dictator. Had such a thing run in the *New York Times*, it would have provoked conservative outrage at liberal saps falling for a Potempkin tour that distracted the world from death camps. For Sheeran wrote that Kim was "self-confident, reflective elder statesman rather than the reclusive, dogmatic dictator he is usually portrayed as in the West."

The *Washington Times* delegates asked about Kim's hobbies in a lengthy Q&A. "So do you have more time now for fishing and other things you enjoy?" they asked of his semiretirement—in which up-and-coming son Jong-Il now handled such government offices as Bureau 39, which handles counterfeiting and the state heroin trade. Replied the elder Kim, "Of course! I have some time to go fishing and I have some time to go hunting. I love hunting and I love fishing also."

A startling amount of newsprint was given to reprinting North Korean officials' thoughts on the state ideology of *Juche*, or "self-reliance." Sample quote, from Kim Il Sung: "We have always paid primary attention to strengthening the driving force and increasing its role in socialist construction and conducted the transformations of nature and society to meet the requirements of *Juche*." Other stories credulously repeated assurances by wordy party members that they'd lost interest in invading Seoul, were rethinking isolation, and, most important of all, welcomed foreign investors.

Fast-forward to 2003, when the Seoul-based *Joon Ang Daily* would wonder how Moon's motor company had won a $55 million exclusive deal to manufacture vehicles for the regime. The paper quoted Hwang Sun-Jo, a church official and head of the Tong-Il conglomerate, who said the good fortune became possible after Moon "sent a *Washington Times* reporter to the North and made the country known to the West with a better image. . . . Since then the North has confided in the church."

Michael Breen, who has drifted away from the church and has written a biography of the Reverend Moon, says the True Father's power to produce a birthday package was more important than the content itself. "As for softening Kim's image, I think that's bollocks," he says. "Moon wanted to show he had white folks calling him 'sir,' and that he influenced

Washington." The newspaper coverage proved to the Kims that Moon was more than just an interested investor.

On December 6, 1992, however, Moon himself claimed to have "softened" Kim's attitude toward America. "After I met with Kim Il-Sung, I sent to him a carefully thought-out plan," he said. "Even to this day, I have received no answer from him. That means he is thinking, 'What is Reverend Moon's idea?' Through the *Washington Times* and the other media which have at our disposal, I introduced this whole concept, even bringing to America an interview with Kim Il-Sung."

In 1994, the *Washington Times* sent Sheeran to Pyongyang for yet another celebration of Kim Il Sung's birthday, though this time her access was no longer exclusive. She did ask a question about human rights, which Kim casually sidestepped. But the dominant note of her stories remained the plea for understanding. Her coverage highlights "wiggly little children" performing a hula hoop dance executed with military precision. Her April 15, 1994, piece was headlined "North Korea Lets Its Hair Down for a Birthday Party." Another *Times* piece was headed "North Korea Pleads for the West's Understanding."

Five months later, on September 9, 1994, an unnamed DIA field analyst discussed the possibility that Moon's paper was serving the purposes of the North Korean government: "Using the Unification Church's perceived influence in such newspapers as the Seil [sic] daily news and the Washington Times, along with church affiliated lobbyists and other personnel linkage, KN [North Korea] will try to deliver its opinions to the governments of the West. The intention is to create a favorable public opinion of KN." DIA cables also noted explosive arms trading allegations that the Japanese press had leveled against the Reverend Moon. Tokyo newspapers had reported that a quartet of men—all four of them married in Moon's mass weddings—were possibly operating on his behalf when, in 1994, they were middlemen in the controversial sale of decrepit Soviet submarines to the North. Supposedly Kim Jong-Il just wanted the scrap metal. But the sale, according to military analysts, offered Kim a chance to study the vessels' missile guidance systems.

The four men from Toen Trading, a tiny Tokyo health food company with improbable connections to North Korea, insisted that there was no Moon link. It may have been solely a coincidence that one of the Toen Trading directors, according to Japanese journalist Arita Yoshifu, was accounting director for the church's "spiritual sales" of astronomically priced religious artifacts to old ladies. A lawyer for the widows, however, told the press that "one cannot help but think that [Toen] is an enterprise of the Unification Church."

Conflicting reports surround the junk trade. The *New York Times* described a small fleet of submersibles hauled off to the North as is, with nonproliferation experts raising eyebrows after the Toen president remarked cryptically, "Nothing is removed." The intrigue heightened that May as North Korea refused to allow Russian weapons inspectors to monitor the supposedly disarmed submarines.

Western experts on North Korea's military technology—including *Jane's Defence Weekly* writer Joseph Bermudez Jr. and John Pike of GlobalSecurity.org—list the scrap sale, whoever was behind it, as a milestone in Pyongyang's quest to build better, more stable missile tubes.

A DIA memo on the subject notes, "Although this transaction garnered a great deal of coverage in the Japanese press, it was not disclosed at the time that Toen is an affiliate of the Unification Church." Reached for comment on the veracity of the cables, a Defense Department spokesperson said they were authentic but not necessarily authoritative. The church insists there has been a misunderstanding. "Reverend Moon . . . spent decades engaged in a global effort to defeat communism ideologically," a spokesperson told me. "He would never, in any way, pass military technology to a Communist state."

• • •

A church that claims the approval of dead U.S. presidents cannot always be taken at its word, at least when it comes to the mortal world. And many of the Unification Church's boasts of influence are undoubtedly wishful, exaggerated, or fantastical. But two new, authoritative sources lend credibility to recent claims by Mr. and Mrs. Moon that the Unification Church, with its exclusive access to Kim Jong-Il, has brokered talks with North Korea.

In 2007, Moon's wife told an audience in Burlingame, California:

> You may not be aware of this, but Rev. Moon has been assisting the Six Party Talks now being held for the sake of resolving the nuclear crisis on the Korean peninsula and reconciling the democratic nations with the communist nations. My husband is presenting a solution based on the principles of peace and harmony rooted in the "Way of the Heavenly Father."

Is the reverend a middleman in U.S. relations with Kim Jong-Il? Bradley Martin, the reigning expert on the Kims, says, "I have no doubt that there are people in the administration who would like to work with Moon. I just imagine most of the State [Department] career people are too professional to number among them."

But new accounts bolster the possibility. According to separate reports by Mike Chinoy (who covered Jimmy Carter's controversial 1994 peace intervention for CNN) and Marion Creekmore (then a diplomat at the Carter Center), it was the Reverend Moon's foreign office, the Summit Council, that permitted the cable network to enter the country. CNN's presence, in turn, is widely credited with giving Carter the chance to talk the regime down from a war footing.

In his book *China Live*, Chinoy describes his encounter with church officer Antonio Betancourt:

> Antonio Betancourt, apparently eager to bolster his organization's clout and prestige by acting as a power broker, was dangling the possibility that the Moonie connection could open a door to North Korea for us at a moment of great international tension. [CNN executive] Eason Jordan and I were dubious, but with the drumbeat of war growing steadily

louder, we were willing to pursue all conceivable options.

Betancourt's proposal was simple. The North Koreans had asked him to organize a goodwill delegation of international VIPs to visit Pyong-yang to mark Kim Il Sung's eighty-second birthday on April 15.

The Summit Council episode wasn't the first time the Moon clergy had played secretary of state. In 1995, the Canadian journal *Maclean's*—which had been investigating a Canadian politician's work with Moon—report-ed that Moon's Summit Council had briefly burrowed into U.S. diplomatic circles before being thrown out. The church group managed to play hosts at a State Department conference room to a gathering of the American For-eign Service Association (AFSA), a group serving eleven thousand profes-sional diplomats. Insiders in attendance included Winston Lord, assistant state secretary for East Asian affairs. After Lord discovered Moon's role, the Summit Council was summarily banished.

When *Maclean's* asked foreign policy expert James Woolsey why he'd participated, he said, "I did not know the Summit Council was a Moon organization." At the time of the meetings, he was Bill Clinton's CIA director.

Kim Il Sung died on July 8, 1994 (official cause of death: "heavy men-tal strains.") The late dictator, in Chinoy's words, had shown on several occasions a "soft spot for messianic religious leaders." Like Moon, the Kims themselves are credited by their followers with magical feats. Wher-ever Jong-Il shows up, according to the state news service, the clouds are chased away; it is also claimed that he is a better golfer than Tiger Woods, scoring three to four holes in one per round.

Could the link between Moon and Kim have something to do with the willingness of Rep. Curt Weldon (R-PA)—a conservative member of the House Armed Services Committee who led delegations to Pyongyang—to play along with Moon's 2004 coronation on Capitol Hill? Could the garish ceremony have been the price of admission to the Kingdom of the Kims?

Should Americans be concerned that the delicate six-way negotiations with Pyongyang could conceivably have been degrees away from a man who, according to the 1978 congressional report, "foresee[s] an apocalyptic confrontation involving the United States, Russia, China, Japan and North and South Korea, in which the Moon organization would play a key role"?

Whatever the truth behind the mystery, the Reverend Moon's preachers consider North Korea the end zone of his lifelong power play. According to a speech at the Washington, D.C., church on February 1, 2004, by Moon minister Michael Jenkins, the northern hinterlands are envisioned by Moon as a the new seat of the "Fourth Israel," a shining theocratic kingdom. "The only thing we lack is we don't have land and Father's searching for that land," he said. "Father must establish a sovereign nation before he goes to the Spirit World." If Korea doesn't work out, according to Jenkins in a March 2, 2003, speech, "all that land in Brazil, the purpose of that was a backup plan in case Korea could not be secured as the Fatherland. Father must have a country . . . [but] Father was able to secure Korea. Korea is going to be secure."

The *Times* publisher claims Kim Jong-Il has invited him to pick up stakes and settle down in his totalitarian paradise. "He tells me," Moon said in 2000, "'I will give you a comfortable place if you come here, and the people will appreciate you more here.'"

• • •

All this time, had the Reverend Moon hated communism for the same reasons the conservatives did? Was it for communism's prison camps and loss of personal liberties—or just its inhospitability to the Divine Principle?

In South Korea, where Moon retains citizenship, doing business up north is considered by some to be patriotic, a step toward reunification. But before American sanctions were lifted in 1999, investment was forbidden by the Clinton State Department as support for a dictatorship that might otherwise collapse for lack of funds.

Dealing with North Korea remains a bizarre proposition for an American media mogul. In 2005, under an executive order from George W.

Bush, Ryongbong, a North Korean company that entered into business with Moon, was blacklisted as a potential producer of WMD parts, whose assets the United States could freeze. "The order is basically the same as imposing economic sanctions," the *Korea Times* heard from an official in the South.

The constellation of financial and political connections between the church and North Korea lends credence to critics who have long insisted that the forces behind the *Washington Times* should register with the Justice Department as foreign-funded political entities.

In the United States, overseas money that funds politics is supposed to be an open book, under the Foreign Agents Registration Act (FARA). The law was passed before World War II to prevent Nazi meddling in U.S. politics. But "foreign agents" as innocuous as the Tea Council of the U.S.A. and the Australian Tourist Commission have had to register with the government under FARA, as required by the law, to forbid secrecy in lobbying from beyond American borders. Moon hasn't.

However, as the Center for Public Integrity reported in 2004, the office in charge of enforcing FARA is an underfunded, decaying dinosaur. Unable to keep up on Saudi influence in Washington, it is running on Windows 95 computers that a spokesperson described as "fragile" and could crash if backed up.

ELEVEN

WE CAN SMASH THE WHOLE WORLD

I feel a great sense of shame and injustice that when I was responsible for the nation I could not teach its many people about God correctly. . . . You must follow Rev. Sun Myung Moon, who has revealed the Divine Principle and Unification Thought. I hope that everyone will consider this most seriously.

—PRESIDENT JAMES GARFIELD
(ACCORDING TO THE REVEREND MOON)

The whole world is in my hand, and I will conquer and subjugate the world. I will go beyond the boundary of the U. S., opening up the toll gate, reaching out to the end of the world. I will go forward, piercing through everything. . . .

When we are in our battle against the whole nation of the U.S.—if you are truly in love with this nation, and if you love this nation more than anyone else, this nation will come into God's possession, and Satan will have nothing to do with it. . . . [W]ith that as the bullet, we can smash the whole world.

—REV. SUN MYUNG MOON, MAY 17, 1973

We will kill you.

We will kill you.

We will kill you.

Two hundred similar cell text messages chimed the week of August 22, 2006, into the phone of Cho Seong-Sik, a Seoul newspaperman. In an irony not missed by his editors at the *Dong-a Ilbo* (a left-leaning newspaper), the messages had been sent by a world peace group. Members of the Rev. Sun Myung Moon's Family Federation for World Peace and Unification were disappointed by his coverage of them.

Cho and his colleagues had alleged that Moon, who'd built a nearby lakeside palace, was rapidly spreading his reach into the country's cultural affairs, politics, religion, sports, and business. One headline asked, "Is He the Messiah or a Pseudo-religious Leader?"

A rival paper estimated that 1,500 riot police arrived to deal with the resulting bedlam. The Federation faithful stormed the lobby through the broken windows. They roughed up a photographer, wrecked computers, and threatened to throw sand into the press. After the police came, they sat stiffly cross-legged in the lobby. The *Daily* editors, vowing not to be intimidated, released a statement: "We will continue to make efforts to fulfill the right of the nation to know."

Former church insider Donna Collins says the incident offered the truest pictures of the Unification Church. "The real deal," she tells me, "is what happened in Korea, not the sugar-coated PR front."

•   •   •

At a Family Federation event held at the Hyatt Regency San Francisco Airport Hotel on May 31, 2007, it's hard to believe this is the identical organization, at least at first glance. The crowd of hundreds of blacks, whites, and Asians could be a congregation at any Bay Area church, joking and gossiping and lining up for cold cuts. Just downstairs from the high atrium and the sports bar, a sign points the way into the "America's Destiny" get-together. It's sponsored by the Universal Peace Federation, the latest of the Reverend Moon's cunning plans to unite the world's religions under him. I have come dressed as an Orthodox Jew, accenting my week's beard with a black yarmulke, in hopes of fitting into the theme.

At the convention tables, a local homeless shelter collects donations, and the guests—not just die-hard Moonists but a variety of friends and interested parties from local religious groups—stream past tables featuring displays hyping the church's worldwide initiatives. The pamphlets hit a touchy-feely note. One bears the smiles of women from varied races, an invitation to "Women of Destiny" tea times where the "Healing Power of Forgiveness" will be considered. A stack of forms invites me to nominate someone for Parent of the Year, the award handed out annually by coronation lobbyist Gary Jarmin. Candidates must exemplify "sacrificial love." One year, high jinks ensued after someone filled out a nomination for Barry Prendergast, a fifty-year-old former leader from the Children of God cult, which was famous for reeling in horny young men by deploying "happy hookers" on the beaches of California. After a newspaper discovered the link, Jarmin defensively said he had no way of knowing from "the information we received." But it is perhaps indicative of who comes to these things.

At the buffet reception, a group of African American ministers, including featured guest Pastor Brondon Reems, confer near the corner of the room. They're talking about the prospect of free trips to Dubai. "Oh, Dubai's beautiful," says one. Then a tall, white man strides into the circle. He wants to tell Reems how and when to give the "Love Offering and Benediction" at the end of the night's keynote speech from Mrs. Moon, the True Mother of Humanity.

Other guests are from a different fringe—perhaps the crowd that attends San Francisco's annual psychic fair. (The Unification Church, after all, has funded a Queens, New York "World Research Institute for Science and Technology" (WRIST), tasked by Moon with inventing a "spirit world machine" that would speak with the dead by discovering their radio frequency.)

On the concourse, boxes contain the framed Ambassadors for Peace certificates that the church will hand out tonight. In 2001, one was handed out to a neo-Nazi named William Baker, an Orange County leader in the racist Populist Party who has advocated segregation and the destruction of Israel. Wondering who else wins awards from the reverend, I am peeking into the box of awards, when I am buttonholed by the perky Japanese lady guarding it—about age forty, in an orange dress.

Her name is Sayuri, and she is part of a local "genealogy group." Is she here to listen to the True Mother? She confides in a disdainful whisper, "I don't believe in that," and goes on to express her hatred of Koreans. Seeing my yarmulke, she changes the subject. She wants to share unshakable evidence she has discovered: that the Hebrew and Japanese alphabets come from identical origins, that the Japanese invented Chinese, rather than vice versa, as is usually accepted. She insists on it. I also gather from her theories that the Lost Ark may be near Tokyo.

A deacon in black robes murmurs "shalom" as he brushes by, and he isn't the first. The Family Federation has been frustrated in its push to unite the religions by a particular deficit of Jews, who have been kept away by Moon's obsessions. "To re-create Israel," Moon said at a 2003 sermon in Arlington, Virginia:

> The church and the state must become one as Cain and Abel. Instead they became one with Rome and captured and killed Jesus. Who are the Jewish members here, raise your hands! Jewish people, you have to repent. . . . Through the principle of indemnity, Hitler killed 6 million Jews. God could not prevent Satan from doing that because Israel killed the True Parents.

Moon has kept to this message since 1978, when he gave a nearly identical formulation: "the Israel people did not care less about [Jesus], that is why they deserve their punishment, genocide of many millions, [because] they did not care for God's property." Because of such pronouncements, the extremist Jewish Defense League "declared war" on Moon in 1976, promising, according to the Anti-Defamation League (ADL), that "no Moon missionary would walk the streets safely."

In 2003, the Family Federation released official guidelines for winning over Jewish people—despite their master's denunciation of Jews as "very cruel people, also very good business people." It is predicated on a questionable theory—that the desecration of Jesus's cross is something Jews will find reassuring—and the missionaries' frank comfort with being two-faced, three-faced, or ten-faced, as the situation requires:

> Put to rest his [the Jew's] fear that he is coming to a "Moonie event." . . . [Show] the 21-minute video, the one that shows the Christian ministers taking down their crosses and the Jews and Christians embracing. . . . This

can be extremely moving to Jews. . . . Do not show the shorter versions of the video, which lack the taking down the cross theme and [are] overwhelmingly Christian."

Sure enough, standing at the hotel doors, it isn't too long before a woman from the Family Federation spots my black kippah and invites me into the shindig. What's it all about? World peace, she says.

• • •

This ballroom seems so familiar—and then it hits me that I saw John Mc-Cain speak here in February 2000 at the state convention, two weeks before his Waterloo in South Carolina, when you could still believe he was the next president. Next door, Republicans discussed selling the party message to Latinos—and you could still believe that was possible, too. On stage, John McCain compared himself to Luke Skywalker battling his way out of the Death Star.

But tonight a Cal Berkeley student is on that stage, reading an opening prayer from a Reverend Moon supporter who wasn't able to make it tonight—former president James Madison. Though the Father of the Constitution has been six feet deep for 171 years and disdained religion as a source of "ignorance and servility in the laity . . . superstition, bigotry and persecution," the Moon flock claims he has endorsed our meeting. The young woman, reading Madison's Message from the Spirit World, is reading in such a flat, breathless mumble that few ears perk up. Madison, according to Moon, says that "the people of America must follow the teachings" of the True Father "so that America will not lose its status as an eternally powerful country."

The ballroom's packed with people. At every place setting is a small plastic packet of Holy Juice, the mystery fluid that Moon says will cleanse the blood of those who drink it. Rows of Second Generation youth sit in the back rows, slouching like students stuck at a class assembly. They catch packets of Holy Juice thrown to them by their friend, an acne-faced usher.

Asked what's in it, the usher says, "I think it's just wine." A moment later he is at my side again and says, "I think it's just grape juice."

Every guest gets the text of Hak Ja Han Moon's speech in a glossy blue booklet. The words have been tailored to the theme of Hawaii. Hawaii, though, isn't part of the tour. And so it is unclear why it is being read in California. Guests have been told not to be thrown by the Hawaii references and rather to heed the bigger message, which involves the United Nations and the formation of vaguely defined Unification Church offshoots: a new racial "lay organization," the Mongolian Peoples' Federation, as well as a "group of volunteers" calling themselves the "Peace Kingdom Police."

On stage, the James Madison girl gives way to Muslim, then Native American prayers: *hey-ya-ya-ya.* . . . A black woman sings a beautiful Handel piece. A little middle-schooler, bored, is idly running her thumb around the seal of her Holy Juice as a succession of local religious leaders take the stage.

The girl to my left sits beside her white mother and Asian father. She is surprised when a visitor asks what the filmy purple liquid is that she has grown up drinking. She taps on her mother's shoulder to explain. The mother glances over and says, brusquely, "It's part of what we do."

•   •   •

On stage, the master of ceremonies from the Senate coronation, Michael Jenkins, bids the crowd to open the packet and drink. "We believe," he says, that the drink will graft us to God's "original olive tree."

The purple fluid in my hand has an unsettled consistency. I slip two cups into my shirt pocket for later analysis. The recipe, according to typewritten church documents dating to the 1970s, contains three liquors plus "Father and Mother's blood, actual blood." The ingredients have never been identified, though several ex-members swear they were taught it's real blood—that a stockpile of his essence is kept somewhere.

Somehow I couldn't see the Reverend Moon donating that much

blood. The rumor is fueled by other bodily precedents. In *Guidance for the Heavenly Tradition*, a church handbook supplied to me by German sect expert Thomas Gandow, an elite *mooniste* named Young Whi Kim asserts that when Hak Ja Han's first child was born, Young received the special "rebirth" of drinking her breast milk, mixed with dairy.

Whatever was in the juice, Moon follower Gary Fleisher has called it "repugnant" that members have spiked punch, food, and candy with the liquid and served it to audiences unawares. At a March 8, 1998, Women's Federation for World Peace event, he complains—referring to the group that hosted George and Barbara Bush—"there was no explanation to the participants that the juice they were drinking was anything but regular juice." He says the church is just trying to inflate numbers, so it can claim that 3.6 million couples have been purified by Moon, a cheat that could lead to a sort of spiritual Enron.

Weeks later, a laboratory in Van Nuys would get back to me on the Reverend Moon's Holy Juice, which I'd mailed in for forensic analysis. No trace of blood.

• • •

The Rev. Michael Jenkins is talking cheerfully about Moon's proposed reworking of the United Nations. "At the U.N.," the conservative *New York Sun* reported in 2005, "the Unification Church has tried to establish a body made of religious leaders, only to be laughed at." Reporter Benny Avni quoted an expert blaming such defeats on UN liberals' "militant anti-religiosity."

The story Jenkins tells, however, is that it's moving ahead, "but the proposal has been taking too long." That's why, he says brightly, Moon has thought to construct this United Peace Federation: a "parallel United Nations." "We call it the Abel U.N.," he says, as if unveiling the greatest policy proposal in history. (It was plugged by Moon's *Washington Times* and UPI in 2003: "Clerics Rally for Peace at U.N."; "Religious Councils Pushing for U.N. Presence.") The audience listens blankly.

The United Nations, whatever its real-world limitations, is a natural fixture in the imagination of anyone who dreams of world influence. The Reverend Moon has been spending big on a quixotic attempt to knock down the church-state wall of the UN so as to win a special role within.

One prong of attack was the establishment of the church's outrageously named World Association of Non-Governmental Associations (WANGO). Its slick Web site plugs Moon activities and exists to promote the misleading notion that the rest of the world's nongovernmental organizations (NGOs) are rushing to join this church-backed umbrella group.

Using some of the sleight of hand witnessed in the Capitol Hill coronation of 2004, the church has also booked surprising events under the UN imprimatur. Some concerned European observers observed, after a January 27, 2001 benediction, "The mass wedding held in the UN conference room . . . would never have been permitted if the Moon sponsors had honestly announced their intentions." Video of the event shows Moon dressing in the plush garb of a Far East emperor, presiding over a parade of people in traditional costumes, from countries ranging from Paraguay to Latvia, helping the Reverend Moon himself pretend to be a world leader.

Seated behind a chairman's desk, Moon comes across as Kofi Annan–esque, which plays well in his church's high-budget promotional videos. The visual message is that Moon's worldwide acceptance is a fait accompli—even though he remains banned from several countries, including Bulgaria, France, and Fiji, whose government warned Moon midair in 2005 not to land on the little nation. "In short," said Fijian Ministry of Home Affairs chief Lesi Korovavala, "Dr. Sun Moon's doctrines are considered misleading, repugnant and divisive and would affect the peace, good order, public safety and public morality of the Fiji Islands." Bigotry, cried Moon's leaders, especially since shortly thereafter Fiji permitted the touchdown of faith healer Benny Hinn.

Notwithstanding other complaints around the world (including allegations from Paraguayan senator Domingo Laino that Moon was buying land for "control of the narcotics business"), friends in America and at the UN have smiled on the organization. His WANGO held a fund-raiser on June 8, 2007, that was raising as much as $20,000 per table and was attended by UN undersecretary general Ibrahim Gambari.

When money is no object, even Moon's campaign for separate "Cain & Abel United Nations" can be made to look like public policy that has the world listening.

"They keep coming up with these broad plans that never happen," says one young ex-member, laughing at any suggestion that Moon's plans are advancing. At the same time, the church has actually persuaded Jose de Venecia, speaker of the Philippine House of Representatives, to push for Moon's unusual notion of a Security Council for God.

The first signs were in 2003 when Moon, rambling about building "a UN nation," claimed explicitly to be working through the Philippines National Assembly. "We will present a new Resolution at the U.N. general assembly," he said. "Once that resolution is passed, the restored Kingdom of Heaven will open up in front of our eyes. The wild olive tree growing on the other side of the wall will be cut and grated onto the True Olive Tree. And then it will also bear true olives."

Or not. And yet de Venecia—an unabashed fan of the Moon road show who once joked that a mountain in his homeland should be renamed "Reverend Moon Mountain"—was soon declaring, with a straight face, that introducing a "religious council" was a "major objective of Philippine foreign policy," according to the *Washington Times*. On board for the effort, claimed de Venecia, was the Organization of the Islamic Conference, an association of Muslim nations. (In Pakistan, one winner of Moon's Ambassador for Peace award has been the madrassa mufti Qari Muhammad Hanif Jalandhry, who has worked tirelessly to uphold the stoning of rape victims.)

Obediently, the *Washington Times* and UPI ladled hype on the idea. "Hundreds of demonstrators in yellow caps" had descended on the East Side of Manhattan, pleading for "the creation of a new U.N. body, an interreligious council," the *Times* reported. "The Philippines has agreed to sponsor a resolution in the General Assembly to create the new U.N.

organ." In tandem, Moon's newswire alleged that George W. Bush, "a practicing Christian with a keen sense of the power of religion, expressed deep interest" in the idea for an "Interreligious Council at the world body" and "asked his national security adviser, Condoleezza Rice, to study the matter."

In November, the *Times*'s David Sands plugged the Manila plan, disclosing that it "closely tracks a proposal by the Interreligious and International Federation for World Peace, an organization founded by the Rev. Sun Myung Moon." Sands quotes Moon himself, who said, "Serious consideration should be given to forming a religious assembly or council of religious representatives within the structure of the United Nations."

Filipino ambassador Bavani Mercado duly showed up in New York with a proposal for the UN that distantly echoed Moon's idea, resolving that some "mechanism" be set up at the UN for "harnessing interreligious dialogue." He succeeded only in convincing the General Assembly to approve, in 2004, a watered-down version, Resolution 59/23, which promises UN cooperation with "interreligious" groups. Toothless or not, it's a major feather in your cap when you can brag of shepherding your ideas into the UN, especially when you're a wealthy religionist on the make, playing for legitimacy.

Call it a pipe dream, but in his Universal Peace Federation, Moon has established a private diplomatic network claiming friends in 191 countries and making threats to anyone who isn't playing along. "If anyone opposes this suggestion," Moon said of his UN ambitions in 1996, according to remarks published online, "then Father will show the accounting of how many billions of dollars he has spent for various causes and silence them."

In a room full of people sipping mysterious juice, something is happening, and I don't know what it is.

* * *

Sen. Dianne Feinstein (D-CA) has endorsed this thing I'm watching. Or at least that's what the hosts are claiming, making a point of listing Bay Area politicians who have allegedly sent letters of congratulation. (Feinstein's office will claim to have no record of any such letter.)

A screen lights up and plays a video featuring San Francisco housing official Amos Brown, a preacher of the city's biggest Baptist congregation. "The prophet is always misunderstood," Brown says philosophically, ticking off Moon and Martin Luther King in the same breath. "The masses will not see the vision."

Since the coronation debacle of 2004, congressmen seem to have stopped coming to these things. But Henry Lozano, one of Bush's recess appointments, takes the stage tonight. A recovered heroin addict, Lozano's on the board of directors of the Corporation for National and Community Service, which oversees grants to agencies like Americorps. He's the brains behind "Red Ribbon Week," in which high schoolers wear scarlet bands to remember federal drug enforcement agents who die in the line of duty. In 2003, Lozano sat alongside Laura Bush during the State of the Union address.

So Lozano's up there giving a speech about his Aztec heritage and what it meant to join a recent pilgrimage to the Holy Land, as he held the very grains of *la tierra*—the earth—in his hand. It's all a little overcooked. He rouses the crowd with talk of "*nuestra familia* . . . together, one family" before departing the scene as quickly as he came. He will not respond to e-mails about why he was there.

And then, the climax: two speeches from Moon family members, glimpses of two directions in which the Unification Church may go when the Reverend Moon leaves Earth. First on stage is the son Hyun Jin, the Harvard MBA. He is glib, Americanized. He doesn't speak in cryptic talk of Four Israels but in straightforward motivational cant, the language of *How to Make Friends and Influence People*. "Give yourselves a hand," he says. He asks the audience to give it up for his mother, too, and her achievement of bearing over a dozen children by Sun Myung Moon.

After inviting the audience to give themselves yet another hand, he finally introduces his mother, Hak Ja Han, the woman crowned on Capitol

Hill and all over the world, to deliver her keynote address: "A Providential View of the Pacific Rim Era in Light of God's Will: The United States and the Future Direction of the United Nations and the World."

"Ladies and gentlemen!" she begins. "My heart is intense and filled with emotion as I stand before you today."

Unlike at the Rotary Club, there will be no jokes to break this ice. Her speech conveying God's message is delivered in a monotone and has no clear beginning, middle, or end. Her former *Times* columnist, presidential speechwriter Pat Buchanan, would find much to tighten up in the windy language.

The talking points: We find ourselves in the seventh year of the Kingdom that began in 2000. God is in agony. He has "chosen and raised the United States of America as the second Israel." But the grace of the United States has somehow spread to Japan. In between is an ocean. We should tap its resources. Korea is now like Rome. Mrs. Moon recommends that Russians and Americans intermarry to discourage nuclear war between the two. Oh, and Jesus was a failure.

"What do you think the world would be like if Jesus had fulfilled the complete messianic mission during his lifetime on Earth?" she asks. To cope with our fallen world, she says, Mr. Moon has founded the "Peace Kingdom Police Force." A militia? ("A religious thing," a young member explains to me afterward, which is reassuring.) Her progress report also conveys that "through blood, sweat, and tears" she and Moon have succeeded in promoting Jesus to King of the Jews, the last obstacle to her husband's rule. "In 2004," she says, "we were acknowledged as the king and queen of peace both in a United States Office Building and at the Korean National Assembly."

● ● ●

After the speech, an attractive pair of Second Generation members, about twenty-two, linger outside in the hotel concourse. Some other Second Gens have quit the church, fearful of being matched by photograph to a spouse thousands of miles away who doesn't speak English. But these are two Americans, resembling any young Midwesterners who might have met in student government—except that they speak in the language of Moon, whose "ideal family values" they praise. Kirstin says that the Senate coronation of Moon "meant a lot, 'cause Reverend Moon is someone I really respect." Was it right to hold it on Capitol Hill? "Well, it's not like he wants a powerful position," she says.

Their lives, they agree, require not nearly so much sacrifice as those of their forbearers. "Oh, definitely harder," they say of their parents' lives in the 1970s Moonies.

Religious awakening or mind control, true faith or cult—that tired old debate is beside the point. Believers in a coming Paradise, their parents, in the first generation of servants, had suffered untold miseries to build a foundation for a kingdom, so that Moon would change history, so that one day a senator would receive him as the emperor of Washington. Look on his works, ye mighty, and despair.

NOTES

ONE

2   An orange Senate VIP name tag: See media accounts of crowning, ibid., and multimedia at TrueFather.com, the book's official Web site.

2   "I remember the king and queen thing": Eric Zorn, *Chicago Tribune* columnist, quotes Davis in his blog, June 20, 2004. Bartlett is quoted in the *New York Times*, "A Crowning at the Capital Creates a Stir," June 24, 2004.

2   The name of that senator: "U.S. Lawmakers Fete Moon, Church Leader Gets Crown," CBSNews.com, June 23, 2004. For the "defrocked"bishop, see Lloyd Grove, "Moon over Imani," *Washington Post*, May 18, 2001.

3   "There are moments that best play straight": *CNN Newsnight*, June 23, 2004.

4   But through a bait and switch: Author's personal collection of multimedia, gathered at www.tongil.co.kr, a Unification Church Web site in Korea, and www.familyfed.org, the U.S. version; see also accounts from *ABC World News Tonight*, June 23, 2004; author interviews with anonymous guests and an anonymous senatorial spokeswoman, Danny Davis, and Curt Weldon's chief of staff Michael Connallen; and later accounts in the *Washington Post* on June 23 and July 23, 2004, and in the *New York Times*, June 24, 2004.

4   Gripping the podium: *Washington Post*, June 23, 2004.

4   "The five great saints": "Declaring the Era of the Peace Kingdom" sermon, www.unification.net/2004/20040323_1.html.

5   *Moon prevailed*: The church's semiofficial account of its struggles is described in Carlton Sherwood's *Inquisition: The Persecution and Prosecution of the Reverend Sun Myung Moon* (New York: Regnery Gateway, 1991).

5 It was all part of the never-ending awards tour: See "Promised Land," *The Economist*, August 11, 2005; Seamus Mirodan, "Moonies Accused of Involvement in Drugs," *Irish Times*, October 14, 2004. A nearby Bush farm purchase was widely reported in the Latin American press: see "We Hate to Bring up the Nazis, but They Fled to South America Too," *Wonkette*, October 16, 2006.

5 "[W]e want to have the Governor": "Message from Rev. Michael Jenkins Regarding Rev. Moon's 50 State Speaking Tour," February 20, 2001, memo, found at http://unification.net/news/news20010220.html.

5 "When you go get the proclamations": Subcommittee on International Organizations, U.S. Congress, *Investigation of Korean-American Relations* (Washington, D.C.: U.S. Government Printing Office, October 31, 1978), 348, quoting *Master Speaks*.

5 Fed back into Moon's PR machine: See *New York Sun*, December 14, 2004; Harold Paine and Birgit Gratzer, "Rev. Moon and the United Nations: A Challenge for the NGO Community," World Economy, Ecology and Development Association (Bonn, Germany), November 2001; Sun Myung Moon, "Leader's Conference," www.tparents.org/Moon-Talks/sunmyungmoon95/SM950207.htm.

6 In the autumn of 2003: Jenkins sermon video, February 1, 2004 (available on book site). For similar verbiage, see also Jenkins sermon audio, March 21, 2004.

6 "Our American members": Ibid.

7 His followers have said: The "sixteen hours" claim was made to the author by a Moon enthusiast at a San Francisco event in 2005; in Kodiak, Alaska on July 18, 1998, an aide makes the claim—see "Training to Be a Follower" at www.tparents.org/moon-talks/sunmyungmoon98/UM980718.htm.

7 By 2006: "Sushi and Rev. Moon," *Chicago Tribune*, April 11, 2006; "If You Knew Sushi," *Vanity Fair*, June 2007, 120.

8 Moon's Bay Area leader: "Shark-Smuggling Bust Nets $1 Million for Habitat Protection," *National Geographic News* online, February 20, 2007; "The Man vs. Moon: As a Local Moonie Preacher Is Sentenced, Evidence Implicates the Church's Supreme Leader in a Shark-Poaching Scheme," *East Bay Express*, January 31, 2007.

8 Then there's a fortune: See the list of Moon front groups at www.FreedomOfMind.com; for UPI, see Ken Layne, "The Wire That Wouldn't Die," *Online Journalism Review*, May 16, 2000.

8 "Moon can buy a newspaper": "The Nation's Capital Gets a New Newspaper," *Washington Post*, May 17, 1982, C01.

9 "What I don't understand": "A Black Eye for 'Moonie Paper," *Boston Globe*, May 3, 1997.

9 Today the peculiar newspaper: Quoted in "Hell of a Times," *The Nation*, September 21, 2006.

9 The paper's gossip columnist: Ann Louis Bardach, "The Reverend and His Newspaper," in *Killed: Great Journalism Too Hot to Print*, ed. David Wallis (New York: Nation Books, 2004), 145.

9 "How come our media is silent?": E-mail from the Rev. Michael Jenkins, March 18, 2005, to internal church mailing list.

10 The WMA is an allegedly serious panel: Chris Matthews's presence is described at the World Media Association Web site (www.wmassociation.com/proceedings/21wmc/marshall.html), and his fee is discussed in a 1990 panel on "Cults and the Media" featuring former *Washington Times* editors Bill Cheshire and James Whelan.

11 He told his flock: "Serious Moment at Hoon Dok Hae," Sun Myung Moon sermon, various versions, November 23, 2003, www.tparents.org/moon-talks/sunmyungmoon03/SM031125.htm.

11 Just as Karl Marx saw history: Quote from David Brock, *Blinded by the Right: The Conscience of an Ex-Conservative* (New York: Crown, 2002), 24.

11 "We must connect the Bush administration": "Father's Word in Washington, D.C.," May 17, 2003, at the True Parents site: www.tparents.org/Moon-Talks/SunMyungMoon03/SM030517.htm.

11 Specifically, he has lobbied: "Father's Word in Washington DC," May 17, 2003, www.tparents.org/Moon-Talks/SunMyungMoon03/SM030517.htm.

11 "[W]hen the world was adrift": "Mooning the Media," *On the Media*, NPR, August 6, 2004 (transcript at www.onthemedia.org).

12 He has given millions: See Robert Parry, "The GOP's $3 Billion Propaganda Organ," *Consortium News*, December 27, 2006, citing longtime *Washington Times* reporter George Archibald; a more conservative $2 billion estimate is given in the *Columbia Journalism Review*, May 2002. In 1991, Moon said that "literally nine hundred million to one billion dollars has been spent to activate and run the *Washington Times*."

12 During the neoconservative Iran-Contra adventure: See "The Resurrection of Reverend Moon," *Frontline*, January 21, 1992; Sara

Diamond, *Spiritual Warfare: The Politics of the Christian Right* (Boston: South End Press, 1989), 170–71; "Rebel Supporter Linked to North," *New York Times*, June 4, 1987, 15; Scott and Jon Anderson, *Inside the League: The Shocking Exposé of How Terrorists, Nazis and Latin American Death Squads Have Infiltrated the World Anti-Communist League* (New York: Dodd Mead, 1986), 64–66, 125–30, 232–34.

12   "An unsung hero of freedom": See *Insight on the News*, February 18, 2003.

13   And beyond the circle: See Nansook Hong, *In the Shadow of the Moons: My Life in the Reverend Sun Myung Moon's Family* (New York: Little, Brown, 1998); "Surviving Reality TV," *Calgary Sun*, March 31, 2006, G12. For reference to $12,000 watches, see Delroy Alexander and Margaret Ramirez, "Rev. Moon and the Black Clergy," *Chicago Tribune*, November 5, 2006.

14   "There are literally hundreds": See archives of the IIFWP site at http://web.archive.org/ for 2001–2006; Michael Warder, "Bribemasters," *Chronicles*, June 1988.

14   Among the VIPs: Form 990, Interreligious and International Federation for World Peace, filed November 17, 2006.

15   It was after the grandmother: Originally found at www.familyfed.org and in the author's personal collection; also see *Washington Times* anniversary sermon, June 16, 1997, videotaped by C-SPAN and reprinted at www.unification.net.

15   Similar testimonials: Peggy Fletcher, "A Moonstruck Heaven Taps Favorite Son," *Salt Lake Tribune*, Friday, July 12, 2002; Felicity Barringer, "Decisions Differ on Religious Ad," *New York Times*, July 22, 2002.

16   "Please, don't ask me": Mrs. Y. S. Kim, *Dr. Sang Hun Lee's Teachings from Spirit World*, www.unification.org/ucbooks/TSW/tsw-02a.htm.

16   "People of America": James Polk, June 25, 2002; "Messages of Peace from 36 Former American Presidents in Spirit World," available at www.messagesfromspiritworld.info and www.unification.net.

16   To reach the mystical number 36: Author interview with Bruce Herschensohn, October 17, 2006.

17   "The Great Emancipator": "Eric Zorn's Notebook," ChicagoTribune.com, June 20, 2004.

17   "My beloved Son!": Felicity Barringer, "Decisions Differ on Religious Ad," *New York Times*, July 22, 2002. The messages themselves are available at www.messagesfromspiritworld.info.

18   A "nettle in the national consciousness": *People*, December 27, 1982.

18   Evangelist Jerry Falwell: Mary Murphy, "The Next Billy Graham," *Esquire*, October 1978.

18   Her boss: Sojourner Truth, *Narrative* (New York: Penguin Classics, 1998), 61.

19   He assured the flock: William Leete Stone, *Matthias and His Impostures* (New York: Harper, 1835), 171.

19   From Matthias to David Koresh: Paul E. Johnson and Sean Wilentz, *The Kingdom of Matthias* (New York: Oxford University Press, 1994), 173.

19   While the young slaved for him: Josh Freed, *Moonwebs: Journey into the Mind of a Cult* (Toronto: Dorset, 1980), 1–4; "Moon Invokes 5th Amendment in U.S. Civil Trial," *New York Times*, May 27, 1982, B3 (on "questions about his yacht"); Jan Goodwin, "Multimillionaire Minister Woos Children from Their Families to Beg for Him on the Streets," entered into *Congressional Record* 122, pt., 2, January 28, 1976.

19   *Time* attacked Moon: "The Secret Sayings of 'Master Moon," *Time*, June 14, 1976; "Moon Landing in Manhattan," *Time*, September 30, 1974. The "under God's command" quote is also in "Heavenly Tradition," Moon speech, January 20, 1973, at www.tparents.org/ moon-talks/sunmyungmoon73/SM730120.htm.

20   "The world was a different place": Interview with author, June 19, 2007.

20   The $29 million success: Andreas Killen, *1973 Nervous Breakdown* (New York: Bloomsbury, 2007), 4, 8, 112, 129–33, 162–64.

20   Moon told ex-member: Steve Hassan, "The Truth about Sun Myung Moon," www.freedomofmind.com/groups/moonies/moonorg.htm; Robert Boettcher, *Gifts of Deceit* (New York: Holt, 1980), 180.

21   The defense didn't work: Killen, *1973 Nervous Breakdown*, 6, 9, 33, 123–24. See also, as an example of the fascination, the 1978 Flo Conway book *Snapping: America's Epidemic of Sudden Personality Change*, 2nd ed. (New York: Stillpoint, 1995).

21   On the one hand: See "Moonstruck," *The Economist*, February 7, 1976, 39.

22   Speakers said people and families: *New York Times*, February 19, 1976.

22   A piece in the *New Republic*: Carlton Sherwood, *Inquisition: The Prosecution and Persecution of Sun Myung Moon* (New York: Regnery Gateway, 1991), 53–55; see also Stephen Chapman, "Cult-Mongering," *New Republic*, February 17, 1979.

22   Moon had said: "The Secret Sayings of 'Master' Moon," *Time*, June

14, 1976, 49; "Master Speaks: Questions and Answers with Rev. Sun Myung Moon," www.tparents.org; the edition *of Master Speaks* in papers of Ford Greene, 1973–1974.

23 The judge ruled: "Fanshiers Receive No Promise of Moonie Probe in Washington," *Great Bend Tribune*, February 25, 1976, 1; "Sect Sues to Free Follower," *Brownsville Herald*, September 1975.

24 The rallies and marches: William J. Petersen, *Those Curious New Cults* (New Canann, CT: Keats, 1975), 248.

24 For months: "The Resurrection of Rev. Moon," *Frontline*, January 21, 1992.

24 "If you look": Author interviews with Donna Collins and Richard Barlow.

24 Behind his pulpit: Bo Hi Pak, *Messiah: My Testimony to Rev. Sun Myung Moon* (Lanham, MD: University Press of America, 2000), chap. 11; church accounts from www.tparents.org, including "40 Years in America: The Providential Year of 1976," *Rising Tide*, June 7, 1976.

25 "There are critics who say": "The Darker Side of Sun Moon," *Time*, June 14, 1976.

25 Their saintly portraits wobbled: See Freed, *Moonwebs*, 1–4, 166–71.

25 "It worked!": Andrew Ferguson, "Can't Buy Me Love: Is the Unification Church Conservative, or Just Rich?" *American Spectator* 20, no. 9 (September 1987).

25 "A shameless blasphemer": Ibid.

25 "We got kicked": "Public Relations a Factor as Sen. Dole Opens Session," *Washington Post*, February 6, 1979.

26 "Man," Patrick jived: "Breaking the Spell That Binds," *Washington Post*, February 6, 1979, B01.

26 Forrest Wright: Author interviews with Forrest Wright, July 2007.

26 On the Hill: "Cult Wars on Capitol Hill," *Time*, February 19, 1979; Chapman, "Cult-Mongering"; author interview with Wright.

26 Another new church had slain: Reagan Administration attorney John Roberts, now Chief Justice of the Supreme Court, recommended against giving Ryan the Congressional Gold Medal.

26 "It's too bad": From private collection of former constituent Ida Camburn, http://lermanet.com/idacamburn/.

27 On Halloween 1978: *Investigation of Korean-American Relations*, October 31, 1978.

27 Jackie Speier: Testimony from "Information Meeting on the Cult Phenomenon in the United States," February 5, 1979, 318 Russell Senate Office Building, Washington, D.C., 24–30.

27 "The major religious cults": Ibid., 24–30. See also Chapman, "Cult-Mongering."

28 His study of Communist China: Robert J. Lifton, *Thought Reform and the Psychology of Totalism* (Chapel Hill: University of North Carolina Press, 1989).

28 Replying to criticism: See the *Washington Post*, July 17, 1982, A1.

28 The headlines screamed: From the foreword to Barbara and Betty Underwood, *Hostage to Heaven* (New York: Potter, 1979). Also see the TV special "Escape from the Moonies," *P.M. Magazine*, 1981; and "Mom Warns of Moonie Perversions," *Connecticut Post*, April 14, 1994.

28 The church asked its critics: In the 1970s, there was an explosion of books detailing life on the streets as a Moon disciple, including Freed, *Moonwebs*. See also Margaret Singer of the University of California–Berkeley, who has written, "I have had to point out why the United States Marine Corps is not a cult so many times that I carry a list." See "How the United States Marine Corps Differs from Cults," from *Cults in Our Midst* (September 1996), www.rickross.com/reference/brainwashing/brainwashing2.html.

28 Every year: An extensive body of sermons is available at the Web sites www.unification.net and www.tparents.org.

29 It's not in the Bible: See especially Sun Myung Moon's sermon "Purity, Lineage and the Love Organ," February 18, 2001, Tarrytown, New York, www.tparents.org/Moon-Talks/sunmyungmoon01/SM010218.htm.

29 "We have to drain": "Save the Next Generation" youth event video, July 4, 2002.

30 On Blessed Children World: All quotes are from the Blessed Children World Internet group and John Gorenfeld, "Bad Moon on the Rise," Salon.com, September 24, 2003.

30 "When my husband hit me once": "Blessing Candidate Preparation Workshop," *Unification Sermons and Talks*, www.tparents.org/Library/Unification/Talks/Jones/BWKSHP.htm. The source for the material on the *Washington Times* editor is an author interview with Glenn Emery, June 14, 2007.

30   "All men and women in human history": See "The Process of the Blessing and Its Meaning," *Blessing and Ideal Family*, Reverend Sun Myung Moon, www.unification.net/bif/bif-4-4.html. The use of *han* ("grudge") is indicated in chap. 1, pt. 2—"If Jesus has not been liberated, then can God, who sent Jesus, be liberated from His resentment (han)?"—and in pt. 1: "Jesus died leaving his *han* on this earth."

31   "Since this resentment came about": Moon, "The Process of the Blessing,"

31   "The more you love your partner": "All That Heaven Allows: My Sexual Re-education in the Unification Church," Nerve.com, April 21, 2005.

31   "Men and women": Moon, "The Process of the Blessing."

31   So: Woman is on top: See "Instructions for the Three-Day Ceremony," Unofficial Notes Prepared by the American Blessed Family Department, www.tparents.org/library/unification/topics/traditn/3-dayceremony.htm; "Introduction to the Blessing Ceremony," www.unification.org/intro_blessing.html.

32   Novelist Don DeLillo: Don DeLillo, *Mao II* (New York: Penguin, 1992), 1–10.

32   A Montreal reporter: "Satan's Servant Cures Moonie," *Montreal Star*, January 6, 1978; Freed, *Moonwebs*, 120–34.

32   "The world really is our stage": Author interviews with Greene in 2007. See also "Sign of the Cult-Buster," *San Francisco Weekly*, October 5, 2005; and "Ford Greene: Attorney at Odds," *Marin Independent Journal*, January 9, 2005. The Moon quote also appears in *Master Speaks*.

33   Newspaper reports said: See Boettcher, *Gifts of Deceit*, 149; "Ex-Moonies Tell of Suicide Options," *Washington Post*, January 19, 1979; "Religious Cult Destroyed Sonia," *Daily Mirror*, October 23, 1995, 6.

33   "Love me, Benji": Freed, *Moonwebs*, 120–25.

33   "I feel": "Satan's Servant Cures Moonie"; Freed, *Moonwebs*, 121.

34   "Obedience to the law": See *People*, January 3, 1983, 92.

34   "He's a dynast": Author interview with Richard Barlow, June 26, 2007. Barlow and his wife Hazel are listed among the 1,800 Blessed Couples at the very early February 8, 1975, mass ceremony. See www.tparents.org/library/unification/topics/traditn/1800-list.htm.

34   But when Moon made the news: House report, "Investigation of Korean-American Relations," Subcommittee on International

Organizations, October 31, 1978, 327; Fred Hiatt, "Even in South Korea, Few Know Extent of Moon's Empire," *Washington Post*, March 28, 1988.

35 "Moon," writes: Parry, "The GOP's $3 Billion Propaganda Organ."

35 Since 2003: Four-hour Moon sermon, "Victorious True Parents," New Yorker Hotel, January 28, 1993.

35 On the other hand: Companion Web sites, www.tparents.org and www.unification.net, run by churchmen, carry speeches that are a "particularly important source of spiritual inspiration," according to a study by member Sara Horsfall, *Use of the Internet in the Unification Movement*. Before the Net age, she writes, members "waited days, weeks or even months" for these texts, which were "hoarded jealously."

35 "If the Clinton administration fails": Moon sermon, "True Parents' Birthday," January 28, 1993, New Yorker Hotel, January 28, 1993, reprinted in *Unification News*, January 28, 1993, and available at www.unification.net.

36 Moon, according to movement site: Damian Anderson, "Spending Time with True Parents," www.unification.net, September 20, 1999.

36 "After the demise": Sun Myung Moon, "Restoration of True Sonship," sermon at the New Yorker Hotel, February 13, 1997 (www.tparents.org).

36 During the 2000 Gore-Bush: Moon, "Sunday Morning Sermon," December 10, 2000, Tarrytown, New York (www.tparents.org).

36 His son, Hyo Jin: Hyo Jin Moon sermon, "Day of All Things 1992," New Yorker Hotel, June 1, 1992 (www.tparents.org).

36 Moon orders Moonie men: Moon sermon, "Purity, Lineage and the Love Organ of Life," Tarrytown, New York, February 18, 2001, notes by Peter Kim, reprinted in the *Unification News*.

37 At a 1996 event in Buenos Aires: Reuters news service, November 25, 1996: "Moon was in full flow, asking his 700 guests such penetrating questions as, 'Why do sexual organs exist?'"

37 The phrase pops up: Moon and Yang, "Report from East Garden," November 8, 2002 (www.tparents.org).

37 "If the U.S. continues its corruption": "The Secret Sayings of 'Master' Moon," *Time*.

37 He joins Moon: "Dan Quayle then gave a great three-minute speech calling for the 21st century to be the century of peace reconciliation and true love." See *Unification News for March 2003*, www.unification.net. Quayle has also sent birthday greetings in a 2002 "tribute book."

TWO

38   Opening quote: See MessagesFromSpiritWorld.info, www.tparents.org.
38   Some of that money: Damon Darlin, "Legions of Strangers, Guided by
      Moon, Become Seoul Mates," *Wall Street Journal*, August 24, 1994.
38   "Japan is mother and wife": Kevin Sullivan and Mary Jordan, "Once-
      Generous Japanese Become Disenchanted with moon's Church,"
      Washington Post, August 4, 1996, A01.
39   "Your husband is descending": See May 27, 1994, judgment of Fukuoka
      District Court (Japan), case 1990 #1082, against the Unification Church,
      on behalf of two anonymous plaintiffs: two housewives, forty and fifty
      years old.
41   The church denies any wrongdoing: "Judgements Handed Out by
      Court in Japan," www1k.mesh.ne.jp/reikan/english/judement/
      fukuoka/fuku12.htm; the "satans" quote is from Fred Hiatt, "Even in
      South Korea, Few Know Extent of Moon's Empire," *Washington Post*,
      March 28, 1988.
42   "Our Japanese movement": See "Eclipse of the Moon," *Sunday Mail*,
      November 19, 1995, 65; Robert Parry, "Dark Side of Reverend Moon,"
      Consortium News, www.consortiumnews.com/archive/moon4.html;
      Nansook Hong, *In the Shadow of the Moons: My Life in the Reverend Sun
      Myung Moon's Family* (New York: Little, Brown, 1998); Bo Hi Pak, *Truth
      Is My Sword*, vol. 2 (New York: Holy Spirit Association, 1999), 646.
42   In 1992, the same year: Kevin Sullivan and Mary Jordan, "Once-
      Generous Japanese Become Disenchanted," *Washington Post*,
      August 4, 1996.
42   The fliers didn't mention Moon's church: Andrew Pollack, "Moon's
      Sponsor in Japan Is Linked to the Rev. Moon," *New York Times*,
      September 3, 1995, 2.
43   Bush also defied: See "A Letter to George Bush," National Network of
      Lawyers for Counterpoising the Spiritual Sales, www1k.mesh.ne.jp/
      reikan/eletter.htm; and "Celebrities Pulled into Moon's Orbit,"
      Washington Post, July 30, 1996, E01.
43   "[W]hen I found out": Ross Laver and Paul Kaihla, "Ed Schreyer and
      the Moonies," *MacLean's*, October 23, 1995.
43   And Bush himself: Pollack, "Moon's Sponsor"; Michael Isikoff and
      John Burgess, "A Church in Flux Is Flush with Cash," *Washington Post*,
      November 23, 1997, A01.
43   "I sincerely encourage you": Kevin Sullivan, "Addressing Moon

Followers, Bush Touts Family Values," *Austin-American Statesman*, September 15, 1995, A11.

43   The Dome kicked off: Marc Fisher, "Kemp's Moonlighting: Candidate Continued to Speak at Moon Events," *Washington Post*, September 14, 1996, C03.

44   Reuters also reported: "A Capital Coronation," *Los Angeles Times* editorial, June 24, 2004, B14.

44   "The people of Kyushu": From chap. 60 of Pak's book of collected speeches, *Truth Is My Sword*, vol. 2, 647.

44   Those who have encountered: Carolyn Weaver, "Unholy Alliance," *Mother Jones*, January 1986.

44   His admirers include: Pak, *Truth Is My Sword*, foreword.

44   Former disciple: Author interview with Glenn Emery, June 14, 2007.

45   He has also been called the brains: "6 Held in Kidnapping of Rev. Moon Aide, Col. Pak," *Washington Post*, November 28, 1984. See also Hong, *In the Shadow of the Moons*, and www.SaveBoHiPak.org (which has since been taken offline).

45   Editor Seojima Yoshikazu: See *Ampo* (Tokyo) 19, no. 3 (1987); and Isikoff and Burgess, "A Church in Flux."

45   The 1995–1996 Bush-Moon tour: Laver and Kaihla, "Ed Schreyer and the Moonies," 44.

45   During the tour: Barbara Bush's participation is described in "Group Builds Bridge across Racial Divide," *Tampa Tribune*, Bay Life, April 8, 1996, 1; as well as on the Women's Federation Web site, www.wfwp.us/wfwp.html.

46   His conservative policy group Empower America: Fisher, "Kemp's Moonlighting."

46   His recent book *Tempting Faith*: "Book Says Bush Just Using Christians," MSNBC, October 13, 2006, www.msnbc.msn.com/id/15228489/.

47   On February 21, 1991: Moon, "Blessed Couples Conference," New Yorker Hotel, February 21, 1991, www.tparents.org/Moon-Talks/sunmyungmoon91/SM910221a1.htm.

47   Months later: "Let Us Inherit the Realm of Victory of Our True Parents," New Yorker Hotel, April 15, 1991, www.unification.org/ucbooks/Mspks/1991/910415.html.

47   During the 1988 campaign: "The Resurrection of Reverend Moon," *Frontline*, January 21, 1992; and Isikoff and Burgess, "A Church in Flux."

47   "But Bush didn't listen": Moon sermon, "Completion of the
      Responsibilities of True Parents," December 6, 1992, Belvedere, New
      York, www.tparents.org/moon-talks/sunmyungmoon92/921206.htm.

47   The only explanation: Moon, "True Parents' Birthday" sermon,
      January 28, 1993, www.tparents.org/Moon-Talks/sunmyungmoon93/
      930128.htm.

48   A program for the conference: "Brazil Religious Freedom Meeting
      Finds Common Ground," *International Religious Freedom Report* (online),
      Spring 1999, www.ReligiousFreedom.com.

48   A 2006 Japanese TV report: Japanese News Network, June 11, 2006,
      available at the author's Web site, www.gorenfeld.net.

49   Go up Moon's faux Capitol Steps: Original Palace dedication video,
      June 13, 2006.

49   On Mr. Moon's death: Japanese Broadcasting System report, 2006.

49   The Japan News Network: Japanese News Network, June 11, 2006,
      available at the author's Web site, www.gorenfeld.net;
      "Ancestors Liberation Blessing Form, downloaded from the
      Taiwanese Unification Church site, www.unification.org/tw/study/
      cp/img/cplist1.jpg.

49   During the 2005–2006 fiscal year: "$1 Million Moonie Mystery,"
      Houston Chronicle, June 8, 2006; Washington Times Foundation form
      990; Delroy Alexander and Margaret Ramirez, "Rev. Moon and the
      Black Clergy," *Chicago Tribune*, November 5, 2006.

50   But I'm watching: Michael Jenkins May 20, 2007, sermon on video,
      available at the author's Web site, www.gorenfeld.net.

51   Days later, however: Korean-language video, author's collection, at
      the book's Web site.

51   A public relations person: E-mail from Brain Blake, public relations
      specialist at the George Bush Presidential Library and Museum,
      October 15, 2007; e-mail from Jim Appleby, aide to President Bush,
      October 18, 2007.

51   The *New York Times*'s David Brooks: David Brooks, "The Paranoid
      Style," *New York Times*, May 4, 2006.

THREE

52   First opening quote: Quoted in Josh Freed, *Moonwebs: Journey into the
      Mind of a Cult* (Toronto: Dorset, 1980).

52   Second opening quote: "Founder's Address: Absolute Values and the New Cultural Revolution," Fifteenth International Conference on the Unity of the Sciences, reprinted in *Unification News*, November 28, 1986, via www.unification.net.

52   "No one can completely control": Author interview with Cathryn Mazer, March 28, 2007.

52   In 1993, her brother and mother: *Today Show*, November 8, 1993, and November 15, 1993; "NBC Defames CARP and the Unification Church," *Unification News*, May 1994.

53   Gordon Neufeld: Gordon Neufeld, *Heartbreak and Rage: Ten Years under Sun Myung Moon* (College Station, TX: Virtual Bookworm, 2002), introduction.

53   The word *brainwashing*: *Diagnostic and Statistical Manual*, 4th ed. (Washington, D.C.: American Psychiatric Association, 1994), 232: "States of dissociation that occur in individuals who have been subjected to periods of prolonged and intense coercive persuasion (e.g., brainwashing, thought reform, or indoctrination while captive)."

53   Whether the concept: Benjamin Zablocki, "The Blacklisting of a Concept: The Strange History of the Brainwashing Conjecture in the Sociology of Religion," *Nova Religio*, University of California Press, October 1997; see also Louis Horowitz, *Science, Sin and Scholarship: The Politics of Reverend Moon and the Unification Church* (Cambridge, MA: MIT Press, 1978).

54   Moon's take: Author interview with Richard Barlow, June 27, 2007.

54   At Moon's training institute: "Completion of the Responsibilities of True Parents," *The Words of Rev. Moon from 1992*, www.tparents.org/ Library/Unification/Publications/10-Keys99/1_Ten_Keys.htm.

55   "A woman's reproductive organ": Moon, "God Is Our King and True Parent," Harlem, New York, May 8, 2001 (www.unification.net).

55   Under the spell: Emma Andrews, "Mass Appeal of Being over the Moon and in Love," *Newcastle Chronicle & Journal* (UK), May 14, 1998, 30.

56   Nervously, I open: David Ignatius, "Tension of the Times," *Washington Post*, June 18, 2004.

56   "Many comfortable": Moon, "Home Church Is Our Land of Settlement," January 1, 1983, midnight speech, New Yorker Hotel, www.unification. net/1983/830101a.html.

56   I'd read of how Moon: Charlotte Hays, "Moondoggle," *New Republic*, February 17, 1982.

57   In a piece of PBS: "The Resurrection of Rev. Moon," *Frontline*, January 21, 1992; see also Moon testimony before Hearing on Religious Freedom, June 26, 1984, www.unification.org/ucbooks/Mspks/1984/840626.html.

58   It goes on: Also see the WMA Web site (www.wmassociation.com/forums/forums.html); Rory O'Connor, "Toward a 'Faith-Based' Fourth Estate," *AlterNet*, May 24, 2005.

59   "Clearly you have": O'Connor, "Toward a 'Faith-Based' Fourth Estate."

59   Surely Tony Blankley: See the Michael Jenkins video, to be available at the author's Web site, www.gorenfeld.net; and John Gorenfeld, "Dear Leader's Paper Moon," *American Prospect*, June 19, 2005, www.prospect.org/cs/articles?articleId=9868.

59   In the *Times*: Robert Stacy McCain, "Symposium to Honor Lee," *Washington Times*, April 25, 2007, A1; first front-page mention of Park's death was in "Senate OKs Resolution to Honor Parks," *Washington Times*, October 28, 2005.

59   "I have the editorial independence": E-mail to author from Wesley Pruden, May 17, 2005.

60   It has long been known: Katherine Graham, *Personal History* (New York: Knopf, 1997), 597.

60   The paper has bled billions: See Robert Parry, "The GOP's $3 Billion Propaganda Organ," *Consortium News*, December 27, 2006, citing longtime *Times* reporter George Archibald. A more conservative $2 billion estimate is given in the *Columbia Journalism Review*, May 2002. In 1991, Moon said that "literally nine hundred million to one billion dollars has been spent to activate and run the *Washington Times*," in his sermon "Our Mission during the Time of Transition," December 23, 1991. Borchgrave's remarks are from Joan Mower, "Count Moonbeam," *GQ*, March 1990.

60   Even though *Examiner* publisher: Anschutz, at $7.8 billion, ranked ninety-third in *Forbes*'s 2007 list of the world's wealthiest people.

60   A study by the *Columbia Journalism Review*: Allen Freedman, "Washington's Other Paper: Is the Time Right for the *Times*?" *Columbia Journalism Review*, March 1, 1995.

60   Take, for example: Julia Duin, "Suit to Decide Workplace 'Hate Speech'; Flier on 'Natural Family' and 'Marriage' at Issue," *Washington Times*, June 11, 2007. The case is *Good News Association v. Joyce Hicks*, (USDC ND Cal. 2003), Case No. C-03-3542 VRW.

61   Columnist George Will: George H. Will, "Speech Police, Riding High in Oakland," *Washington Post*, June 24, 2007, B04.

62   On a daily basis: Author interview with Craig Maxim, June 7, 2007.

63   "I'm not calling them liars": *The Edge with Paula Zahn,* January 20, 2000.

63   Today the *Times: Washington Times* online media kit, 2007.

63   An example of the paper's power: Brendan O'Neill, "Not a Shred of
      Hard Evidence," *The Spectator,* February 21, 2004, 14–15; Carol Lipton,
      "Wag the Kennel? The Kenneth Joseph Story," *Counterpunch,* April 12,
      2003, www.counterpunch.org/lipton04122003.html.

63   The story begins: Ben Bradlee, Columbia University commencement
      speech, 2007.

63   De Borchgrave: *National Journal,* January 16, 1999, 134; and Joan
      Mower, "Count Moonbeam."

63   He slept: David Jones, "Mullah Omar Speaks," *Washington Times,*
      June 24, 2001, A10, with the writer's memories of de Borchgrave;
      Laurence Zuckerman, "Underdog to an 800-Pound Gorilla," *Time,*
      June 15, 1987.

63   More like the *Times's:* Hays, "Moondoggle."

64   "After shooting yourself": De Borchgrave memo, February 19, 1987.

64   He has published: Lars-Erik Nelson, "The Rev. Moon's New Buddy,"
      Daily News, May 16, 1988, 29; "In Town of Big Egos, Arnaud de
      Borchgrave Stands Out," New York News Service, April 17, 2007;
      de Borchgrave letter to Bill Cheshire, September 9, 1988; Mower,
      "Count Moonbeam."

64   De Borchgrave has done: Speaker's bio, All American Speakers'
      Bureau, www.AllAmericanSpeakers.com.

64   The fired count: Arnaud de Borchgrave and Robert Moss, *The Spike*
      (New York: Crown, 1980).

64   Joseph, the story went: De Borchgrave column filed in Amman, Jordan,
      UPI, March 21, 2003.

64   An emotional personal essay: UPI, March 27, 2003.

65   You could read about Pastor Joseph: "Mugged by Reality,"
      WorldNetDaily.com, March 25, 2003; "Human Shield Wannabe Admits:
      I Was Wrong," NewsMax.com, March 28, 2003, and UPI, March 27,
      2003; "Peace Protesters Shocked Back to Reality," FreeRepublic.com,
      March 22, 2003, www.freerepublic.com/focus/f-news/872426/posts;
      "I Was Wrong about War," *Human Events Online,* April 8, 2003; "Better
      Late Than Never," *Powerline,* March 22, 2003, www.powerlineblog.
      com/archives/002680.php; "Kana's Iraq," *National Review Online,* May
      19, 2004; Jack Kelly, "European Media and Former 'Human Shields'
      Are Beginning to Get It," *Jewish World Review,* March 24, 2003/20

Adar II, 5763; Jeff Gannon, *American Enterprise*, www.TaeMag.com/
issues/articleid.17896/article_detail.asp (via www.archive.org);
"Operation Iraqi Freedom," March 31, 2003, www.whitehouse.gov/
infocus/iraq/news/20030331-11.html.

65   Capitalizing on his fame: "How We're Winning the War on Terror,"
      Sunday Mail (Australia), September 14, 2003, 56.

65   "A former human shield": Fox News, November 3, 2003.

65   But Carol Lipton: Lipton, "Wag the Kennel?"

66   "It transpires": Jonathan Hari, original piece from *The Independent*,
      March 26, 2003; retraction, September 25, 2003.

66   "Lynxgate illustrates": "The Washington Times's Hair-Raising Tall
      Tale," *Extra!* May/June 2002.

66   As if crusading: "An Advertising Department That's on Top of the
      News," *Washington Post*, February 4, 2002, C01.

66   Other national stories: "When Conservatives Smear, Pundits Duck,"
      Extra! update October 2002, www.fair.org/index.php?page=2643.

67   On November 20, 2005: Felix Gilette, "Christmas Sends *Washington
      Times* on a Search for That Slippery PC Crowd," *Columbia Journalism
      Review*, December 1, 2005, www.cjr.org/politics/christmas_sends_
      washington_tim.php.

67   A few days later: "Exclusive: Bill O'Reilly Confronted about Phony
      'War on Christmas,'" *Scoobie Davis Online* (scoobiedavis.blogspot.com),
      December 6, 2005.

67   One of the oddities: Bill Berkowitz, "Mooning Martin Luther King Jr.,"
      MediaTransparency.org, May 14, 2007.

67   *Nation* reporter: Max Blumenthal, "Hell of a 'Times,'" *The Nation*,
      October 9, 2006.

67   In 1995, Coombs: Southern Poverty Law Center, *Intelligence Report*,
      Spring 2005; Blumenthal, "Hell of a 'Times.'"

68   Most outrageously of all: Marian Coombs, "From Safety Valve to Safety
      Net," *Washington Times*, B3. ("Hispanics boast of reconquering
      California. [. . . It] is possible to believe that we too, like Tolkien's
      Aragorn, 'will not let the White City fall.'"). See also "Letters through
      2/5/02," Vanguard News Network, www.vanguardnewsnetwork.
      com/letters/letters87.htm—a Nazi site. "Loved your review of LOTR."

68   One described: Michelangelo Signorile, "That Other Times," *New York
      Press*, www.nypress.com/15/50/news&columns/signorile.cfm.

68   Before coming out: John McCaslin, "Inside the Beltway," *Washington
      Times*, July 3, 2003.

68   In 2007, the FBI: Heidi Beirich and Bob Moser, "Defending Dixie,"
     Southern Poverty Law Center, *Intelligence Report*, Summer 2003;
     "Columnist Receives Deluge of Death Threats," *Monterey County
     Herald*, June 21, 2007; former *Times* writer Robert Redding Jr., "Pitts
     Harasser Linked to the Washington Times," *Redding News Review*, June
     21, 2007.

68   Like Mel Gibson: Blumenthal, "Hell of a 'Times'"; and Roy Reed,
     Faubus: The Life and Times of an American Prodigal (Little Rock:
     University of Arkansas Press, 1997).

68   He has employed: Fred Reed, "It's Time to Face Up to the Coming Race
     War," *Washington Times*, December 16, 1996; bio and writings at his
     personal Web site, www.FredOnEverything.net; "Orwell, with Lots
     More Consumer Goods," www.FredOnEverything.net/King.shtml.

69   Reed, in turn: Steve Sailer, "Q&A with Gary Brecher, 'The War Nerd,'"
     UPI, August 20, 2003.

69   "The evolution": Fred Reed, "On Technology," *Washington Times*,
     February 24, 2005.

70   They "have somehow convinced": Author correspondence with
     George Archibald, June 28, 2007.

70   It went as follows: Gorenfeld, "Dear Leader's Paper Moon."

71   Earlier in the evening: Frank Ahrens, "Moon Speech Raises Old Ghosts
     as the Times Turns 20," *Washington Post*, May 23, 2002, E01.

71   On April 14, 1987: Letters to Arnaud de Borchgrave, August 14, 1987.

71   "I figured all along": Author correspondence with John Seiler, July 4,
     2007.

72   If so: John Seiler, "My Encounter with Tony Snow," *Orange County
     Register* blog "Orange Punch," April 26, 2006.

72   Later Cheshire said: Stated at a seminar, "Cults and the Media," which
     was held in 1990 by the Cult Awareness Network and is available on
     YouTube.

72   One of the departed writers: Seiler, "My Encounter with Tony Snow."

73   Most famous: "The Big Story with John Gibson," Fox News, January
     19, 2007; "Obama Smeared," ThinkProgress.com, January 19, 2007;
     "CNN Debunks False Report about Obama," CNN.com, January
     23, 2007.

73   After attending: "Whitney Houston a No-Show at Moon's Mass
     Wedding Ceremony," CNN, November 29, 1997.

73   [T]hat if a billionaire: From testimony before a Senate panel in 1984;
     see the video at www.gorenfeld.net.

74   [T]hat when a media figure: "Moon's Light Dims," *Vancouver Sun*,
      June 2, 1976; Gorenfeld, "Bad Moon on the Rise."

74   [O]r pined for a holy fire: Moon, "God's Day Speech," January 1, 2004
      (www.tparents.org).

74   A search of the TV news: Vanderbilt Television news archive, tvnews.
      vanderbilt.edu.

74   "Critics say": *The Edge with Paula Zahn*, Fox News, January 20, 2000.

74   "I have seen": Ann Louis Bardach, "The Reverend and His
      Newspaper," in *Killed: Great Journalism Too Hot to Print*, ed. David
      Wallis (New York: Nation Books, 2004), 156.

75   Not one but three: "Mad about Moon," *Time*, November 10, 1975.

75   "The church seems": "Moonstruck," *The Economist*, February 7, 1976.

75   "I was assaulted": "Father Says He Was Beaten by Rev. Moon Men,"
      Daily Review (Hayward, CA), September 29, 1975.

75   Over a year later: "Moonie Kids, Dad Reconciled," *Times Herald
      Record* (upstate New York), January 13, 1977; Carlton Sherwood,
      Inquisition: The Prosecution and Persecution of Sun Myung Moon (New
      York: Regnery Gateway, 1991), 33–35.

75   Josette Sheeran: Her bylines are visible in footage from "The
      Resurrection of Rev. Moon," *Frontline*, January 21, 1992.

75   An ex-Moon leader: Ibid.

76   "I have watched Josette": Author interview with Craig Maxim.

76   Sheeran told the rival: Elisabeth Bumiller, "The Nation's Capital
      Gets a New Daily Newspaper," *Washington Post*, May 17, 1982, C01;
      author correspondence in July 2007 with Emery.

76   The *Washingtonian*: From a State Department bio (www.state.gov/r/
      pa/ei/biog/51686.htm).

77   Says Craig Maxim: Author interview with Maxim, June 7, 2007.

77   Both Hunker and Sheeran: Paula Hunker appears in State
      Department telephone directory, under Sheeran's position; she is
      listed as Paula Gray Hunker in contributions to Moon's periodicals
      The World and I and the *Washington Times*. The apparent connection
      was reported first by reporter Matt Lee of Inner City Press, who
      asked about Sheeran's status at a UN news conference and reported
      on it November 7, 2006. Pak's remarks on the "spiritual counseling
      team" are from his sermon "Wise as Serpents, Pure as Doves," May 1,
      1982, reprinted in his book *Truth Is My Sword*, vol. 2, chap. 40; the
      online edition is at www.tparents.org/library/unification/books/
      tims2/Tims2-40.htm.

77   Fearing embarrassment: "State Department Official Picked to Run U.N. Food Program," *Washington Post,* November 8, 2006; A13.

77   Ironically, according to Robert Boettcher: Robert Boettcher, *Gifts of Deceit, Sun Myung Moon, Tongsun Park and the Korean Scandal* (New York: Holt, Rinehart, & Winston, 1980), 172.

77   When I asked: Author interview, first quarter 2003.

78   There is a story: *Regardie's: The Business of Washington,* November 1988, found in Sara Diamond Collection at the University of California–Berkeley.

78   Michael Marshall: Tom Brown, "Between the Lines" (*Seattle Times* blog), November 28, 2003.

79   UPI columnist: John Bloom "War, Peace and Rev. Moon," UPI, February 24, 2003.

80   It had groaned: "Washington Loses a Newspaper," *Time,* August 3, 1981.

80   "This is going to be": Personal interview with James R. Whelan, July 2, 2004, and successive correspondence. Whelan's story is also described in Jean-François Boyer, *L'Empire Moon* (Paris: La Decouverte, 1986), 261–65, 267–73, 295, 305–10, 319–21, 327.

81   He had been promised: Susan Rasky, "Ex-Publisher Says Moon Church Ran Newspaper," *New York Times,* July 23, 1984.

81 · But Times officials: Letters, *U.S. News & World Report,* April 10, 1989, 7.

81   Columnist Charlotte Hays: Hays, "Moondoggle."

81   To ease the strain: Glenn Emery, "Pay Day!" August 11, 2001, account (www.tparents.org). The $250 million figure is cited in the *Washington Times,* May 18, 1987, 1A. The salary quote is from Bardach, "The Reverend and His Newspaper," 145. For another account of signing paychecks back to the church, see Freed, *Moonwebs.*

82   "The money was fabulous": Bardach, "The Reverend and His Newspaper." 156.

82   "The Moonies operate": Andrew Ferguson, "Can't Buy Me Love: Is the Unification Church Conservative, or Just Rich?" *American Spectator* 20, no. 9 (September 1987). Whelan's comments here are from an author interview.

83   From the church's point of view: "Building a Media Network," a www.tparents.org history of CAUSA.

83   In 2002, Bo Hi Pak: From video of Pak in Washington, September 1, 2002, author's collection, available on the book site.

84   Scaife: Scaife is number 645 in *Forbes's* World's Richest People, October 2004

84   A good many entities: "Scaife Denies Ties to 'Conspiracy,' Starr,"
      Washington Post, December 17, 1998, A2. For various views on the
      growth of the conservative establishment, see Sidney Blumenthal, *The
      Rise of the Counter Establishment* (New York: HarperCollins, 1988);
      Adrian Wooldridge and John Micklethwait, *The Right Nation* (New
      York: Penguin, 2004); Richard Viguerie, *America's Right Turn* (New York:
      Bonus Books, 2004); David Brock, *The Republican Noise Machine*
      (New York: Crown, 2004); Jacob S. Hacker and Paul Pierson, *Off Center:
      The Republican Revolution and the Erosion of American Democracy*
      (Hartford, CT: Yale University Press, 2005).

85   "Mr. Scaife": Karen Rothmyer, "Citizen Scaife," *Columbia Journalism
      Review*, July/August 1981.

85   "I have some influence": Rothmyer, "The Man behind the Mask,"
      Salon.com, April 7, 1998.

85   "And in the deep": Elisabeth Bumiller, "The Nation's Capital Gets a
      New Daily Newspaper," *Washington Post*, May 17, 1982, C03.

86   In one old photograph: "Beating the Odds," *Washington Times* internal
      newsletter from 1983.

87   He has written: Moon's inferno is drawn from "Hoon Dok Hae and
      Sunday Sermon," Tarrytown, New York. May 24, 1998; Larry Moffitt,
      "Blessing Responsibility and Springtime for Hitler," October 3, 2004,
      www.tparents.org/Library/Unification/Talks/Moffit/Moffitt-
      041003.htm.

89   "Nobody would go": "Dr. Sang Hun Lee's Teachings from Spirit
      World," www.Unification.org/ucbooks/TSW/tsw-02a.htm.

89   Moffitt considers: "Moffitt, "Blessing Responsibility."

FOUR

90   Opening quote: "Messages from Former American presidents," church
      Web site MessagesFromSpiritWorld.info.

90   The night of the coronation: Personal correspondence with ABC pro-
      ducer Luis Martinez, June 23, 2004, through 2006.

90   The Catholic Church: "What's behind the Black Rebellion in the Catho-
      lic Church?" *Ebony*, November 1989; "Post Paternalism or Black Black-
      mail?" *Washington Monthly*, February 1990, 1, 8.

91   The D.C. priest angered: Stallings is quoted in *Kenya Times*, July 18, 2006.

91   But then Milingo: "Married African Archbishop," Associated Press,
      September 18, 2006; "Zambian Archbishop Reclaims Korean Bride,"

UK Telegraph, July 29, 2006; "Archbishop Milingo Excommunicated," *Catholic World News,* September 26, 2006.

91   Martinez had just finished: "ADAPT Lie-in," Council for Disability Rights, www.disabilityrights.org/404.htm.

92   His cadence: Michael Jenkins sermon, February 1, 2004, multimedia available at the author's Web site: www.gorenfeld.net.

92   One weekend before: The Jenkins tapes spilling the beans about the coronation on February 1, 2004, and March 21, 2004, both of which have been removed from the church site www.FamilyFed.org, will be available at the author's Web site www.gorenfeld.net.

93   Early in the night: John Gorenfeld, "Moonstruck," *Philadelphia City Paper,* July 1, 2004.

94   Photographs of one: See photographs at the book Web site.

94   In 1986, Moon's daughter-in-law: See Nansook Hong, *In the Shadow of the Moons: My Life in the Reverend Sun Myung Moon's Family* (New York: Little, Brown, 1998).

95   A less well-connected clan: The case is made by Troy Davis, a blogger: "Warren Jeffs Should Have Contributed to the GOP," *Scoobie Davis Online,* August 29, 2006, http://scoobiedavis.blogspot.com/2006/08/warren-jeffs-should-have-contributed.html.

95   When Hong went public: "Reputations: The Rev. Sun Myung Moon, Emperor of the Universe," BBC, August 7, 2001.

96   WashingtonTimes.com would report: "Honor for the Peacemakers," *Washington Times,* March 24, 2004, B01. Reporter Wetzstein's church testimonies can be found via search of www.tparents.org.

96   John Judis reported: John Judis, "Reverend Moon's Rising Political Influence," *U.S. News & World Report,* March 27, 1989.

96   The word *Moonie:* See Don Lattin, "Combatants in Cult War Attempt Reconciliation," *San Francisco Chronicle,* May 1, 2000; "When Scholars Know Sin," *Skeptic* 6, no. 3 (1998).

96   His followers: Moon sermon, "Restoration of True Sonship," New Yorker Hotel, February 13, 1997 (www.tparents.org).

97   "How is it going": E-mail from Peter Elliffe, April 22, 2005.

97   Another young believer: E-mail from teenage Moon follower who asked to be unnamed, April 3, 2001.

97   "The world should follow": Moon sermon, "Rally to Advance the Realization of the Settlement of Cheon Il Guk," March 4, 2005; Moon in a February 6, 2003, speech: "Carrying this card will protect you from Satan."

97   But Moon's influence: Rangel letter in author's collection, posted on the book site.

97   Regardless of how seriously: Moon, "Tradition Centered on God," January 2, 1972, sermon from *Master Speaks* (www.tparents.org).

97   While the rare Democrat: "Ideological Education," www.tparents. org/Library/Unification/Publications/Causa/Causa-03.htm.

98   "Father's [Moon's]": Michelle Goldberg, "The New Monkey Trial," Salon.com, January 10, 2005.

98   As early as 1967: Ibid.

98   The Paris press: Harvey G. Simmons, *The French National Front: The Extremist Challenge to Democracy* (Boulder, CO: Westview, 1996). See "Le Front National Vingt Ans après V.," *Le Monde*, February 8, 1992.

99   But Moon's hand: Jean-François Boyer, *L'Empire Moon* (Paris: La Decouverte, 1986), 292–375; "Pierre Ceyrac, mooniste et deputé s'explique," TV transcript at the French anticult site www. PrevenSectes.com.

99   Several of the black deacons: Rob Boston, "Moon Shadow," *Church & State*, June 2001.

99   "Is there a better icon?": William Reed, *East Texas Review*, June 25, 2004.

99   But Tony Norman: Tony Norman, "A Spiritual Hoodwinking," *Pittsburgh Post-Gazette*, October 26, 2007.

100   "There will never be": Tony Norman, "It's The Second Coming and We Almost Missed It," *Pittsburgh Post-Gazette*, June 22, 2004. See also Michael Warder, "Bribemasters," *Chronicles* (Rockford, IL), June, 1988; Delroy Alexander and Margaret Ramirez, "Rev. Moon and the Black Clergy," *Chicago Tribune*, November 5, 2006.

100   Gary Jarmin: Letters, *U.S. News & World Report*, April 10, 1989.

101   Recalls Desloge: Author interviews May 7, 2007, and October 26, 2007.

101   Early in the year: "Warner 'Deceived,'" *Washington Post*, July 23, 2004.

101   Jarmin, who has complained: Peter N. Carroll, *It Seemed Like Nothing Happened: The Tragedy and Promise of America in the 1970s* (New York: Holt, 1982), 329.

101   The *Charleston Gazette*: Maryclaire Dale, *Charleston* [West Virginia] *Gazette*, January 6, 1999.

101   "Millions of Christians": Quoted at www.ChristianVoiceOnline.com/ about.

101 Jerry Falwell's: Numbers from David G. Bromley and Anson D. Shupe, *New Christian Politics* (Macon, GA: Mercer University Press, 1984), 252–54.

102 Seeking the White House: Mondale on *The MacNeil/Lehrer News Hour*, PBS, September 6, 1984; Jarmin quoted in Doug Bandow, *Beyond Good Intentions: A Biblical View of Politics* (Crossway Books, 1988), 117.

102 Critic Doug Bandow: "The Logic of Hellfire," *Washington Post*, February 12, 1984, B1; Paul Simon, *The Glass House: Politics and Morality in the Nation's Capitol* (Ann Arbor: University of Michigan Press, 1984), 89; Leonard Cargan and Jeanne H. Ballantine, comps., *Sociological Footprints: Introductory Readings in Sociology*, 2d ed. (Belmont, CA: Wadsworth, 1982), 163.

102 By 1996: Ralph Reed, *Active Faith: How Christians Are Changing the Soul of American Politics* (New York: Free Press, 1996), 106.

102 The NCPRR: "The Fear Merchants," *San Francisco Examiner*, February 8, 1998.

103 "Most people": John Judis, "Reverend Moon's Rising Political Influence," *U.S. News & World Report*, March 27, 1989.

103 On Pak's sixtieth birthday: Bo Hi Pak, *Truth Is My Sword*, vol. 2 (New York: Holy Spirit Association, 1999), 612.

103 The name of one: "Global Dominion" references come from FEC records; *Washington Times*, March 13, 2005; and House Clerk's office registry as of 2005 at www.clerk.house.gov.

103 In 1989: Andrew Leigh, "Looking for Cover," *Washington Post*, October 15, 1989.

104 "I rise today": *Congressional Record*, July 27, 1993.

104 Several major media outlets: "Honor Thy Parents," *Washington City Paper*, September 8–14, 1995; "What Is the Truth behind Parents Day?" *Mesa Tribune*, August 9, 1998; "Parents Day Shows Links of Moon's Church to GOP," *Mobile Register*, July 30, 2000; Jeanette Walls, "Moonie Parents?" MSNBC.com, February 15, 1999.

104 "On July 28, 1993": Pak, *Truth Is My Sword*, vol. 1, 477.

105 "Men and women in Congress": Moon sermon, "Our Responsibility in Becoming Children of True Parents," February 16, 1997, *Unification News*, February 16, 1997.

105 The genius: Author interview with Louis Desloge, October 16, 2007.

105 "The 'outside' view": "Who Got the Room for Moon? The Plot

Thickens," Americans United blog, June 30, 2004; Michael Jenkins, "Notes Concerning Father's Comments and Rev. Kwak's Guidance Concerning the Crown," *Unification News,* April 2004 (www.tparents.org).

106   Working there: Ken Layne, "The Wire That Wouldn't Die," *Columbia Online Journalism Review,* May 16, 2000.

106   "Now it's right": "Hoon Dok Hae with True Parents," March 24, 2004, Sheraton National Hotel, Arlington, Virginia (www.tparents.org).

106   In a final, surprising segue: Ibid.

108   "Those who are making": Joseph Farah, "The Fate of UPI," *WorldNet-Daily,* May 22, 2000.

112   "Do you think": "WorldNetDaily RadioActive," June 14, 2004, broadcast.

112   "I'd never been to Korea": Author interview with Joseph Farah, June 18, 2004.

113   While news editors: The Gadflyer.com was first with the story on June 9, 2004. See also "Hail to the Moon King," Salon.com, June 21, 2004; Charles Babington and Alan Cooperman, "The Rev. Moon Honored at Hill Reception," *Washington Post,* July 23, 2004.

113   Both had traveled: Gorenfeld, "Moonstruck."

113   Oddly, while Davis: Ibid.

114   In Florida: "Mrs. Hyu Ja Moon . . . has finished her 40-day fasting condition": *Unification News,* September 2004.

114   "I am going through turmoil": The "anointed one" rationale appears in "3 Utahans off Moon Hook," *Deseret News,* July 1, 2004.

114   "I want people to know": "Iowa GOP Official Steals Journalist's Name for the Moonies," Dailykos.com, July 22, 2005, www.dailykos.com/story/2005/7/22/13024/6833.

114   Not so the e-mail: Rev. Gunnard Johnston, e-mail to author, July 22, 2005.

115   Among the women: John McCaslin, "Inside the Beltway," *Washington Times,* February 5, 1998, A6.

115   "Hey," she told Moon editor: "Stop Dissing the *Washington Times!*" *Washington Monthly,* May 1997.

116   Its e-mail list: See, for example, "Campus Leader," from the YAF e-mail list, April 5, 2007.

116   On July 2: Ken Grubbs, "Moon over Washington: Which Newspaper Proprietor Chats with Hitler and Thinks He's the Messiah?" *Wall Street Journal,* July 2, 2004.

116   Grubbs was axed: See Ron Robinson's official bio on the Young America's Foundation Web site, www.yaf.org/staff/ron_robinson.cfm.

116   He never should have been: Howard Kurtz, "The Ordinary American, under Stress and Oversimplified," *Washington Post*, May 19, 2004, C01.

116   The next month: "Warner 'Deceived' on Rev. Moon Event," *Washington Post*, July 23, 2004; see also "John Warner Was Not 'Deceived,'" *Washington Post*, August 14, 2004, A19.

117   "Welcome home, Jesus": Video of the February 4, 2004, sermon featuring Michael Jenkins and Chris Cannon will be available at the author's Web site, www.gorenfeld.net.

118   "I lent my name": E-mail from Charlie Black, May 6, 2004.

118   This time the cosmic con: "St. Charles Shelter Turns Down Award: Unification Church Had Offered $2,000," *Chicago Tribune*, January 22, 2000.

119   "I lived for those": Moon, "Founder's Commemorative Address," Cannon House Office Building Caucus Room, February 2, 2000 (www.tparents.org); "HDH at East Garden," March 28, 2004, notes by Michael Jenkins (www.tparents.org).

119   Even in his boyhood: Remarks from "Where Do We Go?" sermon in London, September 17, 1978 (www.tparents.org), and "God's Day" sermon in Manhattan, January 1, 1987 (www.tparents.org).

119   This one, at the Marriott: Accounts of the coronation are from multimedia at the author's Web site, which photographs Moon being crowned under a banner with matching date. The Bushes' messages of support are described in Cheryl Wetzstein, "Leaders Call for Unity," *Washington Times*, December 14, 2004, A02.

120   McLeod is also the president: The $1 million is described in "For Ex-Inmates, Getting a Job Is the First Step to Stability," *New York Times*, January 29, 2006. See also "Guests of President Bush and Laura Bush in Her VIP box," Associated Press, January 21, 2004.

120   It would settle the question: Donnie McLeod, "Is Bush's Faith-Based Initiative for Real?" *Washington Times*, December 8, 2004, A17.

120   This cause also occasioned: The Washington Television Center's $250,000 gift is listed in "The Deep-Pocket Donors to Bush's Second Inauguration," *New York Times*, January 15, 2005. The WTC's status as a Unification Church company is described in Marc Fisher and Jeff Leen, "A Church in Flux Is Flush with Cash," *Washington Post*, November 23, 1997.

121   The footage taken in 2002: Multimedia from the cross removal campaign will be available on the author's Web site.

121 God, the church said: For details on the campaign, see Michael Jenkins, "123 Churches Took Down the Cross over the Easter Holiday," *Unification News*, April 2003 (www.tparents.org); BillieAnn Sabo, "One Day DP Seminar in Los Angeles," *Unification News*, April 2003— "[Stallings]'s topic was, 'Trade Your Cross for a Crown.' He spoke for 70 minutes and the guests were screaming with joy, shouting hallelujah, standing, jumping, waving their arms and hands."

122 "The fact that the cross": See www.TrueFather.com photographs. In the Bible, it is actually said that the cross will end enmity between Jews and Christians.

122 "I do not want to spend": "Meet Me at the Empty Tomb," internal e-mail sent March 27, 2005, by Michael Jenkins, quoting Lonnie McLeod. "As one of those African-American ministers that Mr. Gorenfeld seeks to protect—please tell him thanks but no thanks!"

123 One notable in the procession: Bundakji, the Muslim leader, is mentioned seventy-one times on www.tparents.org, a Moon Web site; see Michael Jenkins, "Building Trust with Leaders in the Holy Land," www.tparents.org/Library/Unification/Talks/Jenkins/Jenkins1/Jenkins-050117.htm.

123 "These people don't have": "Whose Peace Is It," *Jerusalem Post*, June 3, 2004.

123 New Jersey minister: Rev. William Whitehead, "Thou Shalt Not Steal Church Members," *Spiked Online*, April 26, 2007.

123 "After the prayer": "Reconciliation of Judaism and Christianity with Repentance," www.FamilyFed.org, June 3, 2003.

124 After breakfast: "Burying the Cross at 'Field of Blood,'" *Unification News* 22, no. 6 (June 2003).

FIVE

125 First opening quote: "Messages from Spirit World" (on churchWebsite), MessagesFromSpiritWorld.info.

125 Second opening quote: "The 25 Most Intriguing People of 1981": "A Direct-Mail Genius Is Funding the Sound Effects for That Thunder on the Right: Richard Viguerie," *People*, December 28, 1991/January 4, 1982.

125 William McKenzie: This and subsequent contemporary quotes are from an author interview with McKenzie, May 2007. See also Jim

Leach, Ken Ruberg, and Bill McKenzie, "Moon's New Horizon: The Theocratic Right," *Ripon Forum*, January 1983.

125 Norquist, twenty-six: Mary Beth Franklin, "Washington News," United Press International, January 5, 1983; Moon sermon, "Home Church Is Our Land of Settlement," January 1, 1983, New York.

126 Norquist arrived: Norquist's "lies" shout from Franklin, "Washington News"; Bill Prochnau, "Ripon Society Decries New Right 'Alliance' with Moon Church," *Washington Post*, January 6, 1983.

126 Having brooded: *Fresh Air*, WHYY (National Public Radio, Philadelphia), October 3, 2004; Susan Page, "Norquist's Power High, Profile Low," *USA Today*, June 1, 2001.

126 But in his salad days: Some of the best accounts on the young radicals are by Michael Levenson, "Roots of a Lobbyist," *Boston Globe*, January 15, 2006; and Nina Easton, *Gang of Five: Leaders at the Center of the Conservative Crusade* (New York: Simon & Schuster, 2002).

126 Figures of the old guard: Prochnau, "Ripon Society Decries New Right 'Alliance.'"

126 "Jack Abramoff": Franklin, "Washington News."

127 "Appealing to the lowest instinct": Ibid.

128 Wrote Leach: Ibid.

128 Richard Viguerie told: Prochnau, "Ripon Society Decries New Right 'Alliance.'"

128 He found *Inchon!*: See the February 13, 1982, entry in *Reagan Diaries* (New York: HarperCollins, 2007).

128 But the Hollywood press kit: *Inchon!* press kit, author's collection.

129 On July 1: Barbara Kantrowitz, "In Moon's Light, Marriage Vows of Members Echo," *Philadelphia Inquirer*, July 2, 1982, A01.

129 In the early 1980s: Quotes from Nina J. Easton, "Abramoff's Grand Aims Came Early," *Boston Globe*, February 6, 2006.

129 Those around him: Ibid.

129 "It was said": "Opposing Forces," *Unification News*, February 2000 (www.tparents.org).

129 On the sidewalk: Lawrence Feinberg, "Soviet Embassy Won't Accept Letter from McDonald's Son," *Washington Post*, September 8, 1983, A25.

130 An ex–FBI agent: Ross Gelbspan, "Documents: Moon Group Aided FBI," *Boston Globe*, April 20, 1988, National/Foreign section, 1.

130 "Can you imagine": "The Report on the Seminar in the Spirit World for 120 Communists," www.unification.org/ucbooks/20020509.html.

130 He made $100,000: William Lanouette, "The New Right— 'Revolutionaries' Out after the 'Lunch-Pail' Vote," *National Journal*, 1978; Sara Diamond, *Spiritual Warfare* (Boston: South End Press, 1989), 57; Bill Berkowitz, "Richard Viguerie: Still Thundering after All These Years," WorkingForChange.com, March 4, 2005.

131 "Before Rush Limbaugh": "A Funding Father," *Washington Times*, September 20, 2003, A13.

131 *People* credited him: "The 25 Most Intriguing People of 1981."

131 "He's been working": "Richard Viguerie's Big Con," Rick Perlstein writing at TomPaine.com blog, May 18, 2007.

131 On August 10: *Reagan Diaries*, August 10, 1982.

131 Lofton was "ever on the prowl": See Letters, *American Spectator*, November 1987; Frank Zappa on *Crossfire*, March 28, 1986 (available on YouTube); Charlotte Hays, "Moondoggle," *New Republic*, February 17, 1982.

132 But before conservatives: Robert Viguerie, *America's Right Turn* (New York: Bonus Books, 2004).

133 "[B]abies are being plucked": Rick Perlstein, "The End of Democracy," *Village Voice*, October 26, 2004.

133 You discover silent majorities: For a liberal take on Viguerie's lessons for fund-raising, see Jerome Armstrong and Markos Zuniga, *Crashing the Gates* (New York: Chelsea Green, 2005).

133 Unnoticed by the mass media: *Booknotes*, C-SPAN, September 5, 2004.

133 Carter Clews: Carter Clews's quote is from Walter Hatch in the *Seattle Times*, "Mainstream Moon," February 12, 1989. On the mid-1980s drought in direct-mail fund-raising, see Ben Franklin, "From Money Magic to Money Misery," *New York Times*, January 14, 1986, 13.

134 In dire straits: Franklin, "From Money Magic to Money Misery." Rees's spy status is described in "Papers Detail Decades of FBI Surveillance," *International Herald Tribune*, June 26, 2007.

134 It was a sweetheart deal: Sara Diamond, *Spiritual Warfare: The Politics of the Christian Right* (Boston: South End Press, 1989), 59–60; see also Franklin, "From Money Magic to Money Misery."

134 The KCFF was raising: Robert Boettcher, *Gifts of Deceit: Sun Myung Moon, Tongsun Park and the Korean Scandal* (New York: Holt, Rinehart, & Winston, 1980), 156. See also Robert Roland, "The Capitol Hill Stalking Dragon," unpublished manuscript (ca. 1975), 204.

134 "The Viguerie letters": Quoted in Leach et al., "Moon's New Horizon";

also "For Many, There Are Big Profits in 'Nonprofits,'" *U.S. News & World Report*, November 6, 1978. The description of the emaciated child is cited in Roland, "The Capitol Hill Stalking Dragon," 206.

134   This enormous gift: Leach et al., "Moon's New Horizon" ; Boettcher, *Gifts of Deceit*, 321–22; Berkowitz, "Richard Viguerie."

135   The con was that there was no fee: The letter is from papers of Adm. Arleigh Burke, in *Investigation of Korean-American Relations*, supplement to pt. 4 (Washington, D.C.: U.S. Government Printing Office, March 15–22, 1978). On June 22, 1977, former KCIA chief Kim Hyung Wook testified before Congress that "Bo Hi Pak . . . proposed to establish 'Radio of Free Asia.'"

135   The investigation also turned up: Boettcher, *Gifts of Deceit*, chap. 12, "Dueling with the Moonies," 307–38; House Subcommittee on International Organizations, *Investigation of Korean-American Relations*, supplement to pt. 4, 23; Roland, "The Capital Hill Stalking Dragon," 12.

135   The letter: *Investigation of Korean-American Relations*, supplement to part 4 (March 15–22, 1978).

136   "Most people who followed": Boettcher, *Gifts of Deceit*, 337–38.

136   His book *Gifts of Deceit*: "Books of 1980," *Washington Post*, December 7, 1980; "Books of the Times," *New York Times*, June 23, 1980; Boettcher's obituary, *New York Times*, May 30, 1984.

136   The Reverend Moon jubilated: Walter Hatch, "Mainstream Moon," *Seattle Times*, February 12, 1989.

136   As scholar Sara Diamond: Sara Diamond, *Roads to Dominion* (New York: Guilford, 1995), 1–16, 228–56.

137   "There were just a handful": *Booknotes*, C-SPAN, September 5, 2004.

137   "The reason we took the money": "Power for Sale: From Greenpeace to the Rev. Sun Myung Moon," *Chicago Tribune Magazine*, April 27, 1986.

137   However, Paul Weyrich: "Moon Buys into U.S. Politics," *St. Petersburg Times*, December 26, 1987, 24A.

138   The only major conservative: Ann Louis Bardach, "The Reverend and His Newspaper," in *Killed: Great Journalism Too Hot to Print*, ed. David Wallis (New York: Nation Books, 2004), 161.

138   In 1997, his Liberty University: Robert Parry, "The GOP's Own Asian Connection: Rev. Moon," *Los Angeles Times*, October 16, 1997; Parry, "Buying the Right," ConsortiumNews.com, 1997; Moon, "International Leaders' Conference," January 2, 1992 (www.tparents.org). A description of Godwin kicking reporter Bardach out of his *Times* office

appears in Bardach, "The Reverend and His Newspaper," 154–55.
50 McCormack also helped: See Billy McCormack's official profile on
the Christian Coalition Web site (www.cc.org/highprofile.cfm);
"Religious Right Joins Rev. Moon at Pro-Bush Inaugural Luncheon,"
Church & State, March 2001; Rob Boston, "Moon Shadow," *Church &
State*, June 2001.

138   According to a House investigation: Feulner's encounter is described
in *Investigation of Korean-American Relations*, final report (Washington,
D.C.: U.S. Government Printing Office, October 1978), 106; the $2.2
million figure is from David Corn and Morley Jefferson, "Made-
in-Korea Conservatives," *The Nation*, January 1989. See also Joel
Bleifus, "Heritage Foundation Tries to Clear Name," *In These Times*,
April 26, 1989.

139   "Under U.S. law": Corn and Jefferson, "Made-in-Korea Conservatives";
Bleifus, "Heritage Foundation Tries to Clear Name."

139   According to *New Republic* editor: John Judis, "Reverend Moon's Rising
Political Influence," *U.S. News & World Report*, March 27, 1989.

139   According to a variety of sources: Confidential Gardiner letter from
December 2006 with matching Heritage Foundation postmark;
transcript, "Lou Dobbs Tonight," CNN.com, January 24, 2006; Joe
Conason, "Joe Conason's Journal," Salon.com, February 3, 2003;
Oxford University alumni notes, http://web.archive.org/
web/20020609142618/http:/pages.prodigy.net/iainkris/union.html:
Gardiner "banned from OUCA [Oxford University Conservative
Association] because of religious discrimination"; confidential
interviews; father Colin Gardiner's participation described on such
Moon sites as "Peace Tour," www.peace-tour.org/tour3_2006/nation/
uk.php; Gardiner's relationship with Nile established in "Recalling
Mystery of Historic Searches for Two Niles," *Washington Times*, October
14, 2001.

140   According to a 1995 article: David and Kathleen Burton, "Digging for
the Religious Foundation at Yale," *Unification News*, March 19, 1995.

SIX

141   The year is 1967: Roland's stories of Moon are drawn from his testimony before Rep. Donald Fraser; see House Subcommittee on
International Organizations, *Investigation of Korean-American Relations*

(Washington, D.C.: U.S. Government Printing Office, October 31, 1978), 40–42 and 45; Jean-François Boyer, *L'Empire Moon* (Paris: La Decouverte, 1986), 128–29; personal interviews with Roland and his daughter, Linda Mattix, June 23–24, 2006; and Robert Roland, "The Capitol Hill Stalking Dragon," unpublished manuscript (ca. 1975).

142 There is even a throne room: As found in the Admiral Burke files, the room is described in an April 15, 1965, issue of *New Age Frontiers*, an early Unification Church newsletter: "a magnificent wing chair covered with rich gold brocade."

142 Meanwhile, at the Rolands' home: Roland, "The Capitol Hill Stalking Dragon," 13.

143 If little is known: Adm. Arleigh Burke papers, reprinted in the supplement to *Investigation of Korean-American Relations* (Washington, D.C.: U.S. Government Printing Office, March 15–22, 1978).

143 In response, Col. Bo Hi Pak: Hearings of the Subcommittee on International Organizations, *Investigation of Korean-American Relations* (Washington, D.C.: U.S. Government Printing Office, 1977), pt. 4, 449.

143 "Marines don't cry": Bruce Petty, "Marines Don't Cry in Public: Robert Roland," in *Saipan: Oral Histories of the Pacific War* (Jefferson, NC: MacFarland, 2002), 117–19.

144 One of the strangest: Bill Gertz, "Russia Tied to Iraq's Missing Arms," *Washington Times*, October 20, 2004; Jonathan Hari, "Ship of Fools," *New Republic*, June 27, 2007.

144 "Thank *God* for Bill Gertz": Video clip in author's possession, dated October 6, 2002, to be available at the author's Web site: www.gorenfeld.net.

145 In 1976, Roland says: Roland, "The Capitol Hill Stalking Dragon," 223–25. For Moon's gambling, see also Nansook Hong, *In the Shadow of the Moons: My Life in the Reverend Sun Myung Moon's Family* (New York: Little, Brown, 1998).

145 He even invited Pak: Roland is described as president of the Men's Council, Potomac Presbytery, in "Christian Laymen's Group Seeking to Aid Witnessing," *Washington Post*, December 31, 1960. He was also a friend of Senate chaplain Bob Halverson; see "Laymen Plan Workshop in Alexandria," *Washington Post*, December 17, 1960.

145 In the twilight: "Little Angels Entertain Eisenhowers," *Gettysburg Times*, September 20, 1995, 1. "In 1964, both presidents Eisenhower and Truman authorized the KCFF to list them as honorary presidents.

Their names were in turn used to convince other celebrities to lend their support": *Investigation of Korean-American Relations*, 357. See also Josh Freed, *Moonwebs: Journey into the Mind of a Cult* (Toronto: Dorset, 1980). Mamie Eisenhower's work with the Angels is also described in an arts column, *Frederick* (Maryland) *Post*, November 20, 1967: "Mamie Eisenhower, who is an angel herself . . . ."

146　They even opened: The Liberace/Little Angels tour is listed in "Las Vegas Show Roundup," *Independent* (Long Beach, CA), June 23, 1976: "HILTON—The Osmonds (close Monday), Liberace, Little Angels (open Tuesday)."

146　One little Angel: *Investigation of Korean-American Relations*, supplement to pt. 4, 2.

146　"Little fragile blooms": *The News* (Frederick, MD), November 13, 1968.

146　Pak had worked: *Investigation of Korean-American Relations*, supplement to pt. 4, 9.

146　Having set foot: See "True Parents' History for Children," www.tparents.org.

146　"Never seen anything": See Freed, *Moonwebs*; Adm. Arleigh Burke papers in the supplement to *Investigation of Korean-American Relations*.

147　"If we use the Little Angels": *Investigation of Korean-American Relations*, 360–61.

147　A single troupe: Ibid., 337.

147　In the Moon publication: Freed, *Moonwebs*; Adm. Arleigh Burke papers in the supplement to *Investigation of Korean-American Relations*.

148　Ike, Moon told his followers: *Investigation of Korean-American Relations*, 348; see also the Adm. Arleigh Burke papers.

149　Born Yong Myung-Moon: Moon's official life story is told in Michael Breen's *Sun Myung Moon: The Early Years: 1920–1953* (New York: Holy Spirit Association Publications, 1997) and is also available at the Unification Church Web site, along with other official biographical material. Also see "Reputations: The Rev. Sun Myung Moon, Emperor of the Universe," BBC, 2001; and Robert Boettcher, *Gifts of Deceit* (New York: Holt, 1980), 34–37.

149　"God does not easily give": Moon sermon, "Today in the Light of Dispensational History," New York, February 23, 1977.

149　"Even God said 'No'": Moon sermon posted on the usenet group alt. religion.unification, November 27, 2001.

149 In 1978, Moon would explain: "Preparation for Blessing," from *Master Speaks*, May 1978, 17 (www.tparents.org).

149 A softer version: "True Parents' History for Children," www. unification.org/ucbooks/Tphc/TPHC-04.htm.

150 "I have lived a chaste life": "Sobbing Moon Aide Calls Panel Chief 'a Liar,'" *Stars and Stripes*, April 13, 1978.

150 He recalled years later: *Master Speaks*, 7.

150 In camps like that: See Bradley Martin, *Under the Loving Care of the Fatherly Leader* (New York: Dunne, 2004), 299.

151 "He could not fulfill": *Master Speaks*, 7.

151 It was all part: Boettcher, *Gifts of Deceit*, 39–40.

152 But Moon told him: Robert Parry, "The Dark Side of Rev. Sun Myung Moon: Hooking George Bush," *Consortium News*, 1997, www. consortiumnews.com/archive/moon1.html.

152 The most powerful early ally: Boettcher, *Gifts of Deceit*, 15, 17–18, 23–25, 38–39; *Investigation of Korean-American Relations*, 354, 355.

152 In a February 26, 1963, report: Carlton Sherwood, *Inquisition: The Persecution and Prosecution of the Reverend Sun Myung Moon* (New York: Regnery Gateway, 1991), 39, 43, 47, 509–10; *Investigation of Korean-American Relations*, supplement to pt. 4, 10.

153 By 1967: Don Oberdorfer, *The Two Koreas* (New York: Basic Books, 2002), 41.

153 It became Japan's official chapter: Scott and Jon Anderson, *Inside the League: The Shocking Exposé of How Terrorists, Nazis and Latin American Death Squads Have Infiltrated the World Anti-Communist League* (New York: Dodd Mead, 1986), chap. 5.

153 Moon called this: Moon, "Day of the Victory of Love," New Yorker Hotel, January 2, 1987 (www.tparents.org).

154 Moon's defender: Sherwood, *Inquisition*, 41.

154 "Directly under Founder/Sect leader": Ibid., 38.

154 Now Prisoner 919: See, for example, the comic book *The Hate Korea Wave* (Tokyo: Shinyusa, 2005–2006).

154 One woman, Yu Shin: Parry, "Truth, Legend and Lies."

154 "I've always wondered": See Hong, *In the Shadow of the Moons*.

154 "Just the thought": Chung Hwa Pak, "Retraction," November 18, 1995, www.tparents.org/Library/Unification/Talks/Pak/Chung-Hwa-Pak-Retraction.htm. Other newspapers in South Korea have

retracted sexual misconduct claims, after the church pursued libel cases against Protestant minister Shin Sa-hun and church critic Tak Myung-hwan.

155   The Senate chaplain: Lisa Getter, "Showing Faith in Discretion," *Los Angeles Times*, September 27, 2002.

156   "Everyone, without exception": Moon, *The Divine Principle* (1973 translation, available at www.unification.net)

156   "Through origin-division-union": Moon, *The Divine Principle* (1996 translation, available at www.unification.net).

157   One day in 1965: *Investigation of Korean-American Relations*, supplement to pt. 4, 405.

158   "I had never heard": Ibid., 217.

158   "Time takes its toll": See appendix to *Investigation of Korean-American Relations* (October 31, 1978).

158   One night after he flew: Roland, "The Capitol Hill Stalking Dragon," 24.

158   "The least I can do": Ibid., 27.

159   The first president, she wrote: Betty Lancaster, "You Are My Sunshine," *40 Years in America* (www.tparents.org).

159   In 1976, she attended: Ibid.

159   "Our brothers and sisters": Ibid.

159   She made the news: "Sect Leaders Arrested for Shooting at 2," *Washington Post*, August 22, 1979, C5.

160   As the van lurched: "Anderson's Ties with Rev. Moon in Question," *Mesa Tribune*, August 9, 1998.

160   Decades after meeting Moon: Lancaster's role as an early church member is described in Peter Maass, "Moon at Twilight," *New Yorker*, September 14, 1998. The quote from Betty Lancaster is in "Switzerland Welcomes National Messiah," *Unification News*, December 1996 (www.tparents.org).

160   Congressional investigator: See Boettcher, *Gifts of Deceit*, 44.

161   In 1987, one of Eisenhower's: "Moon Buys into U.S. Politics," *St. Petersburg Times*, December 26, 1987, 24A; "Ex-Treasury Chief Jailed, Disbarred," *Los Angeles Times*, January 15, 1989, 6.

161   "Life on earth": "Messages of Peace from 36 Former American Presidents in Spirit World" (www.unification.net).

SEVEN

162   January 25, 1974: Vicki Evans, "2,000 Japanese Christians March for Nixon, America," *Stars & Stripes*, January 27, 1974; for Nixon campaign

in general, see also Robert Boettcher, *Gifts of Deceit: Sun Myung Moon, Tongsun Park and the Korean Scandal* (New York: Holt, Rinehart, & Winston, 1980), 151–57.

162 In paid announcements: "Statement by the Reverend Sun Myung Moon," *Charleston Gazette*, January 8, 1974.

162 "When a man has sacrificed": Garry Wills, *Lead Time: A Journalist's Education* (Boston: Houghton Mifflin, 2004), 403.

163 On June 10, 1974: Found in College Republican National Committee Records, kept in fifty-one boxes at the Hoover Institute at Stanford University.

163 "Based on twenty years": Author interview with Wayne Slater, May 9, 2007.

164 And here's a September issue: *Rising Tide*, published by the Freedom Leadership Foundation (ISBN 0364-7668), 1971–1979 issues.

164 In its pages, its liberal enemies: *Rising Tide*, March 7, 1977.

165 Communism "is the true antichrist": *Rising Tide*, April 4, 1977, 6.

165 Karl Marx: *Rising Tide*, August 4, 1975, 4.

165 Bill Gertz: *Rising Tide*, May 1981.

165 In one, he plays: "Reverend Moon Gives 'God's Plan for U.S.,'" *Rising Tide*, December 22, 1975; see also *The Centrality of Science and Absolute Values: Proceedings of the Fourth International Conference on the Unity of the Sciences, November 27–30, 1975* (New York: International Cultural Foundation, 1975).

166 A reliable way: Accounts of prowar and pro-Nixon rallies from Allen Tate Wood, *Moonstruck* (New York: Morrow, 1979); Subcommittee on International Organizations, *Investigation of Korean-American Relations* (Washington, D.C.: U.S. Government Printing Office, October 31, 1978); Michael L. Mickler, *A History of the Unification Church in America* (available at www.tparents.org, www.unification.org/ucbooks/Huca/Huca-05.htm), chap. 5, "A National Movement Attempts to Emerge, 1966–71"; author interview with Allen Tate Wood; Boettcher, *Gifts of Deceit*, 5, 54, 55, 161, 162, 163, 309, 323–24; and various news reports from the period, including humorist Art Buchwald's syndicated column, "Congressman Throggsmutton's Pray-in Encounter," July 29, 1974.

166 A telegram came: Mickler, *A History*.

167 A few years later: See *Investigation of Korean-American Relations*; Wood, *Moonstruck*, 95–105.

168 He was finally insulated: Wood, *Moonstruck*, 68–69.

169 Chuck Colson: See Wood, *Moonstruck*. Colson is quoted in Robert

Roland, "The Capitol Hill Stalking Dragon," unpublished manuscript (ca. 1975), 201, as confirming that Moon's groups "had cooperated with the youth people in the White House in their support of the war effort. So I recommended their cause to some friends who had been helping us."

169 Magruder, who started: Author interview with Jeb Stuart Magruder, July 17, 2006.

169 But Bruce Herschensohn: Author interview with Bruce Herschensohn, October 17, 2006; see also the retrospective in *Rising Tide*, January 6, 1975.

170 That Christmas: Mickler, *A History*.

170 There also hung: Boettcher, *Gifts of Deceit*, 168–77, 339–41.

171 Editor Arnaud de Borchgrave: Eleanor Randolph and Michael Isikoff, "The Washington Times's Mission," *Washington Post*, May 6, 1987.

171 "If we can turn": Boettcher, *Gifts of Deceit*, 147 (for the "secret of our movement") and 163 ("five hundred sons and daughters"); see also *Investigation of Korean-American Relations*, appendices to the report, 1102.

172 There were reports: Boettcher, *Gifts of Deceit*, 149.

172 Here's one account: Boettcher, *Gifts of Deceit*, 149; see also *Investigation of Korean-American Relations*, 105.

172 Steve Hassan: Steve Hassan, "Saving the American Taliban," *Boston Globe*, December 19, 2001.

173 "Someday, in the near future": Quoted in Carroll Stoner and Jo Ann Parke, *All God's Children: The Cult Experience—Salvation or Slavery?* (Radnor, PA: Chilton, 1977), 324.

173 "God Has Given": *Investigation of Korean-American Relations*, 14.

173 "Mr. President": Ibid., as appearing in the July 22, 1977, papers.

173 "We were told": Author interview with Richard Barlow, June 26, 2007.

174 "We practiced singing": *Investigation of Korean-American Relations*, testimony from June 22, 1977.

174 One of Moon's people: Described in Boettcher, *Gifts of Deceit*, 153–54; and *Investigation of Korean-American Relations*, documents entered into the record June 22, 1977.

174 On February 1, 1974: Herschensohn interview. The church account is from Bo Hi Pak, *Messiah: My Testimony to Rev. Sun Myung Moon* (2000), www.tparents.org/Library/Unification/Books/Messiah/0-Toc.htm, chap. 12.

176 On July 31, 2003: Posted at MessagesFromSpiritWorld.info on the church's Web site.

176 "Play Him up": *Investigation of Korean-American Relations* (July 1977), pt. 2.

176 And they warned: Ibid.

176 Chris Elkins has written: See Chris Elkins, *Heavenly Deception* (Wheaton, IL: Tyndale, 1980), and Buchwald, "Congressman Throggsmutton's Pray-in Encounter."

177 "Even if many people": *Investigation of Korean-American Relations*, final report, (October 31, 1978).

177 In July, Neil Salonen: *Charleston Gazette*, July 23, 1974.

177 The Unification Church and Thurmond: On Thurmond, see Boettcher, *Gifts of Deceit*, 157; *Investigation of Korean-American Relations*, 402. On the WACL, see Scott and Jon Lee Anderson, *Inside the League: The Shocking Exposé of How Terrorists, Nazis, and Latin American Death Squads Have Infiltrated the World Anti-Communist League* (New York: Dodd Mead, 1986).

178 Two supporters: "The Resurrection of Reverend Moon," *Frontline*, January 21, 1992; Boettcher, *Gifts of Deceit*, 54, 112. On Sasakawa himself, see "The Curious Clout of Japan's Right," *The Nation*, August 12, 1991.

178 Ex-recruits told the press: "The Resurrection of Reverend Moon"; Supreme Court of the United States, 180 U.S. Briefs 1966.

179 Ted Patrick coined: Andreas Killen, *1973 Nervous Breakdown* (New York: Bloomsbury, 2007), 119.

179 A black San Diego activist: "Breaking the Spell That Binds," *Washington Post*, February 6, 1979, B01; Killen, *1973 Nervous Breakdown*, 111–26, 129, 268. See also Ted Patrick, *Let Our Children Go!* (New York: Ballantine, 1979).

179 "I hit them with things": Killen, *1973 Nervous Breakdown*, 120–25; Flo Conway, *Snapping: America's Epidemic of Sudden Personality Change*, 2nd ed. (New York: Stillpoint, 1995), 56.

180 "Reporter's Project": "Reporter's Project Ruins His Career," *New York Times*, July 17, 2004.

180 He was arrested: Eric Boehlert, "Sleaze and Smear at Sinclair," Salon. com, October 22, 2004.

180 Sherwood argues: Ibid.

180 On the book jacket: See Carlton Sherwood, *Inquisition: The Persecution and Prosecution of the Reverend Sun Myung Moon* (New York: Regnery Gateway, 1991).

181 But PBS's *Frontline*: "The Resurrection of Reverend Moon."

181 "[I]t was as though": Sherwood, *Inquisition*, 23.

182 He finds little sympathy: Ibid., 419–61, 493–522.

182 In a racist flourish: The remarkable "Patrick, Ted" entry appears in *Inquisition* at 31, 52, 92–93, 94, 422–39, 441, 444–45, 451–54, 501–2—which is several pages more than the space devoted to Nixon. The lesbian story appears in *Time*, May 3, 1982.

182 "Sit your ass down": Sherwood, *Inquisition*, 431.

183 "You're not doing": This story is related in Patrick, *Let Our Children Go*, chap. 1.

183 "Unattractive, monotonous": Author interview with Barlow, June 26, 2007.

184 "This world": Audio of the 1974 event from www.Euro-Tongil.org is available at the author's Web site, www.gorenfeld.net.

184 After someone called out: Author interview with Barlow.

184 The appearance was reported: "Reverend Moon Gives 'God's Plan for U.S.' in 'Sermon on the Hill,'" *Rising Tide*, speech given in issue for week of December 22, 1975, found at Graduate Theological Union collection, Berkeley, California; Joseph Levyfeld, "Korean Prays in House Caucus Room," *New York Times*, December 19, 1975.

185 The church would call: On Fraser's hobbies, see Boettcher, *Gifts of Deceit*, 231.

185 In 1978, Moon's chief aide: Boettcher, *Gifts of Deceit*, 313–18. For Pak's testimony, see *Investigation of Korean-American Relations* hearing documents (1977), pt. 4, 321–28; "Sobbing Moon Aide Calls Panel Chief 'a Liar,'" *Stars and Stripes*, April 13, 1978; "The Resurrection of Reverend Moon."

185 But in an SEC probe: "Moon Church, SEC Settle on Fraud Charges," *New York Times*, July 7, 1979.

185 One prong: See Boettcher, *Gifts of Deceit*, and *Investigation of Korean-American Relations*.

186 *Newsweek* had reported: *Newsweek*, June 14, 1976, 60.

186 After Albert retired: Jack Anderson, "Washington Merry-Go-Round," *Daily Times-News* (Burlington, NC), May 5, 1977.

186 On one of the hearing's: *Investigation of Korean-American Relations*, March 22, 1978.

188 Within the week: Boettcher, *Gifts of Deceit*, 324, 384, quoting *Master Speaks*, February 14, 1974; and *Investigation of Korean-American Relations*, 315.

188 The report concluded: *Investigation of Korean-American Relations*, final report (October 31, 1978).

EIGHT

190 Opening quote: Jack Anderson, "Moonies, CIA Cooperate in Sandinista War," *Washington Post*, August 16, 1984.

191 After the Moonies excitedly report: "Moon's Son, 17, Dies after a Car Accident," AP, January 3, 1984; see also Nansook Hong, *In the Shadow of the Moons: My Life in the Reverend Sun Myung Moon's Family* (New York: Little, Brown, 1998); Nancy Cooper, "Rev. Moon's Rising Son," *Newsweek*, April 11, 1988; Michael Isikoff, "Theological Uproar in Unifi-cation Church," *Washington Post*, March 30, 1988.

191 "And you were worried": Lars-Erik Nelson, "The Rev. Moon's New Buddy," *Daily News*, May 16, 1988, 29.

191 "Senator Hatch is after me": *Reagan Diaries* (New York: HarperCollins, 2007), December 24, 1982.

191 And in 2004: On the pardon, see "The Resurrection of Reverend Moon," *Frontline*, January 21, 1992; and Ann Louis Bardach, "The Reverend and His Newspaper," in *Killed: Great Journalism Too Hot to Print*, ed. David Wallis (New York: Nation Books, 2004). The Hatch songwriting connection ("Orrin Hatch/Howard Stephenson/Dan Whitley/Stan Seale") is reported at www.tparents.org and www.PeaceRally.info/album/album.info.

192 Defending a trip to Korea: Jim Leach, Ken Ruberg, and Bill McKenzie, "Moon's New Horizon: The Theocratic Right," *Ripon Forum*, January 1983; "The Resurrection of Reverend Moon."

192 When editor Arnaud de Borchgrave: "The Resurrection of Reverend Moon."

192 Reagan sees fit: *Reagan Diaries*, December 24, 1984.

192 Kim said: Kim Hyung Wook: Richard Halloran, "Former K.C.I.A. Head Says Park Tong Sun Was Korean Agent," *New York Times*, June 5, 1977, A1.

193 "I had extremely extensive powers": House Subcommittee on International Organizations, *Investigation of Korean-American Relations*, hearings, June 22, 1977; Halloran, "Former K.C.I.A. Head."

193 "Anybody who stands up": *World News Tonight*, May 18, 1982.

193 William Martin: Walter Martin, *Kingdom of the Cults* (Minneapolis: Bethany, 2003), 377.

194 In prison, Moon had completed: See Moon, *God's Warning to the World (Book II)* (New York: Holy Spirit Association, 1985).

194 Their mission for 1985: Moon speech, January 1, 1985 (www.tparents.org).

194 In 2007, a young woman: Chris Shott, "Bedbugs Steal New Yorker Hotel's Renovation Thunder," *New York Observer*, September 25, 2007.

194 The hotel also houses: See www.AtlanticVideo.com.

195 Between 1976 and 1979: Robert Boettcher, *Gifts of Deceit: Sun Myung Moon, Tongsun Park and the Korean Scandal* (New York: Holt, Rinehart, & Winston, 1980), 151–52; "Moon Follower Dies in Plunge," *Washington Post*, June 8, 1976; "Moon Follower Falls to Death," UPI, August 24, 1976; "Claims 'Moonie' Was Psychologically Pushed," AP, August 17, 1979.

195 "We have seen many evil things": Moon, "Sermons of Rev. Sun Myung Moon," in *Master Speaks: Questions and Answers with Rev. Sun Myung Moon*, www.unification.org/ucbooks/Mspks/1985/850101b.html.

195 In a widely quoted anecdote: Robert Roland, "Capitol Hill Stalking Dragon," unpublished manuscript (ca. 1975), 453; see also Allen Tate Wood, *Moonstruck* (New York: Morrow, 1979).

195 Hanging over the talks: See Hong, *In the Shadow of the Moons* (excerpts available at www.RickRoss.com); Dan Fefferman at www.tparents.org/library/unification/talks/feffermn/.

196 "We have to give enough": The following quotes from the reverend are from Moon, "Sermons." See also Hong, *In the Shadow of the Moons*.

197 In 1985, D'Souza: Dinesh D'Souza, "Moon's Planet: The Politics and Theology of the Unification Church," *Policy Review* 32 (Spring 1985): 28–34.

197 "What I can't figure out": Eric Alterman, "In Moon's Orbit," *The Nation*, October 27, 1986.

197 That summer: See Dinesh D'Souza, *The Enemy at Home* (New York: Doubleday, 2007); e-mail correspondence with author, June 5–6, 2007.

197 The event: "The Culture Wars in Global Perspective," report from Moon's Universal Peace Federation (www.upf.org). D'Souza's quotes are from June 2007 e-mail correspondence with the author.

198 In October 1981: Durst's quotes appear in Charles Austin, "Bigotry Charge Raised at Rally for Moon," *New York Times*, October 23, 1981; Moon's, "Highest Ownership," June 22, 1986, New York.

198 Questions had lingered: Berkeley Rice, "The Pull of Sun Moon," *New York Times* magazine, May 30, 1976.

198 On October 16: Arnold Lubasch, "Sun Myung Moon Indicted on Taxes," *New York Times*, October 16, 1981. A good overview of the tax case is found in Michael Isikoff, "New Moon," *New Republic*, August 26, 1985.

198   Moon, the *New York Times*'s Arnold Lubasch: Arnold Lubasch, "U.S. Tax Fraud Charge Is Denied by Rev. Moon," *New York Times*, October 23, 1981.

199   "Mr. Stillman is a Jewish lawyer": Bo Hi Pak, "Wise as Serpents, Pure as Doves," in *Truth Is My Sword* (New York: Holy Spirit Association, 1999), vol. 2, 453–73.

199   The Unification empire: David Margolick, "Other Religious Groups Join Moon Church in Its Dispute with the City on Taxes," *New York Times*, April 12, 1982.

200   Moon's defense team: Ian Frazier, "Typewriter Man," *Atlantic Monthly* 280 (November 1997); see also *New York Times*, October 16, 1981.

200   The prosecution called: For Tytell's remarks, see Frazier, "Typewriter Man."

200   The guilty verdict: Arnold Lubasch, "Rev. Moon Is Convicted of Income-Tax Fraud," *New York Times*, May 19, 1982, A1.

200   Judge Goettel rejected : Arnold Lubasch, "Moon Is Sentenced to 18-Month Term," *New York Times*, July 17, 1982.

200   Prosecutor Jo Ann Harris: Joyce Wadler, "Appeal Planned in Tax Fraud Case," *Washington Post*, July 17, 1982.

201   He said of Moon: Michael Serrill, "A Prophet's Unlikely Defender," *Time*, January 23, 1984; *Larkin v. Grendel's Den* 459 U.S. 116; *Heffron v. International Society for Krishna*, 452 U.S. 640.

201   Now, in August 1982: *New York Times*, August 11, 1982.

201   On a smaller scale: The charitable investments are described in a federal lawsuit by Unification Church members challenging a Minnesota soliciting law, *Pamela Valente, et al., v. John R. Larson, et al.*, 1980 U.S. Briefs 1966.

201   For in his ideal world: "A Providential View of the Pacific Rim Era in Light of God's Will," March 17, 2007 (www.tparents.org).

202   [B]ecause Moon was the spiritual leader: Oakes's opinion in *U.S. v. Sun Myung Moon.*

202   Meanwhile, the church set: "The Resurrection of Reverend Moon"; "Sun Myung Moon's Goodwill Blitz," *Time*, April 22, 1985.

202   While "Mr. Moon's tax fraud": John P. McKenzie, "He Too Must Render to the Collector When Income Is His," *New York Times*, May 25, 1984; "Moon Speaks to Panel on Intolerance in U.S.," UPI, June 26, 1984.

202   During the meeting: Video of "Moon Speaks to Panel" at the author's Web site, www.gorenfeld.net.

203   The church made much: Carlton Sherwood writes about the *amicus*

curiae on 388–417 in *Inquisition: The Persecution and Prosecution of the Reverend Sun Myung Moon* (New York: Regnery Gateway, 1991).

203 "We accused a newcomer": "Prude Awakening—Hatch's Squeaky-Clean Reputation Scuffed as Some Question His Work on Behalf of BCCI and Rev. Sun Myung Moon," States News Service, January 17, 1992. NBC news producer Mark Hosenball is quoted: "Hatch might to tone down the moralism"; see "Rev. Moon's Unification Message Coming to Utah," *Salt Lake Tribune*, February 24, 2001.

203 "For all of the histrionics": Author correspondence with Fred Clarkson, June 23, 2007.

203 But daughter-in-law: Hong, *In the Shadow of the Moons*, 141–47.

203 Journalist Robert Parry: Robert Parry, "Moon's Dark Shadow," ConsortiumNews.com, October 1, 1998.

204 She believed: "Reputations: The Rev. Sun Myung Moon, Emperor of the Universe," BBC, 2001.

204 Two years later: David Adams, "In a Remote Corner of the World, Rev. Moon Sees Hope," *St. Petersburg Times*, October 11, 1998; Seamus Mirodan, *Irish Times*, October 14, 2004.

204 "[P]raise in Father's presence": Parry, "The Dark Side of Reverend Moon."

204 Newspapers reported: "Bush: Moon 'Vision Man,'" *Pittsburgh Post-Gazette*, World Briefs, November 25, 1996, A2; *Seattle Post-Intelligencer*, News Briefs, November 25, 1996, A3.

205 Yes, the stranger: See "The Secret Sayings of 'Master' Moon," *Time*, June 14, 1976.

205 In a "goodwill blitz": Richard Ostling, "Sun Myung Moon's Goodwill Blitz," *Time*, April 22, 1985.

205 Inside were videotapes: "Unification Books, Tapes Sent to 300,000 Ministers," *Washington Post*, March 30, 1985, G11.

205 During his prison term: See Hong, *In the Shadow of the Moons*.

205 "In one year": Ari Goldman, "Moon's Jailing May Have Eased Things for His Flock," *New York Times*, July 28, 1985, sect. 4, 7.

205 The Divine Principle: Richard Severo, "Unification Church Acceptance Gains," *New York Times*, July 21, 1984.

206 Sileven demanded: Marjorie Hyer, "Unlikely Coalition Gathers," *Washington Post*, July 28, 1984, B6.

206 "What is most painful": Ibid.; see also Hong, *In the Shadow of the Moons*.

206   With help from $500,000: Beth Spring, "With Their Leader in Prison, Moonies Pursue Legitimacy," *Christianity Today*, September 7, 1984; Sara Diamond, *Spiritual Warfare: The Politics of the Christian Right* (Boston: South End Press, 1989), 69.

206   Attended by about 1,800 guests: Elizabeth Kastor, "Welcome for Moon," *Washington Post*, August 21, 1985.

207   The occasion: Taek Yong Oh, "The Providential Significance of the Inaugural World Convention of the Family Federation for World Peace," www.tparents.org/Library/Unification/Talks/Oh/Ffwp-prp.htm.

207   Former president Gerald Ford: Video available at the book's Web site, originally compiled from the Moon site www.FamilyFed.org. See also Andrew Ferguson, "Can't Buy Me Love: Is the Unification Church Conservative, or Just Rich?" *American Spectator* 20, no. 9 (September 1987).

207   "When I look down": Marc Fisher, "Celebrities Pulled into Moon's Orbit; Speakers Unaware of Conclave's Cult Link," *Washington Post*, August 1, 1996.

208   That year: Carolyn Weaver, "Unholy Alliance," *Mother Jones*, January 1986. The letter excerpted here appears in this article.

210   LaHaye paid Moon: Pak, *Truth Is My Sword*, vol. 2, chap. 45, "Mount Danbury," 513–14.

210   "Your suffering": See Pak, *Messiah: My Testimony to Rev. Sun Myung Moon*, vol. 2 (2002), 168, www.tparents.org/Library/Unification/Books/Messiah/0-Toc.htm.

210   "I'll tell you": Weaver, "Unholy Alliance."

210   Conservatives, say ex-*Times* editorialist: I'll tell you": Author interview with John Seiler, July 11, 2007.

211   Buckley had considered: William F. Buckley, *National Review*, June 16, 1989.

211   He and the Unification Church: "Freedom Group Denies Moonie Control," *National Journal* 20, no. 47 (November 19, 1988): 2942; Bob Grant, "The American Freedom Coalition and Rev. Moon," *Washington Post*, October 29, 1989, B7; Anthony Perry, "Fly Me to the Moon," *Los Angeles Times*, January 17, 1990, B1.

211   "Only Moonies could do that": "Freedom Group Denies Moonie Control."

211   It was announced: Michael Isikoff, "U.S. Ex-Officials Lead 'Contra'

Fund Drive," *Washington* Post, May 9, 1985, A34; Nurith Aizenman, "Stop Dissing the Washington Times! It's Not Just 'That Moonie Paper' Anymore," *Washington Monthly*, May 1997, 26.

211 Just that fall: Selwyn Raab, "FBI Holds 6 in Kidnapping of Moon Aide," *New York Times*, November 28, 1984, B1.

211 But defiant Richard Viguerie: "Freedom Group Denies Moonie Control."

211 They "had an enormous effect": "The Resurrection of Reverend Moon."

212 The story, which two reporters: "Reporter Quits over Story on Dukakis' Health," *Los Angeles Times*, August 12, 1988, 2. See also Aizenman, "Stop Dissing the Washington Times!" 26; Allen Freedman, "Washington's Other Paper," *Columbia Journalism Review*, March 1995, 52; "No. 2 and Trying Harder," *Time*, November 6, 1989, 74.

212 Complained editor: "Reporter Quits"; author correspondence with Michael Dukakis.

212 While the church's dollars: Michael Isikoff, "Moon's 'Lost Son' Sparks an Uproar," *Washington Post*, pt. 5, 1; also see Hong, *In the Shadow of the Moons*.

213 He "seemed to take pleasure": See Hong, *In the Shadow of the Moons*. Other details are from author interviews with ex-members Richard Barlow and others; Michael Isikoff, "Theological Uproar in Unification Church," *Washington Post*, March 30, 1988.

213 "He discovered": Quoted in *Newsweek*, April 11, 1988.

213 According to ex-member: Graham Lester, "Clophas (Black Heung Jin Nim)," from www.tparents.org, originally on members' GVI online church forum.

214 "With my own eyes": Damian Anderson, "Black Heung Jin Nim in DC," *The Words of the Anderson Family*, www.tparents.org, August 10, 2000.

215 First, says Dan Fefferman: Dan Fefferman, "The Words of the Fefferman Family: Clophas [sic] and Dr. Bo Hi Pak," April 22, 1999, www.tparents.org/Library/Unification/Talks/Feffermn/Fefferman-Cleophas.htm.

215 A human rights group: "Human Rights Research Monitor [Zimbabwe]," www.HrForumZim.com/downloads/Monitors/HRMonitor8.rtf.

215 "The Pak beating": William Cheshire, "Reverend Moon and the Witch

Doctor," *San Diego Union-Tribune*, April 3, 1988.

215   The fights became: Moon, "Victorious True Parents," New Yorker Hotel, January 28, 1993 (unofficial notes as Moon speaks for four hours).

215   Such was the AFC's influence" "The Resurrection of Reverend Moon."

216   "An ideology called Godism": David Racer, *Not for Sale: The Rev. Sun Myung Moon and One American's Freedom* (St. Paul: Tiny Press, 1989).

217   "Not only did you allow": Letter from Dave Racer to Bob Grant, November 13, 1989.

217   By 1989: John Judis, "Rev. Moon's Rising Political Influence: His Empire Is Spending Big Money to Try to Win Favor with Conservatives," *U.S. News & World Report*, March 27, 1989.

217   At the last minute: Andrew Leigh, "Inside Moon's Washington," *Washington Post*, October 15, 1989, B1.

217   The fight was over: William Alnor, "TBN Torpedoes Agreement to Expose Moon Funding of Christian Ministries," *Christian Research Newsletter* 3, no. 3; also, *Christian Research Newsletter* 3, no. 2—an online archive provided by the Christian Research Institute, a major evangelical Christian apologetics outfit.

218   He was alluding: Ibid. The link between Christian Voice and Balsiger is described in Sara Diamond, *Spiritual Warfare* (Boston: South End Press, 1989), 68.

218   "But Balsiger had done": Alnor, "TBN Torpedoes Agreement."

218   Balsiger's "conduct": Ibid.

218   After reporter Bob Parry: John W. Kennedy, "Moon-Related Funds Filter to Evangelicals," *Christianity Today*, February 9, 1998.

218   "I think silence": Gary North, "Writing Conspiracy History," LewRockwell.com, March 1, 2002.

219   "The whole thing": Edmond Jacoby, quoted in *Regardie's: The Business of Washington*, November 1988, available in the Sara Diamond collection at the University of California–Berkeley.

219   "CIA, Moonies Cooperate": Jack Anderson, "CIA, Moonies Cooperate in Sandinista War," *Washington Post*, August 16, 1984.

219   There were photographs: See Scott and Jon Lee Anderson, *Inside the League: The Shocking Exposé of How Terrorists, Nazis, and Latin American Death Squads Have Infiltrated the World Anti-Communist League* (New York: Dodd Mead, 1986); and Jon Lee Anderson and John Dillon, "Who's behind the Aid to the Contras?" *The Nation*, October 6, 1984.

219   Someone in Oliver North's office: See John Tower, Edmund Muskie, and Brent Scowcroft, *The Tower Commission Report* (New York: Bantam, 1987); and Thomas B. Edsall, "Report Disputed on North's Authorship of Notes," *Washington Post*, March 3, 1987, A4: "On the bottom are handwritten notes referring to Messing and other individuals and groups, including Western Goals; Linda Guell, former director of Western Goals; CAUSA, the political arm of the Unification Church; and Robert Owen, who has been identified as a key U.S. link to the contras fighting the Nicaraguan government."

220   Liberal president Jimmy Carter: "Bolivia Drug Chief Quits, Clearing Way for U.S. Aid," *Chicago Tribune*, March 5, 1991; Michael Isikoff, "U.S. Protests Bolivia's Pick for Drug Unit," *Washington Post*, March 4, 1991.

220   "I consider the holding": Pak, *Truth Is My Sword*, vol. 1, 510–32 (appendix).

220   Other statements of support: Ibid.

220   There were other scattered reports: Clippings in the Sara Diamond archives at the University of California–Berkeley.

221   "The Unification Church": This and the following quotes are from Anderson and Anderson, *Inside the League*.

221   In San Francisco: "North Fund 'Gave $3.9 Million to Friends,'" *Telegraph*, July 20, 1987; "Charges Urged against Witness Who Apparently Posed as a Priest," *San Jose Mercury News*, May 27, 1987; Diamond, *Spiritual Warfare*, 170; "Contra Witness Exposed," KRON-TV, San Francisco, June 3, 1987; *Hearings before Subcommittee on Western Hemisphere Affairs* (Washington, D.C.: U.S. Government Printing Office, 1985), 304 (available on Google Books).

222   His name appears: FBI document obtained by reporter Gary Webb, originally from the *San Jose Mercury News* site, now at narconews.com.

222   A *Minneapolis Star & Tribune*: John Corry, "'The Africans Renew a Funding Fight,'" *New York Times*, September 14, 1986.

222   "The U.S. government": Moon, "The Standard of the Unification Church," August 10, 1986, sermon (www.unification.net).

222   A few months later: "Under Fire: An Afghan Odyssey," *Los Angeles Times*, October 30, 1987; William G. Blair, "2 Americans Reported Killed in an Ambush in Afghanistan," *New York Times*, October 28, 1987; Ronnie Scheib, "Shadow of Afghanistan," *Variety*, June 12, 2006, 38.

NINE

223 Opening quote: G. K. Chesterton, *Collected Works,* vol. 21 (San Francisco: Ignatius, 1986), 41.

223 The experience: Todd Starnes, *Baptist Press,* January 23, 2001;"Religious Right Joins Rev. Moon at Pro-Bush Inaugural Luncheon," *Church & State,* March 2001.

223 The Christians had agreed: Ibid.

224 "My teaching is wrong": "Notes from Father's January Speeches," January 13, 2001, www.tparents.org/Moon-Talks/sunmyungmoon01/ SunMyungMoon-010113.htm.

224 Remarked the Houston fundamentalist: Todd Starnes, "Evangelicals Unaware Inaugural Event Was Sponsored By Unification Leader," *Baptist* Press, January 23, 2001.

224 Wead was such an intimate: Howard Fineman, "Bush and God," *Newsweek,* March 10, 2003; "Bush Feared Past 'Mistakes' Would Cost Him," Associated Press, February 23, 2005.

224 In fact, according to the Nashville-based: From a report by Brian Kaylor of the Baptist General Convention of Missouri, Center for Ethics, June 29, 2006. at www.EthicsDaily.com.

224 Drake is a pastor: Press release from Wiley Drake, "Pastor Wiley Drake Calls for Imprecatory Prayer against So-Called Religious Liberty Watch Group," August 14, 2007.

224 "[I]f [the Baptist leaders]": Kaylor report.

225 Tonight he would be photographed: Previously reported by the author at "Neil Bush Meets the Messiah," AlterNet.org, December 5, 2005; see also Bill Berkowitz, "The Tumultuous and Tawdry Travels of Neil Bush," MediaTransparency.org, December 23, 2005.

225 He also renewed: Jonathan Kaplan and Hans Nichols, "Moon's Groups Lure Lawmakers to Symposiums and Conferences," *The Hill,* August 4, 2004.

225 One listener: *Taipei Times,* December 2, 2005.

226 "No one was aware": David Helvarg, "Anti-Enviros Are Getting Uglier," *The Nation,* November 28, 1994; "Miners and Environmentalists Clash," *Weekend Edition,* NPR, March 7, 1992.

226 "[P]ublic opinion polls": "Bering Strait Tunnel," from www. PeaceFederation.org, downloaded in 2005.

226 According to the *Manila* Bulletin: Ben R. Rosario, "Moon Praises RP Officials For Interfaith Initiative," *Manila Bulletin*, December 2, 2005; see also Rick Casey, "Sun Myung, Boris and Bush," *Houston Chronicle*, December 15, 2005.

226 Not long after: "No Bush Left Behind," *Business Week*, October 16, 2006.

226 On February 11, 2000: Hank Hyena, "Moonies Rally against Free Sex," Salon.com, February 22, 2000; "Chicago Students Protest Playboy," College Press Service, from University of Houston *Daily Cougar* Web site, circa 2001.

227 They also protested: Ibid. See also Michelle Myers, "Pure Love Alliance National Summer Tour," November 1997.

227 His Rainbow/PUSH coalition: "Abstinence Advocacy Group Kicked Out of Chicago Schools," *Florida Times-Union*, July 24, 2000.

227 At a May 15, 1999, meeting: Minutes taken by Damian Anderson, at www.tparents.org.

228 The Unification Church received: The $1.28 million figure is from Jeremy Learning, "Loss of Faith," *Church & State*, June 1, 2006.

228 "I was sitting in my car": John Gorenfeld, "Bad Moon on the Rise," Salon.com, September 24, 2003.

229 *San Francisco Chronicle*: Don Lattin, "Moonies Knee-Deep in Faith Based Funds," *San Francisco Chronicle*, October 3, 2004.

229 Meanwhile, the Centers for Disease Control: "HIV/AIDS Awareness for Secondary School Students in Lagos, Nigeria," at the FedBizOps (FBO) federal grants tracking site, www.fbodaily.com/ archive/2003/04-April/03-Apr-2003/FBO-00292742.htm, filed as solicitation 2003-N-00739: "The Centers for Disease Control and Prevention (CDC) in Atlanta, GA intends to award a contract on a sole source basis to Inter-religious International Federation for World Peace (IIFWP) in Lagos, Nigeria." The announcement was also posted at the government procurement Web site www.eps.gov, accessed February 26, 2004 (data has expired).

229 "Responses": Author interview with Kathy Harben the week of February 26, 2004.

TEN

230 Opening quote: See www.MessagesFromSpiritWorld.info.

230 They touted: Portions of this chapter were previously reported in John

Gorenfeld, "Dear Leader's Paper Moon," *American Prospect*, June 19, 2005, www.prospect.org/cs/articles?articleId=9868.

231 "We are bound to succeed": Barbara Demick, "Setting Up Shop in N. Korea," *Los Angeles Times*, March 28, 2002.

231 "Some of us": Dave Shiflett, "Mystery of Life Solved," National Review Online, July 24, 2002.

231 "We were taught": Author interview with Richard Barlow, June 19, 2007.

231 Another person: "A Message from Cliff Kincaid," www.usasurvival. org/moon-un.html; see also "The Odd Couple: Sun Myung Moon and Dr. Laura," www.usasurvival.org/moonbyslaura.shtml.

231 When the Swift Boat: Carlton Sherwood, *Inquisition: The Persecution and Prosecution of the Reverend Sun Myung Moon* (New York: Regnery Gateway, 1991), 504

232 The former editor: E-mail from John Podhoretz, May 13, 2005.

232 But its editors: "Kerry's Revisionism on Korea" (editorial), *Washington Times*, October 12, 2004, A18.

233 Involved in 1996: Steve Glain, "North Korea Gives Business Consultant a Mountainous Task," *Wall Street Journal*, July 15, 1996.

233 Michael Breen: Author e-mails with Breen, June 1, 2005.

233 Behind the Bamboo Curtain: Bo Hi Pak, *Truth Is My Sword*, vol. 2 (New York: Holy Spirit Association, 1999), chap. 57.

234 Declassified reports: Defense Intelligence Agency, "Pak Bo-Hi Trip to KN [North Korea]," August 14, 1994.

234 "I told him": "Unification Church official talks about Reverend Moon's visit to North Korea," declassified cable from the U.S. embassy in Seoul to the State Department, February 1992.

234 "Editor Wesley Pruden's: Wesley Pruden, "Lots of Bloviation, Some Signs of Hope," *Washington Times*, April 8, 1992, A4.

234 Her piece highlighted: Josette [Sheeran] Shiner, "Kim Il-Sung Asks for Thaw in Ties with U.S.," *Washington Times*, April 15, 1992, A1.

234 [A] sentence that Sheeran: "Interview with Josette Shiner," *Unification News*, May 1994.

235 For Sheeran wrote: Shiner, "Kim Il-Sung Asks for Thaw."

235 The *Washington Times* delegates: For more on Bureau 39, see Bill Powell and Adam Zagorin, "The Tony Soprano of North Korea," *Time*, July 12, 2007.

235 Replied the elder Kim: "We Don't Need Nuclear Weapons," *Washington Times*, April 15, 1992, A11.

235 Sample quote: Ibid.

235 Other stories: See Michael Breen, "North's Relaxing Hard to Discern," *Washington Times*, April 15, 1992, A12; Marc Lerner, "Leaders Rethink Isolation to Ease Economic Binds," *Washington Times*, April 15, 1992, A10; Michael Breen, "Party Drops Push to Spread to South," *Washington Times*, April 15, 1992.

235 The paper quoted: Min Seong-jae, "Pyeonghwa Motors, Unification Church Do a Deal," October 29, 2005.

236 "As for softening": E-mail to author from Michael Breen, June 1, 2005.

236 "After I met": Moon, "Completion of the Responsibilities of True Parents," Tarrytown, New York, December 6, 1992 (www.unification.net).

236 "Using the Unification Church's": Declassified DIA memo, September 9, 1994, 3.

236 But the sale: See "40 Russian Submarines Go to North Korea: The Japanese Trading Company That Acted as Intermediary Is Linked to the Unification Church," *Shukan Post*, February 11, 1994; *Weekly Bunshun*, February 3, 1994; *Weekly Asahi*, February 4, 1994.

237 A lawyer for the widows: "40 Russian Submarines."

237 The *New York Times*: David E. Sanger, "North Korea Buying Old Russian Subs," *New York Times*, January 20, 1994.

237 Western experts: Bermudez writes about the sub deal in *Jane's Defence Weekly*, August 4, 2004. See also "Report: NK Missiles Could Hit U.S.," CBSNews.com, August 4, 2004 ("North Korea gained some of the technical data for the system when it purchased 12 decommissioned Russian Foxtrot-class and Golf II-class submarines from Japanese scrap dealers in 1993, Jane's Defence Weekly said"). John Pike of GlobalSercurity.org describes the sale at www.globalsecurity.org/military/world/dprk/s-golf.htm ("The 12 submarines in question were reportedly rust-eaten and submerged. But the submarines still had significant elements of missile systems, including launch tubes and stabilization sub-systems. North Korea could nonetheless cannibalize the submarines for parts and insights to improve its own submarine and missile launch technology").

237 A DIA Memo: DIA memo, September 9, 1994, 2–3.

238 "You may not be aware": Hak Ja Han Moon, "Keynote Address: A Providential View of the Pacific Rim Era in Light of God's Will," official program for May–June 2007 speaking tour.

238 Bradley Martin: E-mail to author, May 4, 2005.

238 According to separate accounts: Creekmore's account was vetted personally by Eason Jordan, president of the network. See Mike Chinoy, *China Live* (Lanham, MD: Rowman & Littlefield, 1999), 337; Marion V. Creekmore, *A Moment of Crisis: Jimmy Carter, the Power of a Peacemaker, and North Korea's Nuclear Ambitions* (New York: Public Affairs, 2006), 72.

238 In his book: Chinoy, *China Live*, 337.

239 In 1995: Ross Laver and Paul Kaihla, "Schreyer and the Moonies," *Maclean's*, October 23, 1995.

239 Laver and Kaihla, "Schreyer and the Moonies."

239 Kim Il Sung died: Don Oberdorfer, *The Two Koreas: A contemporary History* (New York: Basic Books, 2001), 340.

240 Should Americans be concerned: Subcommittee on International Organizations of the Committee on International Relations, *Investigation of Korean-American Relations*, Report of the U.S. House of Representatives (Washington, D.C.:U.S. Government Printing Office, October 31, 1978), 387.

240 According to a speech: Video of Jenkins's sermons is available at www.gorenfeld.net.

240 "He tells me": Moon, "Address upon Arrival at East Garden," notes by Tyler Hendricks, April 6, 2000, www.tparents.org/Moon-Talks/sunmyungmoon00/UM000406.htm.

241 "The order is basically": Reuben Staines, "3 NK Firms Targeted as WMD Proliferators," *Korea Times*, June 30, 2005.

241 However, as the Center for Public Integrity: Kevin Bogardus, "Foreign Lobbyist Data Could Vanish," Center for Public Integrity, June 28, 2004, www.publicintegrity.org/report.aspx?aid=332.

ELEVEN

242 First opening quote: www.MessagesFromSpiritWorld.info.

242 Second opening quote: "The Significance of the Training Session," sermon reproduced in *Master Speaks*, May 17, 1973; see also "The Secret Sayings of 'Master' Moon," *Time*, June 14, 1976.

242 In an irony: "Editorial: An Attack on Dong-A Ilbo," *Dong-A Ilbo* (www.donga.com), August 24, 2006.

243 One headline asked: Ser Myo-ja, "Moon's Church Protests Unflattering Coverage," *Joong Ang Daily*, August 23, 2006.

244 After a newspaper discovered: "Mum Defends Son after 'Cult' Claims Award," *The Journal* (Newscastle, UK), August 7, 1999.

244 The Unification Church, after all: "Members of a group dedicated to building a device to facilitate communication with spirits . . . an expressed desire of Rev. Moon for more than 20 years. . . . The group reviewed research by Peter Nordquist of WRIST, a company which Rev. Moon set up for this purpose. . . . [E]ndeavor as follows: 1. Discover what frequency characterizes the mediumistic connection to the spiritual world." See Unification Theological Seminary site, www.uts.edu/index.php?option=com_content&task=view&id=385&Itemid=1.

244 In 2001, one was handed: "Hour of White Power," *Orange County Weekly*, February 14, 2002.

245 "To re-create Israel": "Father's Words and Hoon Dok Hae" (notes by Michael Jenkins), sermon at the Sheraton National Hotel, March 2, 2003, www.unification.net/news/2003/news20030302_1.html.

245 Moon has kept: "Preparation for Blessing" (church document), May 19–20, 1978, 5; ADL, "Backgrounder: The Jewish Defense League," www.adl.com/extremism/jdl_chron.asp.

245 In 2003, the Family Federation: "Preparation for Blessing," 4.

246 "Put to rest": JewishOutreach.doc (from www.FamilyFed.org).

246 Though the Father of the Constitution: Quoted in Garry Wills, *Under God* (New York: Simon & Schuster, 2007), 376

246 Madison, according to Moon: www.MessagesFromSpiritWorld.info.

247 The recipe: For "actual blood," see "Preparation for Blessing, May 19–20, 1978" (church document); for liquors, "Blessing and Ideal Family, Part I" (church publication), www.tparents.org/Moon-Books/bif1/BIF1-4-403.htm.

248 In *Guidance*: "Honor Thy Parents," *Washington City Paper*, September 8–14, 1995; Young Whi Kim, *Guidance for Heavenly Tradition*, vol. 2 (Frankfurt: Vereinigungskirche, 1985), 185.

248 He says the church: "Ashamed of True Parents?" letter to the editor of *Unification News*, Gary Fleisher, March 1998 (www.tparents.org). 18 Weeks later: Forensic analysis conducted in June 2007 by Vetwest Labs, Van Nuys, California.

248 Reporter Ben Avni: Benny Avni, "The Fear of the God-Fearing," *New York Sun*, December 13, 2004.

248 It was plugged: *Washington Times*, October 4, 2003; UPI, October 2, 2003.

249 The Reverend Moon has been spending: Jonathan Kaplan and Hans Nichols, "Moon's Groups Lure Lawmakers to Symposiums and Conferences," *The Hill*, August 4, 2004.

249 Video of the event: Author's collection; see the author's Web site, www.gorenfeld.net.

249 "In short": Fiji Government, "Statement on Dr. Sun Myung Moon," December 7, 2005; ABC Radio Australia, September 12, 2005.

250 Notwithstanding other complaints: Harold Paine and Birgit Gratzer, "Rev. Moon and the United Nations: A Challenge for the NGO Community," GlobalPolicy.org, November 2001. See also "Banning U.N. Corruption," *Washington Times*, op-ed, June 16, 2007. The fundraiser is described in "In Ban's U.N., Sun Myung Moon's Paper Is Praised, While Gambari Raises Him Funds," *Inner City Press*, June 8, 2007.

250 "We will present": "True Father's Word," Tarrytown, New York, May 10, 2003 (www.unification.org).

250 And yet de Venecia: "Maybe we should rename this mountain, *Reverend Moon Mountain!*"—see Church's *World CARP News* 2, no. 1 (August 2001). The *Times* story is David Sands, "U.N. Office on Interfaith Dialogue Eyed," *Washington Times*, November 23, 2003.

250 In Pakistan: Khalid Hasan, "Madrassa Time in Washington," *Daily Times* (Lahore, Pakistan), July 1, 2007; "Ulema Convention Calls for Repeal of WPA [Women's Protection Act], *The Nation* [Pakistan], December 15, 2006.

250 "Hundreds of demonstrators": "Clerics Rally for Peace at U.N.," *Washington Times*, October 4, 2003.

251 In tandem: Martin Walker, "The UN and the Churches," UPI, July 14, 2003.

251 In November: David Sands, "U.N. Office on Interfaith Dialogue Eyed," *Washington Times*, November 23, 2003, A07.

251 Filipino ambassador: For the UN resolutions, see T. J. Burgonio, "RP Proposal on Interfaith Dialogue Gets UN Nod," *Inquirer News Service* (Philippines), November 15, 2004; "Interreligious Dialogue and Cooperation," UN General Assembly draft resolution A/58/L.13, November 3, 2003; "Promotion of Interreligious Dialogue," UN General Assembly draft resolution A/59/L.15/Rev.1, November 8, 2004; "Promotion of Interreligious and Intercultural Dialogue," UN General Assembly Resolution 61/221,; "UN General Assembly Adopts

RP Resolution on Interfaith Cooperation for Peace," press release, Permanent Mission of the Republic of the Philippines to the United Nations, December 20, 2006 (www.un.int). For de Venecia's work with Moon on "interreligious," issues see the *Manila Bulletin Online,* February 12, 2005, in which he attends a church event in Seoul and praises "contributions to the Inter-faith Dialogue by one of the foremost advocates of peace in our time, the Rev. Sun Myung Moon." See also "UN Passes Resolution on Interreligious Dialogue," from Moon's organization UPF, http://upf.org/programs/un/briefings/ irdialogue/index.php?report_id=425&event_id=116.

251   "If anyone opposes": Moon sermon, "The Grand Clean-Up Period in the History of Good and Evil," Belvedere, New York, June 23, 1996 (www.tparents.org); the "191 nations" boast is from the official Web site, www.upf.org.

252   He's the brains: Claire Vitucci, "$600 Million for Drug Treatment," *Press-Enterprise* (Riverside, CA), January 30, 2003.

ACKNOWLEDGMENTS

It's been a long road to the publication of this book, and I'd like to thank Peter Richardson and Scott Jordan at PoliPointPress for making it happen; Phil Wentz for his astonishing powers of research; Joe Conason; *The Gadflyer*'s Paul Waldman and Tom Schaller, for printing my first story on the Moon coronation; ABC's *World News Tonight*; Laura Larson and the folks at Michael Bass Associates; Jan Frel and Max Blumenthal; for speaking out, Donna Collins, Richard Barlow, Craig Maxim, Gordon Neufeld, Cathryn Mazer, Louis Desloge, Ford Greene, Graham Lester, Forrest Wright, and many others who will remain anonymous; James Whelan, Bill Cheshire, and John Seiler, all true gentlemen; a special thanks to the Roland family; Bob Parry, Rory O'Connor, Fred Clarkson, Dan Junas, Steve Hassan, Bill McKenzie, Ann Louise Bardach, and Larry Zilliox, for working this beat before I did—shoulders of giants, et cetera—and helping me get up to speed; decades of *Washington Post* journalists to whose reporting I owe a great debt, especially Michael Isikoff; Sara Diamond; Robert Boettcher; Norman Solomon; Joseph Farah; Rick Ross; Salon.com; Kazumoto Ohno; Michael Tomasky; dozens of bloggers including Scoobie Davis, Len Rojas, Ron Gunzburger, and Duncan Black; David Greenberg, Rick Perlstein, Dennis Roddy, and Tony Norman; Eric Ritezel; Steve Meretzky; James Tapp Jr. for telling me how to deliver my message; Matt Pendleton and Patrick Runkle, for their friendship; Bob Carney, Bob Pease, and Steve Pollock, my grade school writing teachers and above all, my own family, to whom this book is dedicated.

Index

About the Author

John Gorenfeld lives in the Bay Area, where he's written feature articles for *Radar*, Salon.com, the British *Guardian*, the *American Prospect*, *Reason*, and other publications, about everything from monster movies to fugitive Internet tycoons.

OTHER BOOKS FROM PoliPointPress

The Blue Pages: A Directory of Companies Rated by Their Politics and Practices
Helps consumers match their buying decisions with their political values by lsting
the political contributions and business practices of over 1,000 companies.
$9.95, PAPERBACK.

Jeff Cohen, *Cable News Confidential: My Misadventures in Corporate Media*
Offers a fast-paced romp through the three major cable news channels—Fox CNN,
and MSNBC—and delivers a serious message about their failure to cover the most
urgent issues of the day.
$14.95, PAPERBACK.

Marjorie Cohn, *Cowboy Republic: Six Ways the Bush Gang Has Defied the Law*
Shows how the executive branch under President Bush has systematically defied
the law instead of enforcing it.
$14.95, PAPERBACK.

Joe Conason, *The Raw Deal: How the Bush Republicans Plan to Destroy Social Security
and the Legacy of the New Deal*
Reveals the well-financed and determined effort to undo the Social Security Act
and other New Deal programs.
$11.00, PAPERBACK.

Kevin Danaher, Shannon Biggs, and Jason Mark, *Building the Green Economy:
Success Stories from the Grassroots*
Shows how community groups, families, and individual citizens have protected
their food and water, cleaned up their neighborhoods, and strengthened their local
economies.
$16.00, PAPERBACK.

Reese Erlich, *The Iran Agenda: The Real Story of U.S. Policy and the Middle East Crisis*
Explores the turbulent recent history between the two countries and how it has led to a showdown over nuclear technology.
$14.95, PAPERBACK.

Steven Hill, *10 Steps to Repair American Democracy*
Identifies the key problems with American democracy, especially election practices, and proposes ten specific reforms to reinvigorate it.
$11.00, PAPERBACK.

Yvonne Latty, *In Conflict: Iraq War Veterans Speak Out on Duty, Loss, and the Fight to Stay Alive*
Features the unheard voices, extraordinary experiences, and personal photographs of a broad mix of Iraq War veterans, including Congressman Patrick Murphy, Tammy Duckworth, Kelly Daugherty, and Camilo Mejia.
$24.00, HARDCOVER.

Phillip Longman, *Best Care Anywhere: Why VA Health Care Is Better Than Yours*
Shows how the turnaround at the long-maligned VA hospitals provides a blueprint for salvaging America's expensive but troubled health care system.
$14.95, PAPERBACK.

Christine Pelosi, *Campaign Boot Camp: Basic Training for Future Leaders*
Offers a seven-step guide for successful campaigns and causes at all levels of government.
$15.95, PAPERBACK.

Sarah Posner, *God's Profits: Faith, Fraud, and the Republican Crusade for Values Voters*
Examines corrupt televangelists' ties to the Republican Party and unprecedented access to the Bush White House.
$19.95, HARDCOVER.

William Rivers Pitt, *House of Ill Repute: Reflections on War, Lies, and America's Ravaged Reputation*
Skewers the Bush Administration for its reckless invasions, warrantless wiretaps, lethally incompetent response to Hurricane Katrina, and other scandals and blunders.
$16.00, PAPERBACK.

Nomi Prins, *Jacked: How "Conservatives" Are Picking Your Pocket—Whether You Voted For Them or Not*
Describes how the "conservative" agenda has affected your wallet, skewed national priorities, and diminished America—but not the American spirit.
$12.00, PAPERBACK.

Norman Solomon, *Made Love, Got War: Close Encounters with America's Warfare State*
Traces five decades of American militarism and the media's all-too-frequent failure to challenge it.
$24.95, HARDCOVER.

John Sperling et al., *The Great Divide: Retro vs. Metro America*
Explains how and why our nation is so bitterly divided into what the authors call Retro and Metro America.
$19.95, PAPERBACK.

Daniel Weintraub, *Party of One: Arnold Schwarzenegger and the Rise of the Independent Voter*
Explains how Schwarzenegger found favor with independent voters, whose support has been critical to his success, and suggests that his bipartisan approach represents the future of American politics.
$19.95, HARDCOVER.

Curtis White, *The Spirit of Disobedience: Resisting the Charms of Fake Politics, Mindless Consumption, and the Culture of Total Work*
Debunks the notion that liberalism has no need for spirituality and describes a "middle way" through our red state/blue state political impasse. Includes three powerful interviews with John DeGraaf, James Howard Kunstler, and Michael Ableman.
$24.00, HARDCOVER.

FOR MORE INFORMATION, PLEASE VISIT WWW.P3BOOKS.COM.

About this Book

This book is printed on Cascade Enviro100 Print paper. It contains 100 percent post-consumer fiber and is certified EcoLogo, Processed Chlorine Free, and FSC Recycled. For each ton used instead of virgin paper, we:

- Save the equivalent of 17 trees
- Reduce air emissions by 2,098 pounds
- Reduce solid waste by 1,081 pounds
- Reduce the water used by 10,196 gallons
- Reduce suspended particles in the water by 6.9 pounds.

This paper is manufactured using biogas energy, reducing natural gas consumption by 2,748 cubic feet per ton of paper produced.

The book's printer, Malloy Incorporated, works with paper mills that are environmentally responsible, that do not source fiber from endangered forests, and that are third-party certified. Malloy prints with soy and vegetable based inks, and over 98 percent of the solid material they discard is recycled. Their water emissions are entirely safe for disposal into their municipal sanitary sewer system, and they work with the Michigan Department of Environmental Quality to ensure that their air emissions meet all environmental standards.

The Michigan Department of Environmental Quality has recognized Malloy as a Great Printer for their compliance with environmental regulations, written environmental policy, pollution prevention efforts, and pledge to share best practices with other printers. Their county Department of Planning and Environment has designated them a Waste Knot Partner for their waste prevention and recycling programs.